MEN'S BODIES

Edited by Judith Still

For Keith and Michael

Contents

(Re)presenting Masculinities: Introduction to *Men's Bodies* JUDITH STILL	1

SECTION I Re-posing Men

Masculinity and Muscularity: Dr Paul Richer and Modern Manhood ANTHEA CALLEN	17
Kitsch and Classicism: The Male Nude in the Twentieth Century EDWARD LUCIE-SMITH	42
Morimura/Duchamp: Image Recycling and Parody KERSTIN BRANDES	52
Show Your Wounded Manliness: Promises of Salvation in the Work of Joseph Beuys CORINNA TOMBERGER	65
Tom's Men: The Masculinization of Homosexuality and the Homosexualization of Masculinity at the end of the Twentieth Century GUY SNAITH	77
Freak Flag: Humour and the Photography of George Dureau MELODY D. DAVIS	89
In Conversation: Photographer Ajamu and Cultural Critic Anita Naoko Pilgrim AJAMU X AND ANITA NAOKO PILGRIM	107
What is a Man? Looking at the Traces of Men's Sexuality, Race and Class in the Work of Some Contemporary Photographers JUDITH STILL	119

Fellas in Fully Frontal Frolics: Naked Men in *For Women* Magazine
CLARISSA SMITH   134

Underexposed: Spectatorship and Pleasure in Men's Underwear Advertising in the Twentieth Century
PAUL JOBLING   147

The Language of Bodybuilding
JEREMY STRONG   163

'Support our Boys': AIDS, Nationalism and the Male Body
JOHN LYNCH   175

A Genealogical Approach to Idealized Male Body Imagery
ROSALIND GILL, KAREN HENWOOD AND CARL McLEAN   187

SECTION II Moving Men: Masculinity and the Moving Image

Reclaiming the Corporeal: The Black Male Body and the 'Racial' Mountain in *Looking for Langston*
CHI-YUN SHIN   201

Exposing Himself: Sweet Sweetback's Body
DOROTHY C. BROADDUS   213

The W/hole and the Abject
PHIL POWRIE   222

Queer Masculinity: The Representation of John Paul Pitoc's Body in *Trick*
NIALL RICHARDSON   232

Racing Forms and the Exhibition(ist) (Mis)Match
CALVIN THOMAS   245

Mainstreaming the Money Shot: Reflections on the Representation of Ejaculation in Contemporary American Cinema
GREG TUCK   263

Homosexual Prototypes: Repetition and the Construction of the Generic in the Iconography of Gay Pornography
JOHN MERCER   280

(Re)presenting Masculinities:[1]
Introduction to *Men's Bodies*

The papers collected in this volume are some of those given at the 'Men's Bodies' conference held at the University of Nottingham 29–31 March 2001, co-organized by myself, Keith Fairless and Michael Worton.[2] The pieces brought together in the first section 'Re-posing Men' all have as a focus the male body posed, or somehow captured, in a fixed and immobile representation. The second section 'Moving Men: Masculinity and the Moving Image' will instead take as its theme men in motion, men on screen. In this Introduction I shall attempt to outline briefly a few of the issues involved in analysing the sexual politics of looking at pictures of men. One issue which I shall simply take for granted is the dissolving (or at least disturbing) of disciplinary boundaries which this enterprise entails. For instance, the aesthetic focus of traditional Art History, and the canon of traditional Art History, are inevitably challenged by a focus on (sexual) politics whether that comes from feminism, or the newer realm of men's studies, or indeed from cultural studies or critical theory.[3] The section title 'Re-posing Men' brings together two major questions that we should ask when we analyse pictures of the male body: one is captured in the term *repose*, the question of passivity or stasis; the other is the question of *posing* and the gender masquerade. Moreover, in this volume, we are re-posing certain questions usually asked of women. In the second section six articles address the question of men on screen, film and pop video, men whose bodies as *objects* may be screened by *action*. The drive to screen (display or disguise) the male body by showing it to be engaged in willed activity may of course be traced in representations long pre-dating the advent of the movies. One of the challenges of earlier forms is how to evoke an appropriate mental or physical dynamic in a necessarily frozen and silent moment. Motion (and sound) apparently solve that problem — and yet we incessantly cut back to the questions posed by representation as such, and by representation of men's bodies in a particular historical moment.

Representation: the Gendering of Images and the Imaging of Genders[4]

We need to consider the relative place of the visual historically, and the relative place of masculinity and femininity within visual culture at different times. Representation is not necessarily visual — it is possible to represent some one or thing with words or even in music. However, in this double volume, we shall focus on the visual — a form of representation that has a long and important history. Its pre-eminence is unsurprising in times when the majority of the population was illiterate, and yet our age of mass literacy is also the age of the mediatic spectacle, and so visual representation has renewed vigour. The question of representation involves three terms, which can be analysed according to different theories which bring with them different sets of vocabularies. The first term is the producer of the representation (in their micro- and macro-context), what we could otherwise name the conditions of production, or the producing intertext or of course the artist. The second term is the material image itself, that which has been produced and placed in a particular location (whether tabloid newspaper or Art-house cinema) and is then consumed, and probably cannot be analysed outside its consumption. So finally the third element is the consumer, the spectator, the gaze (again in micro- and macro-context) — another intertext.

It is not possible to analyse the places of the masculine, or the places of men, without analysing those of the feminine or of women. This is true not only because they mutually define each other, but also because masculinity is bound up with power. Lynne Segal writes:

The closer we come to uncovering some form of exemplary masculinity, a masculinity which is solid and sure of itself, the clearer it becomes that masculinity is structured through contradiction: the more it asserts itself, the more it calls itself into question. But this is precisely what we should expect if (...) masculinity is not some type of single essence, innate or acquired. As it is represented in our culture, 'masculinity' is a quality of being which is always incomplete, and which is equally based on a social as on a psychic reality. It exists in the various forms of power men ideally possess: the power to assert control over women, over other men, over their own bodies, over machines and technology.[5]

It has often been argued that our culture is ocularcentric, and that this is crucially linked to the structure of patriarchy, and to the prizing of intelligibility *rather than* sensuality.[6] This can be referred psychoanalytically to the visibility (and so relative privilege) of the male sexual organ.[7] And yet one could cite a range of feminist analyses claiming that, throughout most of the twentieth century, man is typically an active spectator (and a producer of images) and the woman a passive spectacle, the object, indeed commodity, to be consumed.[8] Thus masculine sexual or biological visibility has

(Re)presenting Masculinities: Introduction to Men's Bodies 3

been rendered invisible by our culture. And it can be argued that, where the penis is represented only symbolically, phallic power is just as, or all the more, potent.[9] In *The Nude: A New Perspective*, Gill Saunders claims that: ' "Nude" is synonymous with "female nude" because nakedness connotes passivity, vulnerability; it is powerless and anonymous'.[10]

However, the series of binaries implied above need to be treated with some care. This is a somewhat time-bound perspective, which is convincingly historicized by Margaret Walters in one of the rare monographs on *The Nude Male*.[11] She reminds us that: 'The male nude remained the basis of art training — in a sense, of art itself — from the fifteenth century almost to the present day. Renaissance artists often used male models for their female figures; even those later artists whose sole interest was in women or animals or landscape had to begin their studies with the male nude' (7). The position of the male nude in the plastic arts was only seriously challenged in the nineteenth century, and with this challenge came a reconceptualization of the significance or signification of the nude:

> Over the centuries of Western civilization, the male nude has carried a much wider range of meanings, political, religious and moral, than the female. The male nude is typically public: he strides through city squares, guards public buildings, is worshipped in Church. He personifies communal pride or aspiration. The female nude, on the other hand, comes into her own only when art is geared to the tastes and erotic fantasies of private consumers. (*The Nude Male*, 8)

This brings us to the issue of what is the rule and what is the exception. To take one example of a strategy which has been popular amongst feminists in the last few decades: in *Male Subjectivity at the Margins*, Kaja Silverman looks for texts that subvert the dominant fictions of normative masculinity. But Abigail Solomon-Godeau would argue contra Silverman that the 'crises' in masculinity 'are closer to the rule than to the exception'.[12]

One issue then is that of the male object: what does it look like? What can be shown? And what does it signify? But if the image can only be read via consumption we must also ask who looks at (which) pictures of men? In this volume, many authors have focused on the naked or almost naked male body — the desirable body — which appears to cathect many of the important questions about historical change. But who produces these pictures, and who do they produce them for, and even if they are produced for a specific market, are they now available more generally?

Some articles in this volume focus on explicitly homosexual images, contexts, and, by implication, consumers (such as John Mercer on gay porn, Guy Snaith on Tom of Finland or Niall Richardson on the 1999 film *Trick*). In some less marked contexts there is nevertheless an assumed homoerotic gaze — obviously in the photography of Robert Mapplethorpe or even in advertising strongly influenced by his work, and this is one aspect of Paul Jobling's article on the history of men's underwear advertising. This brings us of course to the question of women and scopic desire (for the male body). This is treated by Clarissa Smith in this collection in relation to erotic magazines specifically addressed to women (although not necessarily consumed only by them). Smith points out that many models and indeed specific images drift between erotica produced for women and for men. And it may certainly be contended that far more women will consume images of men who are (or who might be) gay, produced by men who are (or who might be) gay, that exist in a variety of more readily available locations, as will consume visual pornography produced explicitly by women for women — rather harder to lay your hands on.[13] What then is the specificity of the female or feminine gaze? And what could be the possible mutual interference of the hetero- and homo-erotic which might be productive of desire? There has been useful work on the queering of film spectatorship — where the apparently fiercely heterosexual lead is perfectly accessible to homosexual desire if only within the darkened chamber of the cinema. It may be asked whether, in a weak sense, the actively desiring female gaze is always a little queer (queer by definition) — such is the strength of the conventions of activity and passivity that we have inherited. A third question of course is that of the straight-identifying man's gaze on the desirable male body. Straight men can easily gaze on naked men in contexts where desire is deemed to be left out of the picture (for instance, in the showers or changing rooms after strenuous physical exercise). But looking at pictures of naked men which might be produced *in order* that they be desired (rather than, to take a different example, to draw the viewers' attention to their victimhood) is another ball game.

Representation is fascinating, powerful and dangerous. Why might it be dangerous? On a philosophical and psychic level, representation can be deemed to entail a loss of immediacy. We are often represented by others and usually for others. Jean-Jacques Rousseau, one of the earliest great modern men, was notoriously (as notoriously analysed today) anxious about (mis)representation. In his last work, the *Rêveries of the Solitary Walker* he paints himself and, he writes, only for himself.

Yet as soon as the signs are on the paper they are accessible to others, and, of course, his self-portrait has been studied by millions since his death. We cannot have that face-to-face, silent, transparent union and communion with Rousseau for which he longed.[14] In the face of death, mediation is all we have. The mediation which Rousseau dreaded was not only that of writing in the narrow sense, but also pictorial — he hated the paintings produced of him — and, above all, political.[15] Yet Rousseau's acute sensitivity to the danger that any representation can be a loss as well as a misrepresentation and that any self-representation might be (seen as) a pose, has not been universally recognized.

Representation and Power

We have to ask how both representation and power function, and what is the relationship between them. If representations can be produced by power, can shore up or reflect power, can they also undermine the power structure at least in a particular context or via a particular dynamic between observer and image? The images analysed in this volume may be static, or action fixed forever on celluloid and bounded by its form, but there is a certain mobility of the look.

Representation, and the control of representation, has long been a *sine qua non* for those in power.[16] They wish to disseminate their words and physical images of themselves as widely as possible. However, the key is perhaps control: powerful men wish their physical images to be appropriately serious, potent, awe-inspiring. The body has had to be the image of the mind. As feminists have been insisting since before the term feminism was coined, women (and to some extent other races) have born the burden of embodiment, of material support, of physicality. However, this sexual distinction has taken a wide range of forms. At certain historical moments (classical Greece is a favourite example) men's self-judgement as mentally superior has been accompanied by admiration for an idealized nude male body as the appropriate envelope or, at least, companion, for the beautiful mind. At other moments, for example the nineteenth and twentieth centuries, male power is supported by a sense that the beautiful body is (erotic and) quintessentially feminine.[17] Men may be judged by their words and their works; women can be judged by their appearance. Consequently liberation movements have often adopted the strategy of reclaiming representation as serious. Feminists have demanded women newscasters or political commentators, dressed in suits, as opposed to exotic dancers, love-interests and the like; those struggling for racial equality have also wanted ethnic minorities represented positively and seriously not only as entertainers, sporting stars or criminals. Thanks largely, but not solely to feminism, a serious amount of work has been done on the visual representation of women; far fewer studies exist which address the construction of masculinity in visual culture.[18] Nevertheless the image of the (ideal) male physique is a product of ideology and fantasy just as the images of perfect womanhood have been shown to be.

Representation and the Loss of Power

Whatever changes there have been in masculinity in the final decades of the twentieth century have been both reflected in, and influenced by, visual culture — in particular a new freedom in ways to represent the male body. Ros Gill *et al*'s article in this volume places this new freedom in the context of feminism and the New Social Movements. It includes a flood of images of men unclothed or half unclothed, erotic images, feminine images, comical images ... This variety, this liberation, has been enthusiastically greeted by some as evidence of a more general liberation of masculinity from the trappings and constraints of patriarchal and homosocial power. It can be argued that uncautious readers of Judith Butler's *Gender Trouble*, and indeed of Bakhtin's theory of the carnival, have been too swift to detect liberation in various forms of sexual masquerade.[19] This welcome stems in part from the fact that we are emerging from a period (the nineteenth century and the first three-quarters of the twentieth century) when the male body was very hard to represent at all — as body rather than as clothing for the mind or soul — and it has been the female form that has born the burden of embodiment. But we must remember that at other historical moments the male body, albeit an idealized male body, has been presented as the body — just as 'man' can stand in for humanity. The idealized male body has, moreover, had two dominant forms: the active, heroic form (associated with the Classical and Renaissance periods) which epitomizes adult virility, and the passive, sometimes suffering (Christ and the saints), sometimes boyish (Classical again), form. This dual possibility reminds us that the representation of the male body apparently disempowered, indeed feminized, can co-exist quite comfortably with patriarchal power.[20] If we have emerged with an explosion of representations of men, with or without clothing, both in high and in popular culture, this time round it has not, however, been accompanied by any significant diminution of fascination with the female form.

The relationship between high and so-called low culture is currently a complex one of inter-penetration. Perhaps this has made easier a focus on the sexual male, previously relegated to low cultural forms. One thinks for example of the role of the over-proportioned phallus in popular festivals and comedy throughout the centuries, while classical statues or neo-classical paintings typically presented modestly proportioned male genitalia evoking the mortality of the body (*Male Trouble*, 36–8). Meanwhile the symbolic labour of evoking the phallus was often performed by bunches of drapery or swords. Postmodern irony and disturbance of genres has no doubt facilitated the increase in production and consumption of certain kinds of previously censored images. However, relaxed and sophisticated secular audiences are not necessarily a result of, and do not necessarily bring about, real political change.

Alongside the focus on the nudity or otherwise of the body, on which part of the body is privileged, on action or stasis, on serious or comic tone, we can also consider the male body with respect to solidity or fluidity. Conventionally, at first glance, the male body should be hard, and it is the female body that is associated with softness or fluidity. Certain fluids are of course prized—usually because they are associated with work or struggle and/or they are precious and scarce. For instance, men's blood can be seen to exist in an economy of scarcity—either in a warrior culture or in a society dominated by genealogical concerns (the two not mutually exclusive but not identical).[21] In this volume Phil Powrie, Greg Tuck and Calvin Thomas all address the question of the fluids that are produced by men's bodies, and the problem of abjection. In what context is sperm a precious fluid, ejaculation a pro-ject in a way that Sartrean existentialism could understand? And when is ejaculate, by contrast, in its physical materiality, an abject product?

Representation and the Show of Strength

Apparently patriarchy demands that men are strong, active and serious, the subjects rather than the objects of desire. To this end there has been a preference for heads over bodies, or clothes (the trappings of power, of a distinctive place in the hierarchy) over nakedness. However, Solomon-Godeau shows from the perspective of French Neoclassicism that this is a historically contingent strategy. (A different argument could focus on Christian iconography through different periods.)

What does it mean that men are represented as strong and active? This question is asked by a number of contributors to this volume. Anthea Callen looks back at the early days of photography, and the preference for male models with well-developed muscles. She carefully shows how the photographs intimate to their reader that they are not showing working men — whose muscle development through labour would most likely be imbalanced. Instead the photographs show the idealized perfectly muscled nude body which has been constructed by professional exercise. Thus the photographs refer to an aesthetic other than Naturalism. Is the sculpted body then an erotic object? The erotic is apparently deflected by the sporting activity also referenced in the images. Snaith analyses another historical moment, another art form, and an overtly erotic representation of the muscled body — the drawings of Tom of Finland. He shows how life imitated art as (gay) men's clothes and (gay) men's bodies followed Tom's prototype clone look.[22] Tom's unleashing of the fantasy of the hypermasculine has been said productively to disempower this apparently patriarchal force, and gay men's relatively explicit self-fashioning has been echoed more generally. Jeremy Strong asks related questions of the contemporary cult of bodybuilding with its implicit revelation of the plasticity of the body. Another related instance would be the example of audience fascination with the way in which actors such as Robert de Niro re-sculpt their bodies in a range of different films.[23]

Feminists have often sought to destabilize patriarchal power by privileging a certain androgyny. How should we react to the fashion for the muscled male body amongst both gay and straight men? It appears to threaten in a classic way — *Raging Bull* not only shows us the boxer in the ring, but also domestic violence. Does the fact that the masculine body is recognized as 'built', explicitly constructed rather than natural, make it less phallic? If muscles narcissistically developed in a gym are another version of the myriad changes (from cosmetics to surgery) that have been imposed on the feminine body does that make them better or worse? Or are these questions simply pointless outside a very specific socio-political context — which often means: I can enjoy playing with the gym or with stilettos because I am an enlightened (middle-class) person — but the oppressed others may be precisely oppressed by these dangerous games. It can be argued that the muscular body represents temporary and provisional power because it is purely physical and operates in an erotic, domestic, private kind of space—one on one, no weapons. In our society, real and lasting power is economic and political rather than physical. In desiring the muscled body, we may be desiring 'safe' domination, someone who has *provisional* power over us—the classic 'bit of rough'. While this seems to me to have some purchase, we should not forget the specific (and global) reality of the experience of 'battered wives'.[24]

Multiple Individuals

Any represented individual (or group of individuals) is a subject crisscrossed by different, sometimes contradictory, texts. Each exists in a complex and mobile fabric of relations. If we borrow the vocabulary of systems theory, as Jean-François Lyotard does, we could say: 'Young or old, man or woman, rich or poor, a person is always located at "nodal points" of specific communication circuits, however tiny these may be'. Importantly, Lyotard adds: 'No one, not even the least privileged among us, is ever entirely powerless over the messages that traverse and position him at the post of sender, addressee, or referent.' [25] This relative mobility is even solicited by the regulatory mechanisms. These relations, apart from gender, include race, sexuality, nationality, culture and class.

The question of race or cultural difference is posed by a number of contemporary artists working on the male body—Ajamu, Rotimi Fani-Kayode, the Harris brothers and Sunil Gupta were all exhibited in *Typical Men!*, and are briefly discussed in my article in this volume. Yasumasa Morimura's work is analysed by Kerstin Brandes.[26] John Lynch's article raises the question of the relation between the nation and the male body in his analysis of two images in *The Sun*. The sexually and racially ambiguous body of Freddie Mercury is juxtaposed to the apparently unambiguous nationalist image of a soldier saluting the flag. The Harris brothers, like Ajamu, evoke many nations to which you can adhere more or less problematically—not only the USA or the UK but also including the black nation and the Queer nation. In Thomas's examples the black male body is produced for white consumption *as* the phallus. *Having* the phallus is the prerogative of the white man. Dottie Broaddus and Chi-Yun Shin also foreground the intersections of race, sexuality and nationality in their analysis of two very different American films (*Sweet Sweetback's Baadasssss Song* and *Looking for Langston*).

Class is a key factor, alongside sexuality and race, affecting visual experience and representation, access to certain images, and particular forms of self-fashioning. Laws on censorship, or at least their application, often withhold images from the lower orders, however conceived (sometimes a definition inflected by sex or race), even while they are privately available to an elite. The body of the working man or the body of the proletariat has at certain times been particularly on display, available to the gaze, unable to withdraw from visibility. Just as the exotic bodies of the National Geographical magazine were available to the 'scientific' or titillated reader, so the 'criminal' or 'insane' were displayed without being able to withhold permission. At the same time, these bodies were often deemed undesirable to display, and the reality of labour or class was to be hidden as in eighteenth-century landscapes. The question of the status of models and actors should also not be elided. Feminists have repeatedly addressed the exploitative conditions under which images can be produced, and not only in the porn industry, but it is important not to forget that not all of the men's bodies we see in print or on screen belong to highly paid Hollywood stars.

The meanings and power of autobiography should also not be forgotten. The traces of personal or social history in images can act against the force of universalizing idealization. Corinna Tomberger, in this volume, suggests the importance of the mingling of life, body and work in Joseph Beuys. Self-expression in a public forum can be particularly important for those who identify with a historically silenced 'nation'—such as the African-American nation. It may of course be argued—though it may seem paradoxical to many feminists—that men in general have been repressed in that it has historically been difficult for them to represent themselves or other men in a number of ways. They have been framed by the trappings of power, the limitation of potency.

Expected and Unexpected Moves

Finally we should end with the role of the consumer of images: how much freedom/power do we have as desiring subjects to re-write, re-frame, re-position the bodies in the images? Here we need to analyse the game of representation and the play of glances: representation is powerful and dangerous, but commensurately weak; it always exceeds or falls below the intentions of those behind its production, reproduction and consumption. There can be a reactive oscillation of looks between men posed or screened and those looking at them, a certain ocular eccentricity.[27] Any one shift in representation—whether it be Langston Hughes introducing softness and androgyny to the idealized

African-American male[28] or Tom of Finland wishing to escape stereotypes of effeminate gay men — requires a counterbalance. However, these very qualities make representation all the more worth analysing in its complicated relationship to the changing structures of power in our society, in particular in relation to sex and sexuality.

JUDITH STILL
The University of Nottingham

NOTES

1 See Diana Saco, 'Masculinity as Signs: Poststructuralist Feminist Approaches to the Study of Gender' in *Men, Masculinity and the Media*, edited by Steve Craig (Newbury Park, Sage Publications, 1992, 23–39): '*(re)presentations of gender*. This phrase parenthetically conveys the idea that gender is constructed (...) (presented) as if it were direct knowledge of real objects (as if it were representation)' (25).

2 The conference formed part of the project *Real Men and Others: Towards New Masculinities*. We should like to express our thanks for the financial support given to the project by the AHRB. The conference also received a subvention from the British Academy for which we are grateful. Speakers want to thank all participants for their contribution to the debate.

3 The conference took place in the University Arts Centre, used facilities belonging to the Department of Art History, and was timed to accompany an exhibition, *Typical Men! Recent Photography of the Male Body by Men* curated by Michael Worton and myself. (See my article in this volume.) Nevertheless the majority of papers were given by speakers from Departments of Literature or Sociology.

4 This section title plays on an expression used by Jeff Hearn and Antonio Melechi in 'The Transatlantic Gaze Masculinities, Youth and the American Imaginary' in *Men, Masculinity and the Media*, (215–32). They argue that 'Images and imaging involve references to culturally assigned meanings of looking, showing, being looked upon, being shown' (216) and that 'images are (only) produced in their consumption' (217).

5 *Slow Motion: Changing Masculinities Changing Men* (London, Virago, 1990), 123.

6 See Martin Jay, *Downcast Eyes: the Denigration of Vision in Twentieth-Century French Thought* (Berkeley, University of California Press, 1993) for an account of the critique of this privileging of the visual, of light and illumination. Luce Irigaray argues that, instead of prizing one over the other, we should seek a *sensible transcendental*.

7 Of course the long debate over the significance of the penis and/or phallus in Freud and Lacan immediately complicates the relationship between literal

and figural which is a major issue in discussing representation. Jean-Francois Lyotard argues, in 'One of the Things at Stake in Women's Struggles', translated by Deborah J. Clarke et al, *Sub-Stance*, 20 (1978), 9–17, that feminism (and he cites Irigaray in particular) has helped to undermine the neat distinction between symbolic and referential. He writes: 'When a "feminist" is reproached for confusing the phallus, symbolic operator of meaning, and the penis, empirical sign of sexual difference, it is admitted without discussion that the metalinguistic order (the symbolic) is distinct from its domain of reference (realities). But if the women's movement has an immense impact equal to that of slaves, colonized peoples, and other "under-developed" groups, it is that this movement solicits and destroys the (masculine) belief in meta-statements independent of ordinary statements' (15).

8 John Berger and Laura Mulvey are two names that will reoccur throughout this volume. The work of Luce Irigaray could also be invoked of course.

9 In a now classic article, Richard Dyer gives a neat account of the inadequacy of the penis as a representative of phallic power in photographs of male pin-ups; he points to the hysterical massing of phallic symbols in certain famous examples as well as the importance of flexed muscles. See 'Don't Look Now — the Male Pin-Up', *Screen*, 23: 3–4 (1982), 61–73. He also draws our attention to the modalities of the gaze — the male gaze able to stare boldly (at women) in public spaces, or stare boldly out of a photograph, and yet also able to look up or to the side in (a show of) its disinterest for its female interlocutor. Women meanwhile must gaze demurely down, particularly in public, coyly invite male attention, or gaze in rapt attention while the man speaks.

10 London, The Herbert Press, 1989, 7.

11 *The Nude Male: A New Perspective* (New York and London, Paddington Press, 1978). To be fair, Saunders does later complicate her picture with a brief invocation of ancient Greece.

12 *Male Trouble: A Crisis in Representation* (London, Thames and Hudson, 1997), 35.

13 Political and economic factors (such as the changing relative cost of production) are of course crucial to this dynamic, which is sometimes incorrectly represented as relating largely to the question of taste e.g., the polemical claim that 'most women don't like (visual) pornography'.

14 See Jean Starobinski, *Jean-Jacques Rousseau: Transparency and Obstruction*, translated by Arthur Goldhammer (Chicago, 1988).

15 For instance, the mediation of the Member of Parliament who deputizes for us. Quentin Skinner has pointed out, in an analysis of Thomas Hobbes ('Burying the Body of the People', John Coffin Memorial Lecture, 8 May 2003), the shifting meaning of political representation and representative. The former refers to a visual or theatrical sense of the production of a likeness whereas the latter is chosen to represent us, to speak and decide on our behalf.

However, both senses produce real anxieties and their interpenetration or confusion in so many texts only add to this.

16 Control over representation, as Rousseau already suggests, is both a reality for those in positions of power, and an illusion since representations by definition can escape both those who produce and those who receive them. Representations can always be re- or mis-appropriated. Even Nazi iconography, rightly associated with extreme control, has been reappropriated in the service of sado-masochistic sexual games or the imagery of 1970s punk fashion. This example also perhaps serves to illustrate the danger in placing too much confidence in the iconoclastic power of a reappropriated image.

17 Abigail Solomon-Godeau argues that: 'The "crisis" of the book's title is the historical turning-point during which the beautiful male body ceded its dominant position in elite visual culture to the degree that the category "nude" became routinely associated with femininity. It also refers to the transition from earlier courtly models of masculinity to recognizably modern, bourgeois ones, a transition fostered by the expulsion of femininity (and women) from increasingly masculinized cultural and political domains' (7–8). I am grateful to Michael Worton for drawing this book to my attention.

18 Exceptions include the work of Edward Lucie-Smith or Melody Davis.

19 See Michel Foucault's *History of Sexuality* translated by Robert Hurley (Harmondsworth, Penguin, 1978), volume 1, for a clear warning about the dangers of celebrating our own openness and liberatedness relative to the past. There is a profit (for speaker or writer) to be had in maintaining such a stance, but it usually entails presenting power in the past (and indeed present) as monolithic, top down, purely repressive and censoring. It ignores the many ruses and complexity of power. Hearn and Melechi, for example, are rather optimistic about the effect of popular culture: 'we conceptualize this popular imaginary as a space in which fantasy can unfix the status of sexual identity, collapsing the binary oppositions between masculine/feminine, homo/hetero, and narcissism/voyeurism into polymorphous desires. It is precisely in this sense that there is no text of masculinity. In the imaginary, the dialectic of the gaze, there is always difference, where the subject is consumed and reproduced in and through a multiplicity of desires' ('The Transatlantic Gaze', 230).

20 See, for example, Tania Modleski, *Feminism without Women: Culture and Criticism in a 'Postfeminist' Age* (London and New York, Routledge, 1991) on men incorporating female power. Solomon-Godeau refers to this in *Male Trouble*, 38.

21 Leaking blood, in particular menstrual blood, is of course rather less valorized in many social contexts as numerous feminist analyses have pointed out. See, for example, Irigaray on *sang blanc* and *sang rouge* in *This Sex Which Is Not One*, translated by Catherine Porter and Carolyn Burke (Ithaca, Cornell University Press, 1985).

22 A look undoubtedly also influenced by other artists and art forms such as Hollywood action movies.
23 A great deal has been published in this connection; for example, on *Raging Bull*, see Pam Cook, 'Masculinity in Crisis?', *Screen*, 23:3–4 (1982), 39–46.
24 I am using this expression metonymically to represent those terrorized by physical power in a 'private' context.
25 *The Postmodern Condition: A Report on Knowledge*, translated by Geoff Bennington and Brian Massumi (Manchester, Manchester University Press, 1984), 15.
26 Amongst others, see also Segal on the sexual reading of race (*Slow Motion*, 175ff.).
27 Is this Martin Jay's 'multiplication of a thousand eyes' (591)?
28 See Chi-Yun Shin in this volume for analyses of Langston Hughes in film.

RE-POSING MEN

Masculinity and Muscularity: Dr Paul Richer and Modern Manhood

This essay examines scientific photographs of naked men. It focuses on the visual 'evidence' widely deployed by later nineteenth-century Western industrialized societies to study and control the human body. Using a Foucauldian analysis informed by Marxist history, John Tagg[1] found the development of new regulatory and disciplinary apparatuses, including photography, to be closely linked throughout the nineteenth century to the formation of the new social and anthropological sciences. These included not only the obvious field of criminology, but psychiatry, comparative anatomy and, of course, the medical sciences. While endorsing Tagg's general thesis, this paper suggests ways in which it might be nuanced, notably in respect of the naked male body and its representation which, in a predominantly homo-social society provoked issues of conflicted identification, subjectivity and sexuality. The widespread circulation of cheap photographs and the unprecedented proliferation of images of naked bodies (whether artistic, scientific or pornographic), transformed both perceptions of the human body, and the processes of surveillance: paradoxically, these processes were simultaneously enabled and subverted by the flood of photographic nudes. How, in this context, does the naked male body figure? Technological discoveries and innovation were crucial to the changing photographic medium.[2] I shall only touch on some of these but it is important to note them: multi-lens cameras; camera size and efficiency; shutter speed; film speed — improvements in photographic paper and the introduction of celluloid; the use of electrical power and lighting.

I refer to photography in the service of artistic formation and of medical training and diagnosis, but look most closely at its role in anthropometry — Dr Paul Richer's 'science of the nude', and his studies of comparative anatomy. I am particularly interested in ideas of difference, especially normality (or 'health') *versus* pathology, and the ways photography could help define what constituted the normal/healthy body, here, the male body.

Paul Richer (1849–1933) trained as a doctor, and was Jean-Martin Charcot's assistant at La Salpêtrière hospital in Paris. A sculptor and draftsman, too, from 1876 Richer began to record the visible symptoms of Charcot's patients, in line drawings which were published in 1881 in the major volume on Hysteria which made Richer's name.[3] In 1878, Charcot was among the first physicians to establish, at La Salpêtrière, a hospital photographic *Laboratoire* designed to provide both an archive of medical photographic records, and materials for teaching medical students from visual evidence. Projected glass lantern slides were used in the hospital, and also in anatomy classes at the Ecole des Beaux-Arts. Charcot's emphasis on the visual in diagnosis is well known, as are his lectures in which patients were subjected to examination, either singly or comparatively in groups, parading naked before the doctor, his students and visiting *stagiaires* (trainees).[4] This preoccupation with observing and assessing the naked body was a common feature at this period across the sciences, particularly in the medical and in the emergent social sciences, like anthropology. The naked body in question was customarily that of the lower classes or of other, especially non-white, ethnic groups; in the visual arts it was most commonly female. In 1875 Professor Duval recorded his intention to extend the comparative anatomy course at the Ecole des Beaux-Arts, in order 'to confront for the purpose of debate the study of the human races.'[5] For Duval, anthropology was the science of the human races 'which it classifies, defines and describes on the basis of their *anatomical characteristics.*'[6] Paul Richer, who succeeded Duval at the Ecole, took the artistic anatomy syllabus further down the route of comparative anthropology. Both Duval and Richer had long been professionally engaged in this new science, which was founded in France in 1861 by the brain specialist and biological determinist Dr Paul Broca (1824–1880).[7] Comparative anthropological measurement of skulls and skeletons, characteristic of the approach of Broca, gave way under Duval and especially Richer to the study of the live subject.

Richer also shared the contemporary obsession with recording and analysing the mechanics of physical movement now best known through the work of English photographer Eadweard Muybridge (1830–1904) and of Richer's compatriot, the physiologist Professor Etienne-Jules Marey (1830–1904). Although Muybridge's visit to Paris in Summer 1881 predated his studies of human movement (1883–5), his lecture tour doubtless fuelled Richer's passion for the photography of movement. Marey, whom Richer was to assist in 1900 in photographing athletes at the Paris Olympic Games, was a further stimulus to Richer's research. But it was initially due to his contact with Albert Londe at La Salpêtrière, where both men worked under Charcot, that he and Richer began photographing the male

Masculinity and Muscularity: Dr Paul Richer and Modern Manhood 19

body in movement. Richer probably met Marey through Londe, who was a mutual friend.[8] In a sense, Londe's arrival at La Salpêtrière lifted some of the burden of representation from Richer's shoulders; although he continued to draw Charcot's patients, the establishment of the *Laboratoire* marked a shift in the hospital's priorities towards photographic evidence. From 1881, when Londe was appointed to the photographic laboratory (he became its Director in 1884), he and Richer began a long collaboration. Independent of Muybridge, both Marey and Londe had begun developing new photographic techniques and apparatus to capture movement. Londe, one of the century's most important authorities on photography had already, by 1882, independently developed a multiple-lens camera for recording sequential movement; his refined twelve-lenses camera used for the chronophotographs taken with Richer dates from 1893. The lenses were set in a bank of 4 × 3 and uncovered one by one exposing the single plate behind them; the shutters were released electrically and exposure times could be varied. Marey preferred a device he also invented in 1882, the 'gun' camera (*fusil photographique*) which took multiple images through a single lens. I shall return to Richer's work with Marey.

As early as 1893 Marey published, in his *Etudes de physiologie artistique*, plates reproduced from his chronophotographs of male movement. These were made at his *Station physiologique* by his laboratory assistant, Georges Demenÿ (one of the founders of physical education in France), in a collaboration that lasted from 1882 until 1894.[9] Richer's first treatise on human anatomy for artists, *Anatomie artistique*, published in 1890, was based on the traditional, medical study of artistic anatomy and focussed on the superficial anatomy of the male body at rest and in action.[10] In collaboration with Londe, in the early 1890s Richer began systematically to study male models in movement. His subsequent artistic anatomy books were increasingly informed by this close photographic study of the effects of movement on human morphology, which also underpinned his detailed drawings. Male body movement recorded on Londe's twelve-lens camera resulted in chronophotographs which were first reproduced in six *phototypes* plates for Richer's *Physiologie artistique de l'homme en mouvement* (1895). Between 1905 and 1911 Richer also photographed hundreds of male, and then female models — in preparation for his *Morphologie: La femme* of 1915.[11] The twelve-image chronophotographs of moving bodies were all made by Londe, and are all taken outdoors, probably at

Marey's *Station physiologique* in the Bois de Boulogne;[12] those taken by Richer, all single-lens camera shots, are set in an interior: the anatomy theatre at the Ecole des Beaux-Arts. For Marey, chronophotography was a tool for decomposing human movement by reducing it to graphic notations, which revealed for analysis the forces and energy entailed in movement.[13] What Marey failed to recognize was that movement conceived as distinct time-based fragments was an illusion. 'Chronophotography has *constructed* continuous movement as composed of discrete discontinuous "snapshots", rather than *revealed* the discontinuity.'[14] Discontinuity is an effect of the photographic apparatus. However, since Richer's project was to provide accurate anatomical data on human movement normally invisible to the naked eye, for the use of fine artists, the fact that chronophotographs froze movement into discontinuous instants was for him not a problem. He deemed this data essential for an accurate depiction of the mechanics of bodily movement — but not for its reconstruction.

The photographs of men taken by Londe and Richer were originally intended for publication in an *Atlas physiologique*, which was announced as such by Londe in 1895.[15] After Londe's death a sample of the chronophotographs, 64 sheets in total, was published in the 1921 edition of Richer's *Nouvelle Anatomie artistique* (fig. 1).[16] The private, scholarly use of photographic nudes, as in medical or artistic research, had very different connotations to their appearance and use in public circulation, even in the context of an artist's anatomy book. There may have been moral constraints against publishing the *Atlas* in the 1890s; certainly, public circulation of such images was restricted before 1900. In 1887, access to Muybridge's huge work in 11 volumes, seven of which studied human locomotion, was severely restricted by price ($100) and available only on subscription; a smaller and less expensive edition, *The Human Figure in Motion* (1901) permitted wider availability. Periodical magazines distributing photographs of artistic, anthropological or sporting nudes around 1900 were also sold by subscription and not publicly displayed. These included Bayard's *Le nu esthétique* and Rodolphe's body-building monthly *La culture physique*. However, distinguishing between Marey's eye as that of the *physiologist* (scientific and positivist) and Muybridge's as that of the *photographer* (artist and voyeur), Laurent Mannoni regards Muybridge's ambitious publication strategy as unusual for the period. The wider dissemination of Marey's photographs, no matter how scientific their purported intent, may have been inhibited by problems other than a broader public morality. Most obvious among these was the pressing

Masculinity and Muscularity: Dr Paul Richer and Modern Manhood   21

Poins. Arracher de l'haltère. Vue antérieure.

Figure 1. Albert Londe, *Exercices physiques. Weights Snatching the Dumbbells. Front view*, 1894–5. Twelve chronophotographic views with two enlargements, published in Richer, *Nouvelle anatomie artistique* (1924 edition), pl. 32.

need for Marey to secure continued financial support for his research from the Académie de Sciences and the military establishment: he was required to submit his work to the scrutiny of administrators and functionaries. Yet this did not prevent him from publishing in 1893 his *Etudes de physiologie artistique* — arguably some of his more contentious images and specifically aimed at fine artists — which could have compromised his credibility as a scientist. Indeed, Marta Braun argues that these editions, including Richer and Londe's 1895 *Physiologie artistique*, sold widely and became basic reference tools for artists (268).[17] However, *Physiologie*, containing only six chronophotographs, as against 123 in-text drawings by the author, was focussed exclusively on the male body; such images had a less blatant erotic function than did photographs of the female body.

Londe's camera produced a sequence of twelve rapidly-exposed shots, a series of photographs capturing skeletal and muscular movements as if in 'slow-motion'. The chronophotographs fell into three distinct categories destined for separate volumes in the *Atlas physiologique*: Movements; Locomotion; and Varied Exercises. 'Movements', entitled *mouvements partiels* in Richer's 1921 volume, focussed on isolated parts of the body to demonstrate the morphological changes entailed in specific actions, like 'slow flexion and extension of the forearm against the arm' (Richer 1921, plate 1), and the equivalent while lifting weights.

The second category, 'Locomotion', comprized everyday physical actions: different types of walking, on the flat and up an incline; marching; running; jumping, and so on. The *exercices physiques* comprized the specialized, energetic movements associated with particular sports or training exercises, such as weightlifting, shot-putting, ball-throwing, and some gymnastics (fig. 1). Pugilistic combinations (kicks and punches) for both English and French boxing were recorded, as was the sequence of movements involved in kicking a football, seen in the extraordinary chronophotographs of Charcot *fils*, Dr Jean-Baptiste Charcot, which show Londe and Richer using their friends as models.[18]

Studies of models performing the actions of artisans or labourers at work were also included in the chronophotographs of *exercices physiques*; these were given a separate rubric, *mouvements professionnels*, when they were published in Richer's 1921 *Nouvelle anatomie*. Performed on staged sets, these record the characteristic movements of each trade—such as the roles of blacksmith, wood-sawyer, log-chopper, digger. According to the view of positivist physiologists like Marey who conceived of 'man as machine', chronophotographs of labour provided the physiological data for developing an economy of human movement in the performance of specific tasks. These were used to inform the Taylorist 'time and motions' regimentation of an industrialized workforce at the factory conveyor-belt.[19] As Richer himself reported, Marey's chronophotographs of subjects similar to his own had permitted a systematic analysis of the movements, for example, of the coppersmith at work; this enabled Marey's collaborator, the engineer Charles Frémont, to establish in 1887 'the cinematic trace of the sledge-hammer's trajectory', whether in its flight or in the direct hit. Such studies made it possible to ascertain ' "the minimum expenditure of force that, as a consequence, results in the minimum fatigue, which logically explains the instinctive movement of the labourer." '[20] The objective of Marey's images — the analysis of force and energy required in movement — determined his use of models dressed in white photographed against black to show up. In contrast, Richer's 'labourers' were naked because what he sought to analyse were the anatomical changes entailed in movement.[21] A photograph dated to 1894 of Londe operating his twelve-lens camera shows the outdoor setting where these images were taken.[22] The anvil seen on the 'set' in this photograph is the same used by Richer's 'smith' (fig. 2), but different from the one adapted for Marey/Frémont's photographs, with a dial to register the impact of the hammer. The nude model in this photograph of Londe at work also posed for Richer:[23] he used many of the same men repeatedly in his chronophotographs, which suggests they were professional models.

This is the case with *mouvements professionnels* published in 1921; all are performed by one very powerfully-built male model with a military-style crew-cut and an ideal athletic body of a distinctly Aryan worker/soldier type (fig. 2) perhaps a modern 'Labours of Hercules'. Indeed, Richer's 'smith' appears to be the same model as Sallé used in his *Anatomy Class* (which included Richer) painted some seven years previously.[24] This same model performs every *mouvement partiel* and all but the running and jumping actions in *locomotion*; he reappears, too, performing the toughest of Richer's *exercices physiques*: weightlifting and the rings. The model exhibits a musculature well-developed throughout the body and hence unlike genuine labourers, whose repetitive tasks developed specific groups of muscles which resulted in imperfect bodily proportions — where the relation of parts to the whole lacked an ideal harmony. Aptly, then, given his role in both sporting and professional movements, the size and beauty of this model's body removes him from the realms of genuine labour; he is a prototype of the ideal worker of the Third Reich or Stalinist Russia, the very perfection of whose built body effaces all signs of class. This reading is aided by his complete nudity, since it was the worker's coarse, specialized clothes which indelibly marked his social status: as they do when this same man modelled partially clothed for

Le forgeron. Marteau à deux mains. Vue latérale gauche.

Figure 2. Albert Londe, *Mouvements professionnels. The Smith, Two-handed Hammer: Left-side view*. Twelve chronophotographic views with three enlargements, published in Richer, *Nouvelle anatomie artistique* (1924 edition), pl. 60.

Sallé's *Anatomy Class*.[25] It is, indeed, in the *mouvements professionnels* that nudity is the most disconcerting. A combination of the ludicrous and the unashamedly virile gives these bizarre images a more than faintly pornographic quality. Stripped of the trappings of ennobling pugilism or Olympian sport which sanction and civilise male nudity, in worker roles the model is more transparently 'naked', and hence more completely the object of a voyeuristic male gaze than the models in Richer's other photographs of male movement. Accessorized with the tools of labour in a self-consciously theatrical out-door *mise en scène*, in which the fall of natural sunlight on the body is very apparent, this nakedness appears the more starkly incongruous: these *mouvements professionnels* invoke the trope of the homoerotic 'bit of rough'.

As Londe himself admitted, even in artistic compositions one of the gravest defects of photography was that the effect of being 'posed' almost always remained. Yet Londe defended the benefits of artifice in nude photography, of applying 'the general principles of art' in composing the photographic work. Crucial to the credibility of the photographic record was its precision; Londe's twelve-lens camera was renowned for the unusually sharp quality of the chronophotographic prints it produced. This resolved the problem which Marey had experienced with his 'gun', that of blurring — an effect which, by drawing excessive attention to the material process itself and hence the mediation involved in image-making, undermined both the plausibility of the end product and its scientific efficacy.[26] As Londe noted, in photographs where the priority was the legible representation of anatomical form, lighting played the decisive role: 'Studies of the nude are exacting since it's a question of obtaining finely detailed shadows and clearly modelled lights.'[27] Background, viewing distance, focal length, exposure times all entailed careful calculation; judicious printing was often needed to refine the contrasts in order to ensure bone, muscle formation and the morphology of their movement were suitably prominent and discernible. All these factors signalled photography's artifice. New techniques, like the enlargements seen in figures 1 and 2, may have aided the scrutiny of morphological detail frozen at specific points in a movement, but were further evidence of intervention, insistently reminding the viewer of the photographer's agency.

To secure the objectivity of anthropometrical photography, tools for measuring the body were widely employed to give the photographs a comparative statistical credibility. Thus backgrounds with grids or numbered horizontals, or free-standing measuring-sticks, were often included — despite the inevitable inaccuracies due to variations in the angles or distances between model, measure and camera plate. Richer used such measures only in his photographs of athletes, made with Marey in 1900; for his anatomical studies he did not need a visual record of the body measurements, which were kept separately on *fiches* (index cards). In true taxonomic style, Richer underwrote the visual images with statistical evidence to ensure their scientific authority: on these individual *fiches* he recorded standardized sets of body measurements (the same for both males and females). The conventions of this new photographic science of the body also demanded a legitimizing neutrality of setting: anonymous light, dark or grey backdrops helped drain the image of personal or individual associations, and avoided the loaded trappings of a furnished or domestic interior that might overtly eroticize the naked body.

In this respect, the framing and presentation of the photographs was crucial, too. This is particularly evident in images which survive uncropped from Richer's photographic campaigns begun after his appointment to the Chair of Anatomy at the Ecole des Beaux-Arts in 1903. But first I shall outline his aims and procedures. At the latest by 1900 Richer himself had taken up photography; the six albums of instantaneous, single-lens photographs that he made between 1905 and 1911 were designed to display the subject's *morphologie*—Richer's term to distinguish his extensive study of the live model from anatomy of the dead body. He set out to produce systematic photographic records firstly of European male, and then female morphology. Combined with his *fiches*, these data were designed to establish 'mean' body types, as the basis for an aesthetic canon founded on scientific evidence. The photographic data for each model was displayed on a sheet pasted with some 15 to 20 single shots representing a range of poses and movements. Notably, for some of the female models, up to one-and-a-half or even two sheets of photographs were required, since these generally included reclining poses which took up more space. In conformity with the art historical canon of the European nude, male models were rarely posed reclining, but rather in upright, active stances which connoted a virile masculinity.

As in a scientific investigation, the photographic session for each model followed a set procedure. Both male and female models began with three stiff, hieratic standing views (front, back and side), echoing the pose of traditional skeletal or *écorché* anatomical prints. With the male models it also recalled soldiers standing to attention, which Catherine Mathon associates with French anxieties over the sickly state of its nation and armed forces ('Le corps modelisé', 161). These shots were normally followed by a series of rigidly formulaic poses showing the position or use of different muscle-groups in rest or in action: sitting on a box; kneeling, crouching, seated curled up on the floor; bending forward, bending back, twisting (fig. 3). Then there were usually a series of more improvised *contra-posto*-style poses with

Masculinity and Muscularity: Dr Paul Richer and Modern Manhood 27

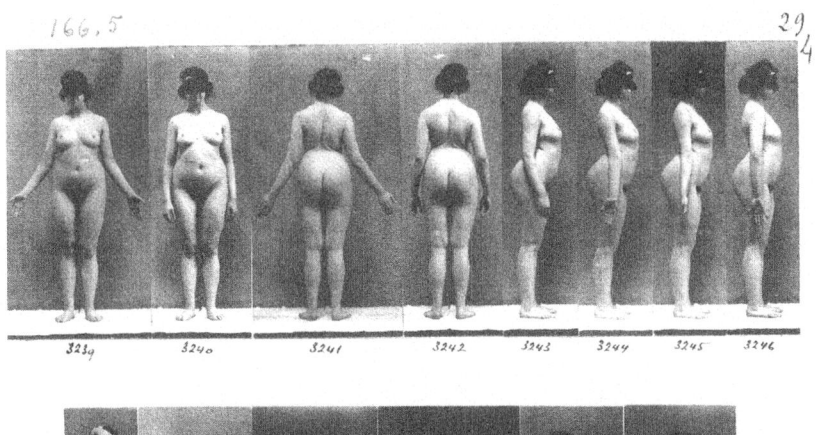

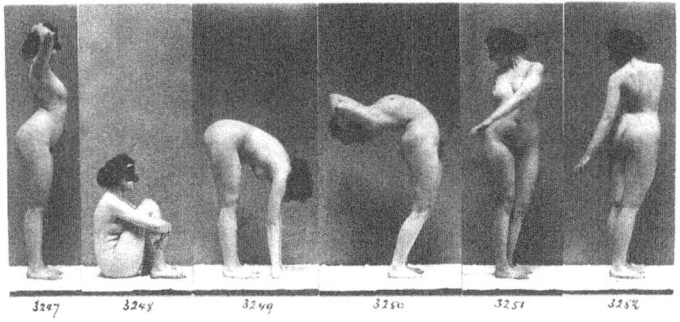

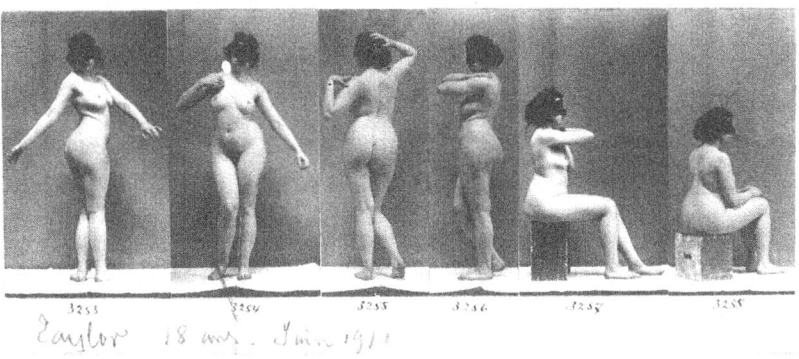

Figure 3. Paul Richer, *Mme Taylor, 18 years old*, c. 1911. Archives photographiques, Ecole nationale supérieure des Beaux-Arts, Paris.

the body-weight shifted onto one leg or the other. It was in these latter, the more free-style poses, that both the individual expression of the model, and a more overt sensuality, tended to emerge. It was also the moment when 'classical' poses were often introduced, probably at Richer's request; these could serve as aesthetic *aides-mémoire* for artists, as well as for anatomical comparison with examples from classical art. Here again, the gendered differentiation of pose becomes most clearly apparent. Male models adopt assertively active, sporting or pugilistic poses, women take more coquettish Venus-inspired standing poses, or passively supine reclining ones.

In the case of Mme Taylor (fig. 3) and several other female models, a mask is worn. Even in a 'scientific' context the mask is an accessory dangerously sited at the potentially transgressive boundary between disguise and revelation. Far from anonymizing the model, the mask eroticizes, making her nudity more obviously 'unnatural' by emphasizing her condition as unclothed, as naked. The mask — especially a fancy, black lace-edged mask — inevitably conjures up the sexually *risqué* world of the contemporary *bal masqué*[28] in which the mask (effective or not) licensed a carnivalesque inversion of normal conventions, including female sexual propriety. This is surely a complicit charade of anonymity played out between photographer and model in the photo-session, and has several layers of meanings. The mask invites, and sanctions, erotic display. In the immediate context, it 'hides' the woman's embarrassment before the intrusive camera/eye. In the broader context, given the ready mass circulation of such images, it creates the illusion of preserving the woman's identity and hence decency in this unnervingly indexical medium, which was already tainted by cheap pornography and the commercial exploitation of women's bodies.[29] Whereas in the artist's studio, the model's nudity is transient and relatively private, and the individual model often unrecognizable in the final art-work, the pose before the camera renders it permanent, public and endlessly repeatable. Relevant, too, is the hierarchy in modelling which gave the artist's model more cachet and status than that of the photographer. Within a discourse of heterosexual desire where the observer is male and the observed is female, the mask could also protect the photographer from the model's direct gaze (whether seductive or resistant) and hence, aided by the controlling, monocular view through the camera lens, to preserve his distance as both scientist and voyeur. In place of the mask, a simple length of cloth was sometimes used in the form of blind-fold; it could entirely cover the model's face.[30] Edward Steichen, who photographed many nudes in Paris, commented of his work '[o]n none of these is the face visible … Even professional models when they posed habitually insisted that their face be not seen'.[31] Some of Richer's female models wore no mask at all, suggesting the choice was left to the individual; all the photographs were apparently posed by professional women models. Not surprisingly, there are no examples of male models in masks: this male nudity confers neither shame nor moral compromise and, in its turn, Richer's athletic manhood solicits the viewer's unabashed, frankly admiring gaze.

This brings us back to the issue of cropping and framing, and its function in minimizing the erotic. Most of Richer's photographs, and hence his figures, were printed to a standard format and cropped close to the extremities of the complete figure; thus the print surface was squarer for a figure with outstretched arms, or tall and narrow for a vertical side-view (see fig. 3).[32] Close-up shots were taken only occasionally by Richer (see n. 32), but in the prints from the chronophotographs, he and Londe often used enlargement to privilege key frozen movements in a sequence (see figs. 1 & 2). In cropping his own prints, Richer removed anything extraneous that might alter or undermine the work's scientific agenda. Surviving uncropped photographs reveal both this process and the unexpurgated actuality. The anatomy theatre setting is explicit; locating the naked body in an identifiable space and time (a clock appears above the model) makes it disturbingly intimate. Off-stage dramas in the uncropped photographs transform the terms of pictorial reference: by exposing the processes of mediation, the cool eye of science is transformed into an overtly voyeuristic one (fig. 4). A male colleague, possibly Albert Londe himself,[33] stands to the left, facing the camera and holding a garment with which to cover the model once the session is over. Fully clothed in formal bourgeois attire, a three-piece suit, collar, tie, handkerchief and fob-chain, with a cigarette in his lips, he stands dwarfed below the imposing raised arm of the huge *Gladiator* cast. The shocking contrast between male dress and female undress combines with the exposure of the photographic process to disrupt the normalization of pictorial nudity: the model is unavoidably *naked*.

The process of trimming aimed to eliminate the anecdotal or narrative. While Richer's photographs are not chronophotographic and do not represent sequential moments of action, they inevitably invoke a narrative reading because of his serial method of posing and presenting them: the Western eye automatically starts top left and 'reads' the images like a text.[34] A narrative reading is affirmed by the evident relationship between photographer and model which can often be seen developing as the series 'unfolds'.[35] More so than in the rapidly-shot chronophotographs, the passage of time entailed in these photographs, and the changes of pose they record, convey, however silently, the dynamic processes of dialogue between Richer

30 *Paragraph*

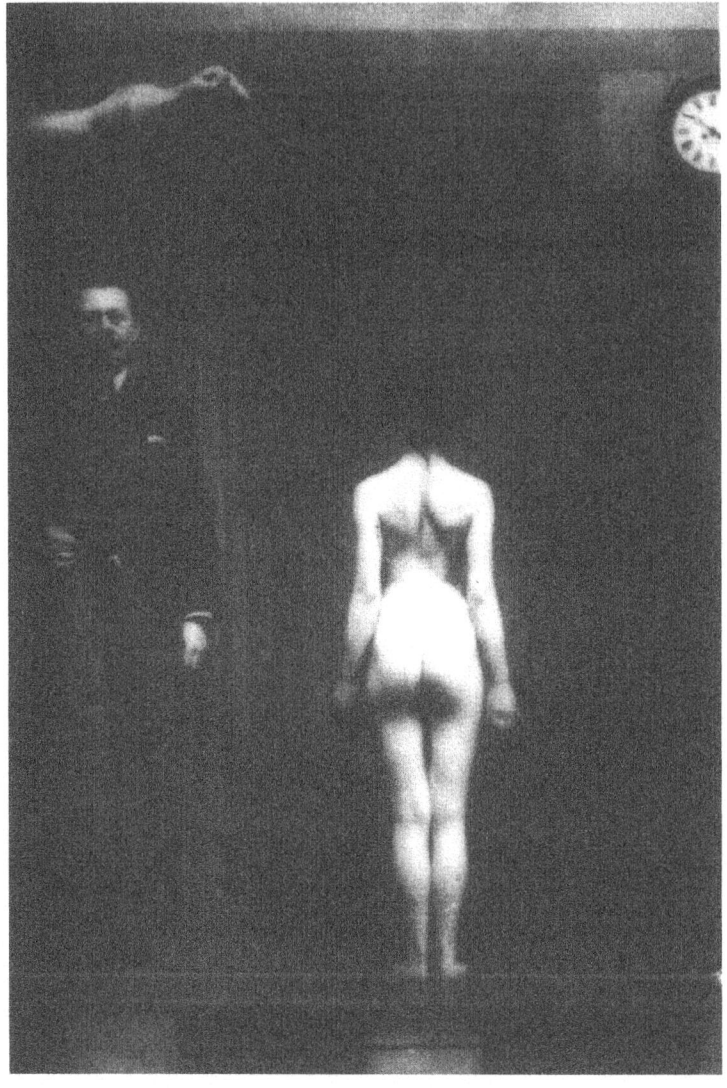

Figure 4. Paul Richer, *Study of a Female Model* (untrimmed), *c.* 1905-11. Archives photographiques, Ecole nationale supérieure des Beaux-Arts, Paris.

and model. Muybridge was far more blatant in his orchestration of a filmic narrative in his chronophotographs of human movement. Not only did he introduce gendered accessories (drapery, garments, urns, sporting equipment) often irrelevant to scientific study, but encouraged his female models to participate *à deux* in voyeuristic scenarios, executing movements of 'a rare extravagance' (Mannoni, 'La Photographie animée', 182) designed expressly to titillate. Sequential shots in chronophotography, as in cinematic narrative, drive forward both action and desire; like strip-tease, it creates anticipation, and leads the (male) spectator towards a climax, a fantasized *jouissance*. Although less explicitly staged, the momentum of an erotic narrative nevertheless emerges in several of Richer's photographic sessions with his female models.

Richer aimed to imbue the artistic nude with a new 'scientific' naturalism derived from the study of the live model. His photographs and resulting anatomical studies of the nude were intended to avoid the tired, classical conventions of academic 'chic'. 'For the aesthetic idea of beauty we have substituted the scientific notion of perfection' he wrote in 1903. Richer's teaching at the Ecole des Beaux-Arts, where he was anatomy professor from 1903, was no longer dominated by the study of the cadaver, by dissection, but 'addressed other sciences' which he outlined in his inaugural lecture. Through the history of art, Richer's courses consulted 'the long experience of artists'. 'We shall ask of *anthropology*', he said, 'the knowledge of races and the science of proportions; of *comparative anatomy*, the differences which can accentuate the human type; and especially of *physiology*, the mechanics of movement' (*Leçon d'ouverture*). Unlike most of his fellow anthropologists, Richer's research into comparative male anatomy was limited almost exclusively to European ('Caucasian') men. The modern ideal body he sought to establish for artists had necessarily to be 'white': none of the Londe chronophotographs reproduced in Richer's *Nouvelle Anatomie artistique* were of the very few black models they had photographed.[36] The expression of Richer's views coincided with the rise in France of national physical education and body-building[37] — the homosocial world of sport. Nationalistic discourses of regeneration for manly health and a superior French race simultaneously provided the opportunity for male bonding and for overt appreciation of the male body. Narcissistic, voyeuristic and potentially homoerotic interest was given legitimacy in the new domains of fitness and hygiene on the one hand, and in the emulation of respectable classical prototypes on the other.[38]

Richer's male models were very carefully selected. Historically, the most sought-after artist's models were soldiers and pugilists, who often turned to professional modelling. Richer discouraged his fine art students from using professional artists' models who through habit lapsed, he felt, into predictable poses which rendered them immobile. Instead he encouraged students to find amateur male models in fairs where weight-lifters performed, or in the circus where acrobats and clowns could provide genuine examples of the well-developed body. Sporting events like football were a good source of young male models, well developed and agile hence able to engage in the most varied and even violent movements. Being fresh and untutored, such models were more natural and vigorous. Historic exemplars of the male anatomical body studied at the Ecole were also athletic or militaristic: prototypes from classical sculpture like *The Wrestlers*, or the *Fighting Gladiator* — which, since the mid-eighteenth century, had been the ideal in physique and proportions which anatomy students were taught to emulate. A cast of the latter was, as we have seen, kept in the anatomy theatre, and it was also available there in print form. Jean-Galbert Salvage's publication, *Anatomie du Gladiator combatant, applicable aux beaux-arts* (Paris, 1812) analysed, in a series of coloured anatomical prints of the *Gladiator*, the underlying flayed form and skeleton of this ideal warrior. Among Richer's sporting models were, as we have seen, Charcot's son, Jean-Baptiste, who posed naked (except for shoes, socks and suspenders) playing football for one of the sheets of 'exercices variés'. Thus Richer profited from his friends' and colleagues' 'aptitudes and anatomies' as Charcot *fils* reported. He added that Richer 'compared and contrasted us, muscular intellectuals, to the beautiful professional athletes he collected in the fairgrounds or public places who served as his models' (cited in Mathon, 160).

Symptomatic of this interest, in 1900 Richer collaborated with Marey to produce an official visual and statistical record of the athletes and their exercises at the Olympic games, a report commissioned by the State Committee of Hygiene and Physiology and published in 1901. As extraneous intimate detail in the untrimmed anatomy theatre photographs suggests, the appearance of items like shoes, socks and suspenders in the chronophotographs of Charcot personalizes them, distinguishing this set from those of professional nude models.[39] Equally, the shots by Richer of athletes, with their *ad hoc* outdoor setting and often incomplete backdrops, lack the pictorial neutrality both of the Londe's chronophotographs and Richer's cropped photographs made at the Ecole. In *Singrossi nu, de face* (fig. 5) Richer stood the athlete in the first of the formal poses used in his Ecole photographs, with lowered arms and palms open towards the camera. Here the athlete bears the signs of an unfamiliar nudity which make him appear more thoroughly 'naked'. The white imprint from his sandals signal their removal, as does the 'negative' left by his sports clothes, where white flesh contrasts with the dark tan from mid-thigh down, and on his arms and face. Referring to his absent clothes, these

Masculinity and Muscularity: Dr Paul Richer and Modern Manhood   33

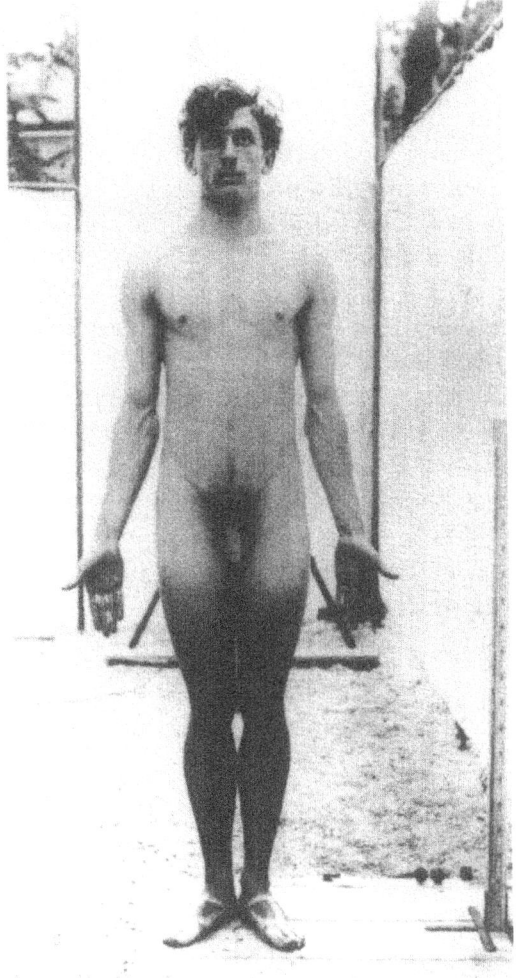

Figure 5. Paul Richer, *Singrossi nude, frontal view*, 1900. Archives photographiques, Ecole nationale supérieure des Beaux-Arts, Paris.

imprints increase the photo's indexicality and eroticize the body: the observer's neutrality gives way to an imaginary rehearsal of the athlete robing and disrobing.

Like many artists, Richer kept a *carnet* (notebook) of his favourite models, one end male, the other female, noting their name, age and address; this was separate from the formal statistical evidence on the *fiches*. His *carnet* re-affirms that Richer was far from neutral in his selection of models; he made personal notes on those he photographed listing the physical qualities he admired in them: 'good proportions, straight legs, pelvis tilted forward, small, blonde, rounded thorax, beautiful arms and legs …' (cited in Mathon, 160). The measurements Richer took aimed at establishing the perfect human morphology based on a 'mean' derived from hundreds of European men or women, and which would result in a modern aesthetic canon. Yet the body proportions he sought through scientific study of nature were based on ideal artistic proportions: following the Antique, his ideal modern body was seven and a half heads. Richer's anthropometric studies of contemporary nudes, however, produced contradictory results: he finally concluded that there were as many human types as there were 'races'.

Richer's male *anatomies*, then, are by no means ordinary, normal specimens: whether driven by notions of physical beauty or scientific perfection, anatomy, or morphology, his work inscribes particular notions of the ideal body which set certain 'better' bodies apart from other 'inadequate' bodies. His male models were all physically trained and developed: body-builders, boxers, soldiers, acrobats, all athletes of one form or another, and all skilled in the use of the body and its public performance. Their poses locate them in a classical tradition of the sporting or militaristic male body, whether directly, through Antique sculpture, or indirectly through its reinterpretation in artistic anatomies. Where, in his role at the Ecole, Richer's brief was to establish modern bodily 'perfection', at La Salpêtrière, with Albert Londe in his role as photographer, they were more overtly concerned with the medical 'norm'. Arguably, the two functions coincided in the healthy athletic male body produced in their *Atlas*, embodied in an idealized, white Caucasian manhood.

It is important, then, to recognize the extent to which fine art practices and signifiers informed Richer's production of 'scientific' photographs of the body, and hence predisposed these images to conform to historical, essentially greco-roman paradigms of ideal manhood: sporting and militaristic paradigms of the built body which underpinned images of the anatomical as much as the 'artistic' body.

Reference to a classicizing past serves to historicize, aestheticize and depersonalize the 'raw' nakedness of the male body, rendering the audience-experience of individual men undressed before the camera less immediate, shocking or comic (we have seen exceptions). Thanks to their physical prowess Richer's male models rarely seem disempowered or objectified by such scrutiny, but rather celebrate this act of exposure. Experienced in bodily self-presentation, these men perform their nudity. Their built bodies are the tools of their trade, displayed like costumes or the armour of war, with pride rather than shame, and even with a vanity more typically identified with the feminine. The issues of sexual shame and women's bodies as sexual commodities are, by contrast, ever-present for Richer's female models. The degree of complicity between photographer and model influences the effect of the model's nudity, whether male or female. Thus the physical beauty and self-assurance of a complicit model often combines with a conventionally artistic pose to render the resulting image more acceptable, and more comfortable to look at than one in which a model's hostility and resistance is palpably felt. In some sense a process of seduction takes place, the photographer responding to the model as an individual subjectivity rather than merely an object of scientific curiosity.[40]

In addition to the social tensions relating to the model's sex (and of course the photographer's), the most notable and obvious distinction in this respect is one of choice: those models who agree to be photographed (whether naked or not) and those coerced into modelling — as was often the case with patients displaying medical symptoms. Thus the medical photographer Félix Méheux's unidentified subject[41] resists submission to the photographer even though he literally 'looks down' on her; she refuses complicity, exhibiting her hostility despite — or perhaps because of — avoiding eye contact with the camera/viewer. In the first category, the complicit, are found the colleagues, students, soldiers, professional artists' models, athletes and circus performers: the few convinced of the scientific value of their collaboration, or the majority, expressly paid for their services. The second category, the coerced, usually comprised the 'under' classes — the poor, the ill, the foreign: the marginalized others in contrast to whom normality was defined. In our present scenario, these were the subjects Richer drew and Londe (or Méheux) photographed at the hospital, rather than those studied at the Ecole des Beaux-Arts.

Whether normal or pathological, the 'truths' of naked manhood are further legitimized by its performance within a conventional scientific framework: the anthropometric study, the measurement of bodily proportions, the diagnostic tool, the record of symptoms, or deformity, or war-wounds. The objective rationale for this study of the male body is a discourse of anthropo-medical enquiry to be deployed in articulating hierarchies of social order; these processes are sanctioned by professional distance embodied in the dual authority of the doctor/photographer.

Degrees of familiarity affect the relations of the protagonists (photographer and model) and hence of the image and its viewers. In this sense it is important to distinguish between the experience of nakedness or near-nakedness in all-male communities—school, sporting, military, bathing—and that of naked women, as models, mostly among clothed men: the photographers, doctors, artists. At this date there is not a single rationale for respectable female undress equivalent to the many for male nudity. Furthermore (and regardless of gender), the boundary between disinterested objectivity and obsessive voyeurism is fragile. Although often at odds with the 'truth' or in Barthes's phrase, 'evidential force' of the photographic image, a classicizing pose for the live anatomical nude does help smooth its physical and discursive irregularities: pose and performance provide a framework to 'clothe' the naked body and legitimize voyeuristic scrutiny.

Sometimes in photographic anatomies the model's body was shaved, or partially shaved, ostensibly the better to distinguish bone and muscle structure. Yet, equally, depilating the male body rendered it closer to pure sculpted form in the classical idiom, closer to the shaved and oiled bodies for which the Greeks were admired—and, more problematically, similar to the smooth skin associated with the 'available' feminine body. Tagg delineates the process by which the observed are constituted as 'passive (...) "feminised" — objects of knowledge ...'; in a passage fired with eloquence he states: '[s]ubjected to a scrutinising gaze, forced to emit signs, yet cut off from the command of meaning, such groups were represented as, and wishfully rendered, incapable of speaking, acting or organising for themselves'. He argues that while as a strategy of control—through precision, measurement, calculation and proof—photographic documentation was not a great success, 'as a strategy of representation its claims and their consequences seem to have gone largely unchallenged' (*The Burden of Representation*, 11).

Yet the range of subjects photographed and the reasons behind it appear less monolithic and unified than this argument might suggest. Certainly the photographs themselves provoke complex and varied readings in which notions of health as well as normality are under negotiation, and where the gender, social position and ethnic origin of the subject crucially inflect how we are invited to read them. Whereas medical photographs at this date mostly offer us fragments representing the whole, and thus patently the silent (if often resistant) oppressed, Richer's anthropometrical studies require the whole for us to read the harmony of its parts. While in some respects his male models are rendered passive, in others they remain active agents:

not just scientific specimens, their virile performance of an athletic perfection renders their bodies eloquent as subjects empowered but also as objects of desire. Differently coerced, perhaps, by even the slightest scent of power, these bodies aim to be victors rather than vanquished. The various ambitions of Richer's comparative anatomy, his aesthetic ethnography, may have been a failure, but its objectives position his enterprise in the vanguard of twentieth-century human engineering, whether Taylorism, or the sinister spread of Western eugenics and social engineering. Yet its more hidden meanings — in the photographs' homosocial and even homoerotic engagement with the (male) viewer — the binary empowered/oppressed breaks down. Instead, these images threaten to subvert (invert) the dominant European norms of ideal heterosexual masculinity.

ANTHEA CALLEN
University of Nottingham

NOTES

1 *The Burden of Representation: Essays on Photographies and Histories* (London, Macmillan, 1988), 5. I am grateful to Michael Hatt for his thoughtful comments on this essay.
2 See e.g., Tagg, or Jonathan Crary, *Techniques of the Observer: On Vision and Modernity in the Nineteenth Century* (Cambridge, MA and London, MIT, 1992), chapter 4 and *passim*.
3 *Etudes cliniques sur la grande hystérie ou hystéro-épileptique*, préface du professeur Charcot (Paris, 1881).
4 A. Souques et H. Meige, 'Jean-Martin Charcot (1825–1893). Les Biographies médicales: Notes pour servir à l'histoire de la médecine et des grands médecins', *Revue médicale illustrée*, 13e année (1939), part I, 333; and see J.-F. Debord, 'De l'anatomie artistique à la morphologie', in J. Clair (editor), *L'Ame au corps: arts et sciences 1793–1993* (Paris, Réunion des Musées Nationaux, 1993), 108–9.
5 *Rapport au Conseil Supérieur par le Directeur de l'Ecole au commencement de l'année scolaire 1874–75* (Paris, Imprimerie National, 1875), 9, Archives de l'Ecole nationale supérieure des Beaux-Arts, Archives Nationales AJ/52/440.
6 M.-M. Duval and A. Bical, *L'Anatomie des maîtres* (Paris, 1890), 3, my emphasis.
7 In 1873, Duval was elected a member of the Société d'Anthropologie. Broca was also a follower of Darwin and founded the French school of anthropology in 1861; in 1876 he established the Ecole Publique d'Anthropologie in Paris. On Broca's death, Duval succeeded him, in 1880, as Director of the

Laboratoire d'Anthropologie in Paris, where he led research in comparative embryology, the laws of development and of heredity. See Etienne Roc, 'Professeur Mathias Duval', *Les Hommes d'Aujourd'hui*, (Paris, n.d. [1886]), 6:273, n.p. [1]. Richer, another Darwinist, was also associated with the Société d'Anthropologie; see Richer, *L'Anatomie dans l'Art, Proportions du corps humain, canons artistique et canons scientifiques* (Paris, 1893), esp. 32–6, and his *Leçon d'Ouverture, 25 November 1903* (Paris, Ecole Nationale et Spéciale des Beaux-Arts, 1903).

8   See for example A. Scharf, *Art and Photography* (Harmondsworth, Penguin, 1974), 368 (and *passim*), where Richer is described as a follower of Marey; on Marey, Richer and Londe, see Marta Braun, *Picturing Time: The Work of Etienne-Jules Marey* (Chicago and London, University of Chicago Press, 1992), 85.

9   L. Mannoni, 'La Photographie animée du nu: l'œuvre de Marey et Demenÿ', in *L'Art du nu au XIXe siècle: le photographe et son modèle* (Paris, Hazan/Bibliothèque nationale de France, 1997), 178 and 182; Marey, unlike Demenÿ, only photographed male nudes. See also Braun, 66–7 and *passim*, for detailed discussion of his collaboration with Marey.

10 The volume was subtitled *Description des formes extérieures du corps humain au repos et dans les principaux mouvements*.

11 Richer remained ambivalent about photography as the best means to illustrate his anatomical treatises, with the exception of his studies of movement recorded in Londe's chronophotographs.

12 See the photograph of Londe using this equipment in 1894, probably at Marey's *Station physiologique*, reproduced in Braun, 90, plate 51.

13 See J.W. Douard, 'E.-J. Marey's Visual Rhetoric and the Graphic Decomposition of the Body', *Studies in the History and Philosophy of Science* (London, 1995), 26:2, 175–204.

14 Douard (196) paraphrasing Bergson's critique of Marey (Douard's emphasis; and cf. Braun, 278–82), and see Douard's analysis, 195ff: Marey makes the 'assumption that movement ... is composed of discriminable fragments, despite appearances to the contrary' (196).

15 Catherine Mathon, in 'Le Corps modelisé', in *L'Art du nu au XIXe siècle: le photographe et son modèle* (Paris, Hazan/Bibliothèque nationale de France, 1997), 160, states that the three-volume *Atlas physiologique* (the original is now in the archives of the Ecole des Beaux-Arts), remained unpublished, as did Michel Poivert, in 'Variété et vérité du corps humain, l'esthétique de Paul Richer', also in *L'Art du nu au XIXe siècle: le photographe et son modèle*, 164; however Braun (85), suggests the *Atlas physiologique* was indeed published in 1895 by Richer and Londe as *Atlas d'anatomie artistique*; I have been unable to locate this publication.

16 I am using the 1924 edition: Richer, *Nouvelle Anatomie artistique, Tome III, Cours supérieur (suite): Physiologie, Attitudes et Mouvements* (Paris, Plon, 7e mille,

1924) plates 1–64. Braun, chapter 6, 228 ff, discusses Muybridge's efforts to enlist Marey's support for his own publications in the 1880s.

17 L. Mannoni, 182–3; he also cites as pertinent in this context the unconventional domestic circumstances of both Marey and Demenÿ, 182.

18 'Lancer le ballon avec le pied', twelve chronophotographic views plus three enlargements, c. 1893–4, reproduced in Richer (1921), edition 1924 (n. 16), plate 54.

19 Taylorism, the engineering of people, is discussed in relation to Marey and chronophotography in Braun, chapter 8, 336–40, 'Marey and the Organisation of Work'.

20 Charles Frémont's 'Etudes de chaudronnerie', *Bulletin de la Société des Ingénieurs Civils de France* (November 1887), cited and paraphrased by Richer in his discussion of 'Quelques mouvements professionnels', in *Nouvelle Anatomie artistique* (1924), 168. Marey's figures, unlike Richer's, were clothed. Two of Marey and Frémont's photographs of hot iron forgers at work, dated 1894, are reproduced by Braun, 325, plate 176. Braun distinguishes Marey's interest in analysing the expenditure of energy, from Frémont's in the quality of tools and the men's skill in using them (324); see her chapter 8, 320 ff, 'Marey and the Organisation of Work'.

21 See the chronophotographs and superimposed exposures by Marey and Frémont of a forger's hammering actions reproduced in Braun, 325, plates 176A and B.

22 Reproduced in Braun, 90, plate 51. The photograph may well have been taken by Richer. Seen in comparison to other photographs showing Marey's *Station physiologique* (see Braun, 105, plate 61), it is not obvious that Londe's set was located there (despite the seated man in this photograph of Londe being identified as Marey by Braun).

23 The same man performed the athletic exercises in the chronophotographs reproduced in Richer (1924), see plates 22–4, 28, 29, 30.

24 In the Sallé the model is more youthful, with longer, darker hair; in the later chronophotographs, where emphasis is on the body, the lower class facial 'characteristics' Sallé chose to stress are less prominent. See my analysis of Sallé's model in Callen, 'The Body and Difference: Anatomy Training at the Ecole des Beaux-Arts in Paris in the later nineteenth century', *Art History*, 20: 1 (1977) 42–3.

25 See also Anthea Callen, 'Doubles and Desire: Anatomies of Masculinity in the Later Nineteenth Century', *Art History*, 26:5 (2003) forthcoming.

26 The insistently phallic and eroticized meanings which appear so blatant in the material practices of photography are not explored in depth here.

27 Albert Londe, 'De l'utilité de certains documents photographiques pour l'art et les artistes', *Bulletin de la Société française de photographie* (1901), XVII, 318.

28 See for example Manet's notorious painting of the equally notorious *Bal masqué à l'Opéra* (1873–4, o/c, 60 × 73 cm, National Gallery of Art, Washington, D.C.); for a background to the ball and the painting, see *Manet 1832–1883* (Paris, Réunion des musées nationaux, 1983), no. 138, 349–5.

29 Even within the Ecole; see the incident from 1893 recorded by Mathon, 155–6, in which the mother of two models complained of an Ecole student taking unofficial photographs of them; the Ecole Director also prohibited the circulation amongst the staff of a photographic album of female nudes made by Duval's anatomy demonstrator, Edward Cuyer.

30 See Richer, 'Pasquiou, 21 ans, modèle féminin masqué', 1907, reproduced in *L'Art du nu au XIXe siècle: Le photographe et son modèle* (Paris, Hazan/BN), 128, cat.243, plate 143.

31 E. Steichen, *A Life in Photography*, New York, 1963, quoted by Hélène Pinet, 'Le masque, l'anonymat du mystère', in *L'Art du nu au XIXe siècle: Le photographe et son modèle* (Paris, Hazan/BN), 124.

32 See for example 'Mlle Gabrielle Vasseur', photographs 2313–2327, 1910, reproduced in Callen (n.24), plate 15: compare photos 2322 and 2315. Close-up shots, giving a bust portrait with the model partially clothed, were used for four photographs on this sheet, 2324–2327.

33 I have not yet seen a photographic portrait of Londe with which to compare this; comparison with his appearance in the earlier portrait in André Brouillet's painting, *Leçon de Mardi* (1887), does make the present identification with Londe plausible.

34 Not all the chronophotographs were taken or presented in a left to right sequence; when they were not, the sequence of movement is much harder to 'read' than in those which do. See for example, Richer (1924), plate 50.

35 This is especially notable in the series of photographs of Sou Gicquel (1909) reproduced in Callen 'The Body and Difference', 49, plate 13; see also plate 15.

36 Richer (1924), plates 1–64.

37 On the rise of body-building in France, see Tamar Garb, *Bodies of Modernity: Flesh and Figure in Fin-de-siècle France* (London, Thames and Hudson, 1998), chapter 2; and more generally, Kenneth R. Dutton, *The Perfectible Body: The Western Ideal of Physical Development* (London, Cassell, 1995).

38 See 'La Beauté moderne: Milo and Milan', a photograph of two body-builders posed after the classical statue *The Wrestlers*, and reproduced in *La Culture Physique* (January 1905), illustrated in Garb, 54.

39 Of course wearing shoes would make sense when kicking a football; however these are the lace-up leather shoes and suspenders of a bourgeois professional man, not sporting or working class attire. The degree of hilarity they provoke is directly related to their incongruity.

40 See the photographs reproduced in Callen 'The Body and Difference', plates 12–15, and compare the male model, plate 11.
41 See for example, the resentful, challenging look of the female patient (who refuses to look at the camera) in Félix Méheux, 'Scars and bone lesions due to syphilis' [1884–96], Service du Professeur Fournier, reproduced in M. Sicard, R. Pujade and D. Wallach, *A corps et à raison: photographies médicales 1840–1920* (Turin, Marval, 1995), plate 44.

Kitsch and Classicism: The Male Nude in the Twentieth Century

The history of the male nude in twentieth-century photography is a peculiarly complex one. High art influences and others from mass culture — often mass culture in its shadier aspects — are intricately intertwined.

From the beginnings of photography, people who used the camera were fascinated by the possibilities it offered for depicting the naked human figure, both in action and at rest. However, their feelings about this category of subject matter were highly ambivalent. On the one hand, photography seemed like a God-given aid to artists. Models need no longer hold tiring poses for hours at a stretch — the camera would provide all the information that was required. The ageing Delacroix, for example, immediately seized upon these possibilities, and commissioned photographs of male nudes from the photographer Eugène Durieu. Soon a trade sprang up in photographs for the use of artists — among the photographers who supplied this material were the Italian Guglielmo Marconi and the mysterious Calavas, a French photographer known for proof sheets showing both male and female figures in a variety of poses. No prints of single figures from these sheets seem to be known. These photographs invariably show the models adopting poses already familiar from the academic studio practice of the day.

They are thus in sharp contrast to the very different photographs made by photographic experimentalists such as Eadweard Muybridge and Etienne-Jules Marey, whose aim was to discover truths about the movement of human beings and animals. Their success with these ventures finished by demolishing many academic conventions, though even here there was a kind of 'classical' residue, which is particularly clearly visible in Muybridge's photographs of young wrestlers and in similar photographs made by the American painter Thomas Eakins.

Throughout the nineteenth century photographs of nude males were much rarer than similar images of nude females. Though the study of the male nude remained one of the staples of the thorough training that was still given to aspiring artists — and this was, indeed, one of the reasons why female painters and sculptors remained at a disadvantage, since it was not considered proper for them to look at completely naked men, even for strictly professional purposes — the male nude was regarded as more threatening than images of the opposite gender. One reason for this, perhaps indeed the chief reason, was that male physiology made the sexual component abundantly visible. This was true even when the male genitalia were in a state of repose.

Photographers, in addition to discovering that photographs could be a useful tool in an artist's studio, also made a discovery that was much more significant from a social point of view. This was that the camera and what it did added a new dimension to erotic representations. The reason is obvious: the photographic image was not simply a picture of something — it was a slice cut through time, and offered a guarantee that what was represented had actually been enacted in front of the camera lens.

From the 1850s onwards there sprang up a huge trade in pornographic photographs. At first these were single nudes, with many more females than males, and little distinction between what was made for 'artistic' purposes and what for purely erotic ones. By the 1870s, helped by the rapid progress of photographic technology, photographers were able to make images of couples and groups engaged in the act of love. In the majority of these photographs the emphasis is still on the female participant rather than on her partner, and trouble is often taken to conceal the features of the male actors in these pornographic scenarios.

In the 1890s, however, European and North American society underwent a subtle shift — a shift which was not concerned with photography as such but with a re-coding of sexual definitions and self-definitions. A number of men, mostly well-off and well-educated, began to see themselves as members of a separate group or class — as 'uranians' who responded sexually to members of their own gender. The camera served some of these as an instrument for defining their own sexual tastes and for communicating these to like-minded spectators. One of the most celebrated examples is a German aristocrat named Wilhelm von Gloeden (1856–1931) who moved to Taormina in Sicily and began to photograph the handsome local youths (fig. 1).

The 1890s saw a strong revival of interest in the classical past, and especially in the Ancient Greeks. Von Gloeden can loosely be defined as a Symbolist photographer — his aim was to recreate scenes from an imagined Greek golden age. The emphasis was not on the mature male, but on the languidly ripening adolescent and it was teenagers rather than young men who formed the majority of von Gloeden's models. A number of other photographers of the period followed his

Figure 1. Wilhelm von Gloeden, *Two Sicilian Youths*, c. 1990.

lead, among them his own cousin Wilhelm von Plüschow and the American F. Holland Day. The rise of gay consciousness since the 1960s has brought with it a revival of interest in the work of von Gloeden and his associates, and their work, once semi-clandestine, now circulates in mass-market editions.

The same period saw a development which I think was in the long run much more significant — the beginning of the modern cult

Kitsch and Classicism: The Male Nude in the Twentieth Century   45

of bodybuilding. The key figure was a near-contemporary of von Gloeden's, the celebrated strongman Eugen Sandow (1867–1925). Sandow belongs to mass-culture not high culture. His impresario in the United States, where he made his reputation and with it his fortune, was Florenz Ziegfield Jr., one of the founders of modern mass-market entertainment. Under Ziegfield's management, Sandow caused a sensation at the Chicago World's Columbian Exhibition of 1894 and was a major celebrity thereafter. The photographs of him made by Napoleon Sarony and others sold in their thousands. These photographs are often based directly on Greco-Roman prototypes. In many of them Sandow figures as the demi-god Hercules, wearing a leopard-skin loin cloth (fig. 2).

Sandow's success triggered a wave of popular interest in the muscular male body. He was not the only exponent of physical strength whose photographs sold in quantity at this period. In particular, there was a great fashion for wrestlers and strongmen in Russia, and many 'real photo' postcards survive to prove it. Among the major stars of the wrestling sub-culture were two muscular Estonians, Georg Lurich (1876–1920) and the long-lived George Hackenschmidt (1878–1968), a powerful wrestler of Estonian-Swedish descent who finished his life with a British passport.

These wrestlers appealed equally to men and to women. They did not carry with them the whiff of brimstone which was attached to the activities of von Gloeden and his associates. True, the photographs which were the medium of their success only occasionally showed them completely naked, and then almost invariably with their backs turned to the audience. There is just one photograph of Lurich posing as Hercules in which he appears completely naked, without even a classical figleaf to cover his genitalia.

The taste for massively muscular men did not survive World War I. It was replaced by a liking for smoother, less rugged physiques, typified by film stars such as Rudolph Valentino and Ramon Novarro. During the inter-war period photographs of nude males nevertheless continued to be made, some by ranking photographers such as the American George Platt Lynes, others in connection with the naturist movement which flourished in Germany during the years of the Weimar Republic.

In the United States, which was to become the new epicentre of the cult of the body, a major revival of interest in bodybuilders and bodybuilding did not take place until the end of World War II. When it revived, it did so with a vengeance. The place where it

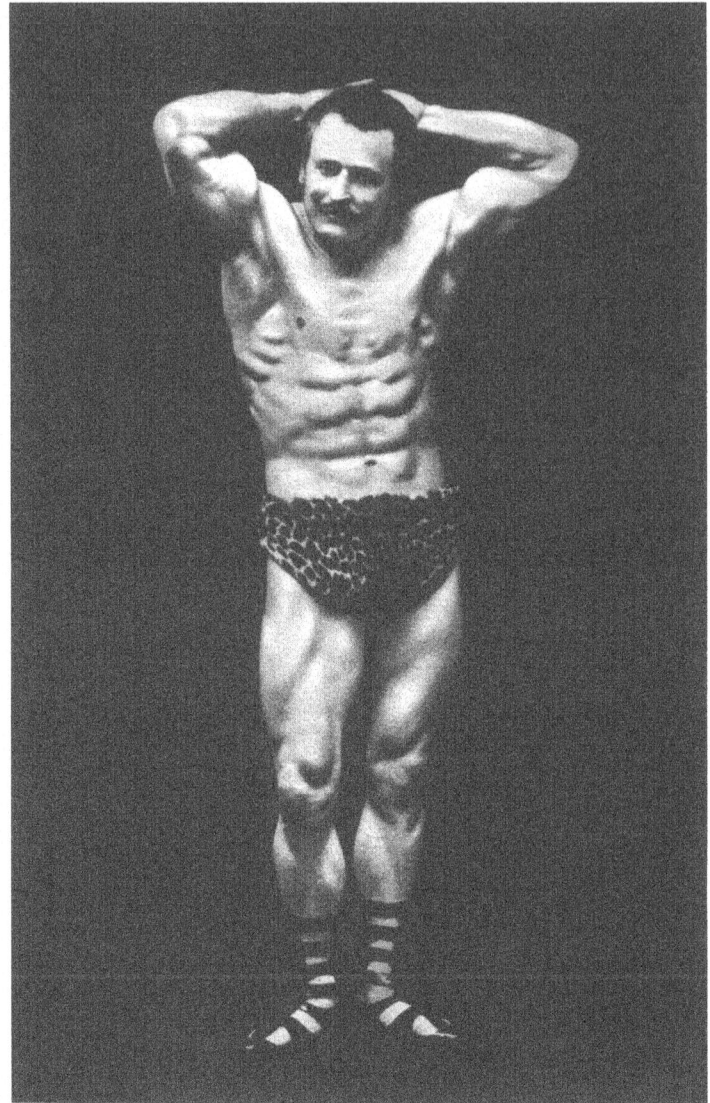

Figure 2. *Eugen Sandow*, full length study, *c.* 1910.

happened was not in New York, the newly anointed capital of the world of contemporary art, but in California, where Los Angeles was the capital of the movie industry. California attracted handsome men who hoped to become movie stars. It also attracted drifters of all kinds, in love with the purely physical life. And in the wake of these came a group of homosexual photographers — among them Bob Mizer of the grandly named Athletic Model Guild, and Bruce Bellas (1909–1974), whose working name was 'Bruce of L.A.'. These catered to a largely clandestine trade in pictures of nude men.

Bruce became a central figure in the world where bodybuilding, the movies and the trade in homosexual erotica met and mingled. He had begun his adult life as a schoolmaster in Nebraska, making photographs of naked men for his own gratification, but also sometimes passing them on to others of the same sexual persuasion. His models were usually hitchhikers picked up on the road, photographed in motel rooms or in the open air. A large number of these early photographs survived in an album Bruce made for himself, and were recently published by the German publisher Janssen under the title *The Naked Heartland*. They are much more informal than most of the images that Bruce made when he turned professional. He became involved in a small scandal, lost his job, moved to California in 1947 and took out a business licence for his California photographic studio in 1948.

He seems to have become aware almost immediately of the opportunities which the new body building studios offered to him. However, he also ran up against restrictions—it was, for example, at that time illegal to send images of naked men with completely visible genitalia through the post—though these were what his most eager customers really wanted. Bruce found ways of getting around these curbs. He would, for example, notify the buyers already known to him in a certain district or region that he would be present at such-and-such a hotel or motel on a given day or days, and would then sell forbidden merchandise out of his suitcase. These travels also gave him the opportunity to recruit new models and find new outdoor locations throughout the west and southwest of America—anywhere, where the light was strong and the climate reliable.

A very prolific photographer, Bruce made pictures of any personable young man who came his way and could be persuaded to pose (fig. 3). Some of these later, commercial photographs were informal shots very like those he had made in Nebraska. Others used props to satisfy the fantasies of his customers (fig. 4). These were often, in turn, based on what Hollywood was then putting out. It was the great age of the Western, for example, and also the time when Marlon Brando made a massive impact with the biker film *The Wild Ones* (1953). Bruce's muscular subjects therefore appeared in association with motorcycles, or wearing cowboy hats and sometimes chaps—the latter had the advantage, when worn without jeans, of leaving the subject's genitalia clearly visible. On occasion, his models carried swords or spears, or

Figure 3. Bruce of L.A. (Bruce Bellas), *John Skaggs*, late 1950s.

leaned against classical plinths. The images show an intermingling of popular culture and half-digested historical references.

The classical references were especially significant because Bruce's career coincided with the reinvention of the so-called 'peplum' movie. The first ambitious films featuring classical and biblical themes had been made at the very beginnings of the cinema industry. The earliest version of *Quo Vadis* was made in France in 1901, followed by others in 1908, 1912, 1913 and 1924.

Kitsch and Classicism: The Male Nude in the Twentieth Century   49

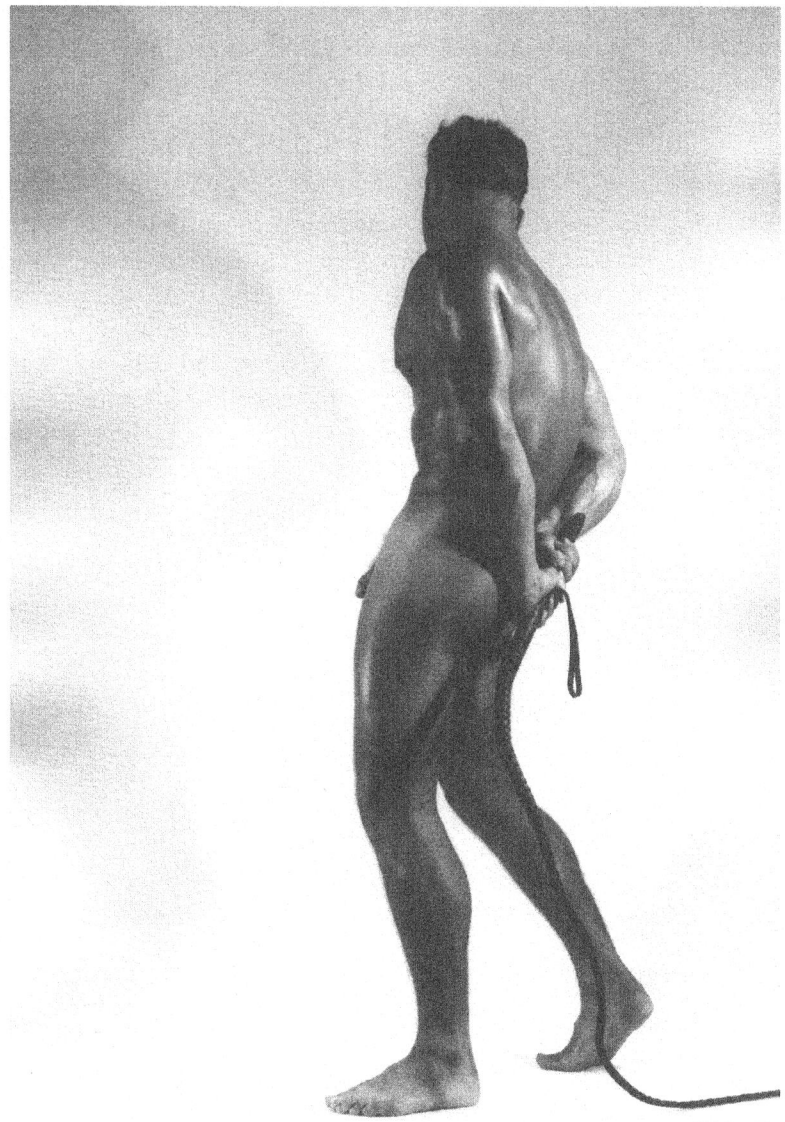

Figure 4. Bruce of L.A., *Nude Bodybuilder with Whip*, 1960s.

In 1958, the spectacular Italian-made epic film *Hercules*, starring the American bodybuilding champion Steve Reeves, took audiences in the United States by storm and triggered a cycle of movies with musclemen as heroes which continued till the beginning of the 1970s. Many of the men who modelled nude for Bruce and his peers appeared in these films, sometimes in starring roles. Bruce made a few photographs of Reeves himself, for example, though never any that showed him entirely nude. Less inhibited was the model who went by the name of 'Ed Fury' (fig. 5). Frequently photographed by Bruce, he was also the hero of four Italian-made classical films shot in the early 1960s.

Stills from these films — often better and more dramatic than the movies they were connected with — are close in style to some of Bruce's photographic compositions. They differ from the work put out by the Californian homoerotic studios in two respects. First, the subjects are just a little bit more clothed. Second, the sado-masochistic content, already present in some of Bruce's photographs, is much more overt. In stressing the physical sufferings of their muscular protagonists, the peplum movies and the publicity material issued in connection with them were in fact reverting to venerable traditions in European art. The direct ancestors of these still are the spectacular scenes of martyrdom painted by the great artists of the Baroque for churches in Rome and Antwerp.

Figure 5. Ed Fury in *Ursus*, *c*. 1964.

Bruce's work is significant in several respects. His more considered images were well-known to the new generation of gay photographers who emerged in the 1970s and preferred to carve out positions for themselves in the art world rather than in that of popular culture. This seems to have been especially the case with the most celebrated of them, Robert Mapplethorpe. There are close parallels for some of Mapplethorpe's best known images to be found in Bruce's output. A case in point is the famous Mapplethorpe self-portrait which shows the subject with the handle of a bullwhip pushed into his anus. There is a very similar image by Bruce where the model, considerably more muscular than Mapplethorpe, simply holds the whip behind his back, but in close proximity to his buttocks (fig. 4). These resemblances have tended to pull Bruce, posthumously, into the realm of high art, and his prints, which once changed hands for very small sums, are now increasingly expensive and sought after by collectors.

Bruce also has another role, however. Paradoxically, he, and the camp gay world he inhabited, became the guardians of classical ideas and values at a time when these were scorned elsewhere. If the male figure is now once again a vehicle for creating expressive artworks, and especially through its encounters with photography, this is largely due to Bruce and the other gay photographic studios of the 1940s, 1950s and 1960s. They in turn possessed an ancestry in popular culture which can be traced back at least as far as the early triumphs of Eugen Sandow. Which amounts to saying that the male nude has played a significant role in mass-culture almost since it began.

EDWARD LUCIE-SMITH

Morimura/Duchamp: Image Recycling and Parody

Whether appreciative or critical in their intent, re-visiting and re-visualizing the archives of Western cultural imagery are a declared focus of contemporary art practice and central to the work of Japanese artist Yasumasa Morimura. Using photography and his own body, Morimura re-images some of art history's so-called masterpieces — like Manet's 'Olympia', Rembrandt's 'The Anatomy Lesson of Professor Nicolaes Tulp' or Goya's 'The Third of May' — as well as images drawn from popular culture such as stills of female movie stars like Marilyn Monroe, Jodie Foster, Vivien Leigh or Marlene Dietrich.[1] He also plays on artistic styles as in his 'Mother (Judith II)' (1991) which is part of a series on Judith and Holofernes and portrays the figures à la Cranach revisualized in the style of Arcimboldo.[2]

Morimura's 'Doublonnage (Marcel)' (1988) appropriates Marcel Duchamp's photographic self-representations as Rrose Sélavy from the early 1920s. Within the range of Morimura's photoworks, 'Doublonnage' is special in so far as it refers to a piece of work that itself intentionally plays with cultural imagery. Moreover, Morimura comments on an artistic gesture which has paradoxically been neglected by American discourses that term Duchamp the paternal origin of postmodernism and define that postmodernism as antimasculinist.[3] By playing upon an image that itself occupies a somewhat striking position in art history, Morimura invites the critic to ask what kind of effect this might have on our reading both of his work and of Duchamp's; even more so, as Morimura inevitably finds himself situated within contemporary discourses that celebrate multiculturalism, but differ in acknowledging multicultural artistic practices in terms of 'minority art' on the one hand, and as a challenge to the dominant politics of representation on the other.[4]

From a feminist perspective, Duchamp's 'Rrose Sélavy' portrait has been analysed as an intervention into ideas of photographic 'truth', of gender as a stable and coherent category, and of authorship as it underlies the traditional canon of art history (see Jones, *Postmodernism*). Morimura's 'Doublonnage' shifts and complicates the level of that analysis by altering the image, employing modes of doubling and introducing ethnicity. What is at stake here, is the signification of the male body as the site of its own interrogation and the ways in which this is linked to the concept of the artist/author as a masculine instance. It seems worth, therefore, doing a close reading of 'Doublonnage (Marcel)' through Duchamp's Rrose Sélavy gesture, in order to explore the strategies that are at work in the production of meaning of those visual representations and how they are played out as a mode of de/constructing 'identity'. The idea is to provide an interrogation not of 'the "image" of the person, but (...) of the discursive and disciplinary place from which questions of identity are strategically and institutionally posed' that, as Homi K. Bhabha has argued, is exactly what is transformed in the postmodern perspective.[5]

The two terms 'image recycling' and 'parody' in my title, are meant to map the field within which Duchamp's and Morimura's work is to be situated. Sigrid Schade has argued, that the interplay of the circulation of images and their technical reproduction performs an institutional rhetoric that participates in the production of its own object of investigation.[6] The process of meaning production, as Schade states, involves the systems within which the images circulate and the technical means of recycling: that is, the institutional discourses and apparatuses which are processing the social meanings and within them — as an effect — the 'meaningful' subject (Schade, 'Charcot', 465). The recycling of images or icons of Art into and within contexts exterior to Art (like mass media and advertising) — and, one could add: back into Art — therefore, has its very precondition in the art historical *dispositif* itself which then makes recycling possible.

Parody is discussed as *the* postmodern strategy. It is theorized with regard to concepts of gender and sexual identities as performative acts[7] as much as to aesthetic practices. Linda Hutcheon, who has extensively worked towards a theory of parody, its poetics and politics, defines parody as a 'repetition with critical distance, which marks difference rather than similarity.'[8] According to Hutcheon, it is to be understood as a new form that 'develops out of the old, without really destroying it'; it operates 'as a method of inscribing continuity while permitting critical distance. It can (...) function as a conservative force in both retaining and mocking other aesthetic forms; but it is also capable of transformative power in creating new synthesis (...)' (Hutcheon, *A Theory of Parody*, 35, 20). Moreover, in that it 'seems to offer a perspective on the present and the past which allows an artist to speak *to* a discourse from *within* it, but without being totally recuperated by it', parody 'appears to have become (...) the mode of (...) the "ex-centric", of those who are marginalized by

54   *Paragraph*

a dominant ideology.'⁹ And therefore, it 'has certainly become a most popular and effective strategy of the other ex-centrics — of black, ethnic, gay, and feminist artists — trying to come to terms with and to respond, critically and creatively, to the still predominantly white, heterosexual, male culture in which they find themselves. For both artists and their audiences, parody sets up a dialogical relation between identification and distance' (Hutcheon, *A Poetics*, 35). Taking the former of those two set-ups — image recycling and parody — as the structural conditions of picture politics and the latter in terms of the appearance of images as potential subversion of those politics, we will now trace how they are interlinked and can be put to work in an interpretation of the artworks in question.

Rrose Sélavy has come to be known as Marcel Duchamp's female alter ego. She made her first appearance in Duchamp's semi-readymade 'Fresh Widow' in 1920 as a legal stamp of copyright — then still spelt with a simple 'r'. Later she became Rrose Sélavy spelt with double 'r' — being a pun on 'ars, c'est la vie', 'eros, c'est la vie' or 'arrose la vie'. Apart from other pseudonyms like 'Totor', 'M. Dee', 'Marcel Douxami', 'R. Mutt', or just 'Marcel', Duchamp also used 'Rrose Sélavy' to sign his works (see Jones, *Postmodernism*, 134, 154). Thus, 'Rrose Sélavy' at the same time signifies a play upon words and a 'person' who owns a copyright, has her own signature and even got her own picture. In a series of small black-and-white photographs[10] taken by Man Ray in 1920–1, Marcel Duchamp presents himself in female drag, wearing contemporary bourgeois ladies's fashion (fig. 1).[11] The mode of representation corresponds to contemporary conventions of portrait photography as it was also used in cosmetic advertisements and celebrity photos of the time.[12] In the particular portrait Morimura plays upon, adopting a pose somewhere between coyness and coquetry, Rrose Sélavy looks into the camera with her hat drawn deep into the face and her hands holding the fur stole close around the neck. Pose, jewellery, white powdered face and make-up, all accentuate an image of femininity which is highlighted by the camera's soft focus and the retouching of the print.

In 'Doublonnage (Marcel)', this image has turned into a huge colour print (fig. 2).[13] Morimura dressed all in black poses against a green background. His face is covered with unevenly applied white make-up that makes the eyes, which are surrounded by greenish eye-shadow and black eye-liner, and the red painted mouth stand out. The face is framed by a black fur stole and two identical hats

Figure 1. Man Ray, *Marcel Duchamp as Rrose Sélavy*, 1920–21. © Man Ray Trust, Paris/VG Bild-Kunst, Bonn 2003.

put on top of each other. More striking even than the doubled hats is the double set of arms: two light-skinned hands holding the fur stole are themselves held at their wrists by two darker-skinned hands which — one might suggest — belong to Morimura himself; the left hand of each pair wearing a massive ring. The camera position has been shifted from face level to a view from slightly underneath; soft focus is replaced by a sharp outlining of picture elements; instead of a single source of light, we have diffuse lighting; and the photographed subject's look is no longer directed at the camera — and thus at the viewer —, but passes by the camera's lens into an uncertain distance.

Comparing Duchamp's 'Rrose Sélavy' to Morimura's 'Doublonnage', Jennifer Blessing has argued that while Duchamp played with binary distinctions along the lines of sexual difference, Morimura works towards a multiplication of binaries beyond that male/female axis by including 'ethnic and cultural dimensions and the manner in which these terms are sexualized.'[14] The convergence of gender and ethnicity in Morimura's piece, indeed, effects more than a multiplication of binaries and a cross-referencing in terms of mutual influence; it evokes an interrogation of identity categories themselves. Referring to Duchamp's self-representational strategies as Rrose Sélavy, Amelia Jones observes: 'gender itself is played out as a system of shiftable codes, a socially ordained structuring of sexuality that is "neither true or false, but ... only produced as the truth effect ... of a discourse of primary and stable identity"' (Jones, *Postmodernism*,143). Morimura intervenes into that very system of shiftable codes making the truth effect itself a topic which also involves the notion of 'truth' so deeply installed within the photographic image.

According to Blessing, Morimura's strategy of multiplied doubling, combined with the introduction of a marginalized perspective, represents an act of self-inscription into Western Modernist history that he employs to reveal modernism's ideology in terms of how race and ethnicity are taken for granted. By forcing 'the margins to the center', as Blessing puts it, Morimura unveils the ideological to the viewer (Blessing, 'Rrose', 86). Rather than working as a mode of retrospective critical 'unveiling', though, 'Doublonnage' performs a critical productivity. By operating a strategy of doubling in terms of playful displacements — one could say 'dis-play-cements' — of what 'Rrose Sélavy' has played upon, Morimura's piece works towards a destabilization of the viewer's position in that it explicitly states a refusal of closure. Moreover, the strategy of pushing the marginal to the centre has been identified in or applied to a great deal of work by contemporary non-male, non-Western and/or non-white artists — i.e. artists speaking from marginalized positions, Hutcheon's 'other ex-centrics' —, and this has quite rightly been linked to the question of authorship.[15] It needs to be considered, however, that the very notion of authorship itself has undergone a significant shift within modernism which conceptualizes the marginal as being always already inscribed.[16] Blessing's statement, therefore, repeats a concept of avant-garde that Morimura's 'Doublonnage' re-imaging Duchamp's 'Rrose Sélavy' challenges rather than exemplifies.

Duchamp and Morimura with their 'portraits' both produce a text that works deconstructively in simultaneously confirming the given-to-be-seen and calling it into question. This, however, happens differently in each piece and is to be followed along the lines of the closely linked discursive fields of 'pose' or 'posing', 'masquerade', and 'authorship'. As Sigrid Schade has pointed out, the moment of immobility in the process of being photographed hits the subject's consciousness as posing. The pose is a posture that indicates a viewer[17] and it proves the existence of an image or visual trope prior to the actual photograph which the sitter is trying to imitate.[18] The gesture of posing in the process of being photographed is a *mise en scène* of the gaze of the Other in the scopic field as it was theorized by Jacques Lacan.[19] Posing, as Craig Owens has observed, appears as an activity that is deeply concerned with desire and representation and, therefore, 'has everything to do with sexual difference.'[20]

In Duchamp's 'Rrose Sélavy' image, nothing seems to disturb the idea that the photographed person is a 'true woman'. Looking more closely, though, as Blessing rightly observes, the angle of Rrose's arms in relation to her body seems somewhat odd, and perhaps the arms and hands seem a bit too small in relation to the face (Blessing, 'Rrose', 23). Rrose's arms indeed belong to a female friend of Duchamp. Yet, the point to be made here is not whether those arms were inserted into the picture by photomontage — as Blessing says — or by positioning the woman behind Duchamp when the picture was taken — as others have stated. The point is that a coherent and perfect image of femininity is created exactly through half-obvious manipulation and works in spite of anatomical mismeasurements. Its subversiveness, therefore, lies exactly in its seeming perfection. In this sense, Duchamp's self-representation as 'Rrose Sélavy' can be read as a deliberate act of mimicry. Looking into the camera, she presents herself as a desired and desirable subject. 'Rrose Sélavy' visualizes an ideal that was to be achieved by an instance of correction — that is, those female arms —, and thus, her 'pose-made-perfect' must be read as a revised result of photographic distortion. Duchamp's playing takes place between the poles of appearance and knowing, which, however, do not refer to each other as equation in the way a traditional construction of photography as evidence and document would have it,[21] but in terms of 'fake'. The fake is actually revealed in the photograph itself: in the lower right of the picture, we find a handwritten dedication and signature saying 'lovingly Rrose Sélavy alias Marcel Duchamp'. The knowledge that the artist Marcel Duchamp hides 'behind' the resulting picture — which is laid open and proved by the signature — signifies the image of perfect femininity as masquerade. As such, the Duchampian representation foregrounds an oscillating between the femininity of the pose and the male artist or sitter.

Morimura's self-representation exposes the pose itself by reiterating the projection of an image of femininity onto the body; mimicry both adopts and counters the anticipated effect of its representation. The light-skinned arms held by the darker-skinned hands allow for a number of interpretations that mark this ambivalence: the gesture of covering oneself is associated with femininity; but it remains impossible to decide whether the 'white' arms are actually being held towards the fur stole or being pushed downwards — thereby likely to uncover what is underneath or 'behind' the costume. The arrangement of the two sets of arms/hands metonymically represents a convergence of 'gendered Other' and 'ethnicized Other' that works beyond assumed 'facts' like skin colour or bodily appearance. The dark-skinned hands being just as carefully manicured as the other two and decorated with jewellery, reiterate Rrose's 'femininity' whose artificiality is simultaneously indicated by the wax-like appearance of the 'white' arms. And, moreover, the gesture of 'hands-holding-hands' signifies and uncovers the 'deceit' in Duchamp's 'Rrose Sélavy'.

Whereas the 'Rrose Sélavy' photograph appears as a contained and coherent portrait, 'Doublonnage' seems fragmented. Its colouring increases the impression of disparity that is first induced by the doubling of arms and hat. In 'Rrose Sélavy' we find a careful modelling of tones and can assume three-dimensionality, the green background and the black clothing in 'Doublonnage' seem two monochrome and 'flat' areas with those sets of arms stuck on as in photomontage. The face, however, contrasts with the colour-caused flatness. While Duchamp's whitened face appears as a smooth surface, Morimura's make-up is clearly recognizable as such. Its irregular application makes the skin colour more or less shine through. Due to the huge format each single pore is visible and thus the traces of make-up are additionally emphasized. If Duchamp's white make-up refers to conventions of the representation of ideal femininity (Blessing, 'Rrose', 86), in Morimura, combined with those differently coloured arms/hands, it signifies implications of gender(ed) identity within the construction of ethnicity — first, by playing on the European imaginary's feminization of the Asian male[22] and secondly, by stressing 'whiteness' as such.

Moreover, the very 'imperfection' of Morimura's makeup evokes a different notion of masquerade. In its ambivalent appearance as neither 'coherent' nor fragmented, nor doubled (in the way hat and arms are), the impression of 'masking' seems to be stamped upon the face, raising the question of what might be hidden 'behind' — which now does not so much refer to the artist or sitter, but to the facial image itself. The mask, as we have first learned from Joan Rivière,[23] is neither an actual nor a stable object, and femininity is a masquerade that conceals a non-identity — that is, nothing is hidden 'behind' the mask. If masquerade is all about the constructedness of sexual difference and exposes gender as a set of identities produced in the social or symbolic realm,[24] then Morimura's 'doublonnaged' face, here, metonymically performs an extended and undecidable 'masquerading' in terms of hiding and/or being 'someone', signifying femininity and/or masculinity and marking and/or unmarking ethnicity. Thus, Morimura's face offers itself as a 'screen' — a surface for the projection of the spectorial gaze — and simultaneously rejects this offer. Its identificatory promise directed towards the observing, desiring look of the viewer is caught and returned — but continues as a promise.

In the Duchamp photograph, the handwritten 'lovingly Rrose Sélavy alias Marcel Duchamp' reminds us of the photograph as personal present or celebrity autograph; at the same time it explicitly indicates that 'Rrose Sélavy' and 'Marcel Duchamp' are one and the same person. Giving the alias-name first, 'Rrose Sélavy' becomes the 'real' name of the female person photographed; the woman in the photo *is* Rrose Sélavy who *is* 'alias Marcel Duchamp' — i.e. literally, another Marcel Duchamp. Duchamp's representation of a 'person' named Rrose Sélavy exposes the instability of gender identity by linking it to the signature, and thereby questioning authorship. As Michel Foucault has argued, the author is always a product of discursive formations. It is a function that is 'tied to the legal and institutional systems that circumscribe, determine, and articulate the realm of discourses',[25] it is changeable and gives way to a plurality of authorial subjects. Using alias-names, Duchamp plays upon the notion of the author as a single and coherent entity who is identified with a creative individual existing prior to the text it produces and who is always thought a masculine instance.[26] Duchamp's usage of pseudonyms, as Jones argues, brings forth a play with the power of signature that makes transparent the non-identity of author and individual (Jones, *Postmodernism*, 136 ff). The Rrose Sélavy gesture extends the highly complex author-function of Duchamp by splitting it along the axis of gender (Jones, *Postmodernism*, 142, 160). Rrose Sélavy is the *non*-opposite of Duchamp (Jones, *Postmodernism*, 160, 180). Simultaneously, she is him and she is not. She becomes an author by way of her signature being herself authorized by her 'other' — i.e. Duchamp. Thus, Duchamp's 'Rrose Sélavy' works as a parody on a traditional notion of authorship.

'Doublonnage (Marcel)' lacks a signature, but nevertheless doubles Duchamp's authorial strategies by splitting them along the axis of cultural identity and sexuality. The word 'Marcel' put in brackets in the work's title refers as much to one of Duchamp's alias-names as it performs a citation of the artist's 'real' first name. It gets a dedicatory function similar to the signature in 'Rrose Sélavy', addressed to the instance of the author, to an imaginary 'real' Duchamp and to the viewer. Morimura's '(Marcel)' becomes an equivalent of Duchamp's 'Rrose' signifying 'eros' by transforming the stammering repetition of the 'r', which first made that pun possible, into brackets that simultaneously emphasize and dis-emphasize the meaning of what they provide the 'frame' for. Referring to Foucault's author-function read through Freud, Amelia Jones describes the signature as the 'site of *transference* where the interpreter makes the dead author "present" by projecting her or his own desires into and onto the text, allowing it to be read' (Jones, *Postmodernism*, 136). Morimura's interpretation of Duchamp's image works as a signification of desire that oscillates between 'Rrose' and a doubled 'Marcel'. The author-function 'Morimura' itself is produced through referencing the author-function 'Rrose Sélavy'. In the very act of exposing to the viewer that he represents himself as Marcel Duchamp as Rrose Sélavy, Morimura evokes a parody of parody. This — as we have seen — is not an effect of 'simple doubling' (in terms of 'splitting' or 'adding something'), but of a simultaneous 'shift in direction' that explicitly blurs the notion of a clearcut difference between terms constructed as binaries — in short, by installing a concept of hybridity. With regard to Linda Hutcheon's definition of parody as 'repetition with critical distance' which can be as much an homage as an ironic critique, Morimura's 'Doublonnage (Marcel)' exactly holds the balance between the two by deconstructing Duchamp's deconstructive strategies and challenging the very effects of photographic mimicry.

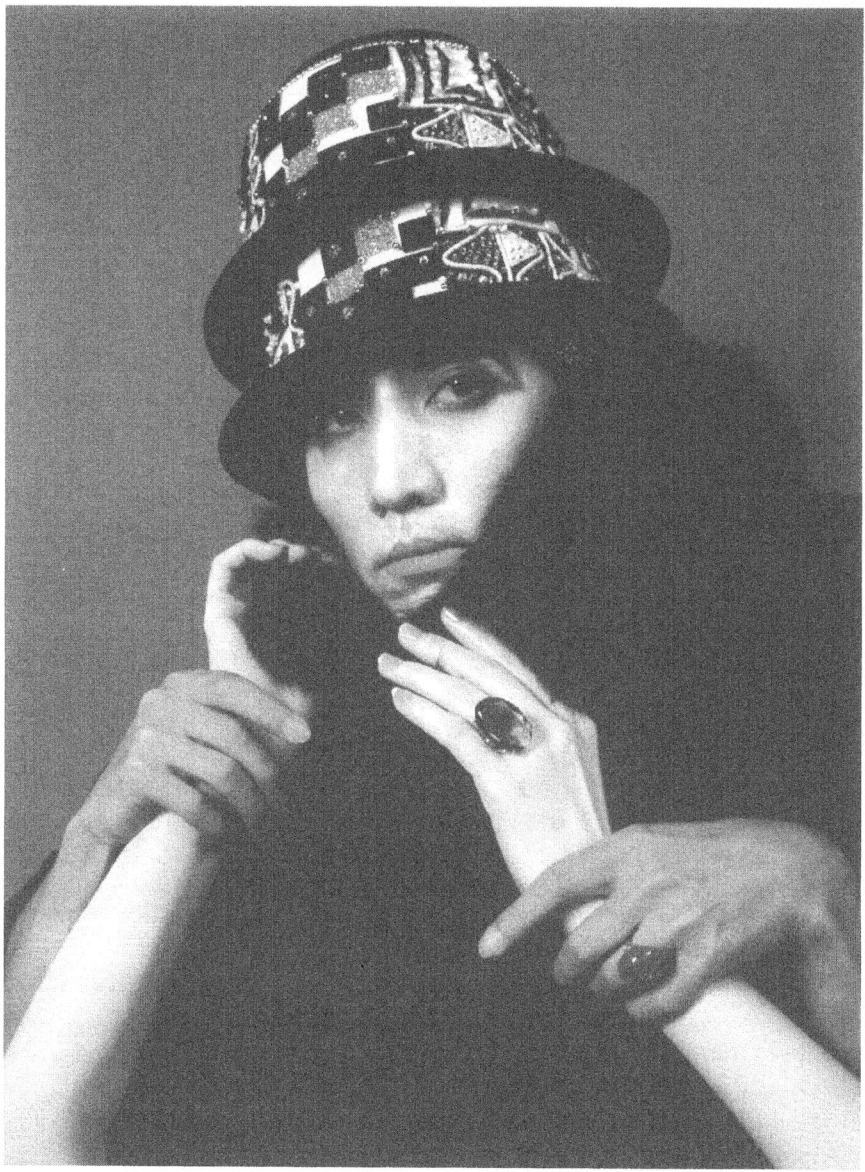

Figure 2. Yasumasa Morimura, *Doublonnage (Marcel)*, 1998. Permission of the artist.

Just as Morimura's work can be considered to function as a kind of reminder of Western visual archives making visible the art historical *dispositif* seen through the eyes of an Eastern Other, it simultaneously reminds us that parody in order to be recognized — that is: readable — as parody, needs that archive as its essential precondition.

Subverting picture politics always needs and depends on modes of affirmation. Whereas in the 'modern times' of Duchamp, the 'ex-centric'—and, that is, feminized—artist was still conceptualized as a male subject (see Schade and Wenk, 'Inszenierunge', 361–4), and as such the central figure of a dominant art discourse, the contemporary 'ex-centric' cultural practitioner has gained access to certain critical aesthetic discourses. The honour of being acknowledged is always combined with the danger of being functionalized as Other. Here, Morimura's work—and especially 'Doublonnage (Marcel)' and the context it refers to—also might provide some input towards a thinking of art discourse that includes the questioning of its own construction—that is, an interrogation of its conditions and boundaries.

KERSTIN BRANDES

NOTES

1 See *Lust und Leere—Japanische Fotografie* Exhibition Catalogue (Kunsthalle Wien, 1997).
2 See Norman Bryson, 'Yasumasa Morimura, Mother (Judith II)', *Artforum*, 32 (1994), 70–71.
3 See Amelia Jones, *Postmodernism and the En-Gendering of Marcel Duchamp* (Cambridge, New York, Melbourne, Cambridge University Press, 1994); see also Amelia Jones, 'The ambivalence of male masquerade: Duchamp as Rrose Sélavy' in *The Body Imaged: The Human Form and Visual Culture since the Renaissance*, edited by Kathleen Adler and Marcia Pointon (Cambridge, Cambridge University Press, 1993), 21–31.
4 With regard to art exhibition politics this was problematized by Abigail Solomon-Godeau. See her essay 'Mistaken Identities' in *Mistaken Identities*, exhibition catalogue edited by Constance Lewallen and Abigail Solomon-Godeau (Santa Barbara, 1992), 19–65.
5 Homi K. Bhabha, 'Interrogating Identity' in *Identity—The Real Me* edited by Lisa Appignanesi, ICA Documents 6 (London, 1987), 5–11 (5).
6 Sigrid Schade, 'Charcot und das Schauspiel des hysterischen Körpers', in *Denkräume—Zwischen Kunst und Wissenschaft*, edited by Silvia Baumgart et al. (Berlin, Reimer, 1993), 461–84.
7 See Judith Butler, *Gender Trouble* (New York, Routledge, 1990).
8 Linda Hutcheon, *A Theory of Parody: The Teachings of Twentieth Century Art Forms* (London and New York, Routledge, 1985), 6.
9 Linda Hutcheon, *A Poetics of Postmodernism: History, Theory, Fiction* (London and New York, Routledge, 1992), 35.

10 They are $8\frac{1}{2} \times 16\frac{13}{16}$ inches in size.
11 The model for Duchamp's self-representation was probably a photograph of the Countess Elsa von Freytag-Lornighoven with whom Duchamp was suspected of having some sort of love affair. See Dickran Tashjian, 'Vous pour moi?', in *Mirror Images/Women, Surrealism, and Self-Representation*, exhibition catalogue edited by Whitney Chadwick (Cambridge, MIT Press, 1998), 36–65.
12 See Jones, *Postmodernism*, 147; also Jones in *Body Imaged*, 26.
13 The format is 60 × 48 inches.
14 Jennifer Blessing, 'Rrose is a Rrose is a Rrose — Gender Performance in Photography' in *Rrose is a Rrose is a Rrose — Gender Performance in Photography*, exhibition catalogue edited by Jennifer Blessing (Solomon R. Guggenheim Museum, New York, 1997), 18–119 (86). Both the Morimura and the Duchamp image were presented in that exhibition. On Duchamp as Rrose Sélavy, see 19–23.
15 Solomon-Godeau argues that it is especially artists speaking from marginalized positions who work towards the 'demise of the universal artist and the birth of a specific and historical one'. See Solomon-Godeau, *Identities*, 24.
16 See Sigrid Schade and Silke Wenk, 'Inszenierungen des Sehens: Kunst, Geschichte und Geschlechterdifferenz' in *Genus: Zur Geschlechterdifferenz in den Kulturwissenschaften*, edited by Hadumod Bußmann and Renate Hof (Stuttgart, Kröner, 1995), 340–407 (361–4).
17 Sigrid Schade, 'Der Schnappschuß als Familiengrab. Entstellte Erinnerung im Zeitstil der Photographie' in *Zeitreise: Bilder/Maschinen/Strategien/Rätsel*, edited by Georg Christoph Tholen et al. (Basel and Frankfurt, Stroemfeld, 1993), 287–300 (298).
18 Sigrid Schade, 'Posen der Ähnlichkeit. Zur wiederholten Entstellung der Fotografie' in *Mimesis. Bild und Schrift — Ähnlichkeit, und Entstellung im Verhältnis der Künste*, edited by Birgit Erdle and Sigrid Weigel (Köln, Böhlau, 1996), 65–81 (74).
19 Jacques Lacan, *The Four Fundamental Concepts of Psychoanalysis* (New York, Penguin 1978), 106: 'In the scopic field, the gaze is outside, I am looked at, that is to say, I am a picture. (...) The gaze is the instrument through which light is embodied and through which (...) I am *photo-graphed*'.
20 Craig Owens, 'Posing' in *Beyond Recognition — Representation, Power, and Culture*, edited by Scott Bryson et al. (Berkeley, Los Angeles, London, University of California Press, 1992), 201–17 (212).
21 'It [documentary, K.B.] is a genre of photography which is dependent upon the simple equation between appearance and truth, and between description and knowledge' David Green, 'Veins of Resemblance: Photography and Eugenics' in *Photography/Politics: Two*, edited by Patricia Holland et al. (London, Comedia Publishing Group, 1986), 9–21 (13). On the history of

photographic evidence see John Tagg, *The Burden of Representation: Essays on Photographies and Histories* (Houndsmills and London, Palgrave 1993).
22 See Norman Bryson, 'Morimura: 3 Readings', *Art & Text* 52 (Sept. 1995), 74–79.
23 Joan Rivière, 'Womanliness as Masquerade' (1929), in *Formations of Fantasy*, edited by Victor Burgin et al. (London, Routledge 1986).
24 See Jacques Lacan, 'The Signification of the Phallus', *Ecrits: A Selection* (New York, W.W. Norton, 1977), 281–91 (288).
25 Michel Foucault, 'What is an Author?', *Screen* 20:1 (Spring 1979), 13–33 (23).
26 Jones, *Postmodernism*; see also Schade and Wenk, *Genus*, 346–70.

Show Your Wounded Manliness: Promises of Salvation in the Work of Joseph Beuys

Show your Wound

A broad, inhospitable room: in it are carefully arranged mortuary tables, two sorts of metal tools, framed editions of the Italian newspaper *La lotta continua* (The Fight Goes On) and blackboards. Each element is displayed twice. Written on the blackboards, is the request which forms the title of this environment, created by Joseph Beuys: *Show your Wound*. The artist explains this work as follows: 'Show your wound, because one has to reveal the wound which one wants to heal. The room talks about the illness of society'[1] and: 'Of course, the traumatic character is mentioned. A wound which is shown can be healed'.[2] The art work does not stop at the wound it also contains, according to Beuys; 'allusions, that the deadly paralysis can be overcome (...) something (...) which indicates a way out' (*Süddeutsche Zeitung*). Thus the environment indicates the therapeutic intention which characterizes the whole work of Joseph Beuys.

Show your Wound — whose wound is exhibited here? Who or what has to be healed, and from what? I want to suggest that the continuous theme of the wound in Beuys's work latently deals with a wounded manliness in crisis in postwar Germany. The war-injured body of the artist, its use in artistic performances, and the specific materials Beuys used in his work, demonstrate and symbolically go through healing processes which promise salvation from the fascistic past for German society.

In a critique of *Show your Wound* the artist's body itself appeared as a wounded one. A photograph of Beuys (posing without hat) in a popular daily was entitled: 'The man with the hat shows his wounds' (*Die Abendzeitung*). Beuys's hat was not just a lasting accessory and thus a trademark of the artist, but also a sign for the head injury he suffered during the Second World War. This injury is said to be the initial reason for Beuys wearing a hat. As time went by this head-gear gained symbolic meaning. The war wound in turn is part of the personal myth of Beuys being wounded and rescued during the Second World War, the myth founding his artistic career.

The Tartarian Legend

One has to make clear in advance that Beuys's life and work are tightly associated in a mythical narrative which several authors have contributed to. The 'Life Course/Work Course', first published by Beuys in 1961, particularly establishes this connection. Labelling several biographic dates as 'exhibitions' they are presented as stations of Beuys's artistic development. The entry for the year 1921, for instance, the year of Beuys's birth, says: 'Cleves exhibition of a wound drawn together with plaster',[3] and with this a reproduction of *Bathtub*, a work from 1960, is shown. In this work Beuys added stripes of sticking-plaster and fat-soaked gauze to his former bathtub. 'Life Course/Work Course' has served as a basis for the only biography authorized by Beuys and for several other publications.[4]

Following the mythical narrative, one of Beuys's key experiences was his experience during the Second World War. In action as an aircraft radio operator and a combat pilot, Beuys crashed with his plane in the Crimea in 1943 where he was found and nursed back to health by Tartars. In Beuys's words:

> Had it not been for the Tartars I would not be alive today. They were nomads of the Crimea, in what was then no man's land between the Russian and German fronts, and favoured neither side. (...) it was they who discovered me in the snow after the crash (...) I had bad skull and jaw injuries. (...) I was completely buried in the snow. That's how the Tartars found me days later. (...) They covered my body in fat to help it regenerate warmth, and wrapped it in felt as an insulator to keep the warmth in. (Tisdall, *Joseph Beuys*, 16–17)

This treatment with fat and felt is retrospectively interpreted as a shamanistic healing ritual. An early collector, admirer and friend of Beuys, and at the same time a frequent commentator on his work, Franz Joseph van der Grinten, described this cure as an 'experience of naturalness', an encounter with the 'mystery of unity', in which Beuys was granted 'magic instead of method, wisdom instead of knowledge'.[5] The way Beuys saw himself as an artist later on seems to be founded on his salvation by the Tartars, for the figure of the shaman was crucial in Beuys's performance of being an artist.

Beuys's Shamanistic Initiation

According to Mircea Eliade, the shaman is a formerly sick person who healed himself and thereby became capable of healing others.[6]

Beuys's depressive crisis in the years 1956–7 is being characterized as his shamanistic initiation in this sense. In 'Life Course/ Work Course' this phase occurs as follows: 'Beuys works in the fields' (Tisdall, *Joseph Beuys*, 8). Beuys indeed is said to have spent a few months on van der Grinten's farm doing agricultural and manual work. In Adriani *et al*'s biography, they quote Beuys describing this phase as follows:

Certainly incidents from war produced an after-effect on me, but something also had to die. I believe this phase was one of the most important for me in that I had to fully reorganize myself constitutionally; I had for too long a time dragged a body around with me. The initial stage was a totally exhausted state, which quickly turned into an orderly phase of renewal. The things inside me had to be totally transplanted; a physical change had to take place in me. Illnesses are almost always spiritual crisis in life, in which old experiences and phases of thought are cast off in order to permit positive changes. (...) This was the stage I began systematic work on certain basic principles [his *Theory of Sculpture*]. (Adriani, *Joseph Beuys*, 56–7).

In a revised edition from 1994 there is another explicit reference to his artistic work: 'During the crisis, I slowly began to restart drawing. When I returned from the field in the evening, I drew. Especially this time was a very fruitful time for my drawing.'[7] Mentally working through his war experience is supposed to have been a cathartic period during which Beuys not only became an artist—this period also founded the specific way he saw himself as an artist: 'For me it was a time when I realized the part an artist can play in indicating the traumas of a time and initiating a healing process. That relates to medicine, or what people call alchemy or shamanism ...' (Tisdall, *Joseph Beuys*, 21). Thus working through his war experience becomes the founding myth of the artist Beuys, a connection which is repeated on the level of the artistic material.

Fat and Felt as Means of Transformation and Survival

Fat and felt, the materials the Tartars treated him with, function as the main substances in Beuys's *Theory of Sculpture*. Whereas felt is used for its isolating quality, fat is an element which can be transformed energetically. Beuys used the melting and hardening of fat for his sculptural work interpreting the former as a temporal chaotic state which can dissolve and thus 'heal' crystalline solidification. In Beuys's words: 'Chaos can have a healing character, coupled with the idea of open movement which channels the warmth of chaotic energy into order or form' (Tisdall, *Joseph Beuys*, 21). Beuys described the artistic process, for example the production of his famous fat corners, as the transformation of 'a chaotic, indefinite quality of energy' to an ordered, definite form: 'the two poles definite and indefinite', Beuys continued, 'are being mediated through the action and through the motion, this means: chaos, motion, form' (Schneede, *Joseph Beuys*, 73).[8] This transformation of substance was not only meant to be a forming of the material, but also a broader spiritual renewal which Beuys converted into sculpture. Beuys extended idea of art intended to form a social sculpture in the sense of reshaping society, in his own words: 'how we mould and shape the world in which we live' (Tisdall, *Joseph Beuys*, 6).

Although Beuys strictly refused to associate his *Theory of Sculpture* directly with his mythical salvation by the Tartars, his use of material often made allusions to this event. This is obvious when considering the object *The Pack* from 1969. It consists of a Volkswagen bus with twenty sleds each of them equipped with a roll of felt, a lump of fat and a flashlight. Beuys commented:

This is an emergency object: an invasion by the Pack. In a state of emergency the Volkswagen bus is of limited usefulness, and more direct and primitive means must be taken to ensure survival. (...) Each sled carries its own survival kit: the flashlight represents the sense of orientation, then felt for protection, and fat is food. (Tisdall, *Joseph Beuys*, 190)

Wintry conditions, a state of emergency of vital significance, in which high technical equipment breaks down, army grey felt, the uniform equipment of the series of sleds — the work suggests associations with the Russian Campaign of the German army during the Second World War. The equipment of the German army had proved to be insufficient in wintry weather conditions. Soldiers stumbling through snowstorms, tanks getting stuck in snowdrifts — *The Pack* recalls images of the German defeat at the Eastern front from the collective memory. At the same time it refers to the myth that the German army was not defeated by the military force of the enemy but by the cruel Russian winter, which means by a natural force. Fat and felt as means of survival do not only refer to Beuys's mythical salvation by the Tartars, they also seem to promise a belated healing to the German army which suffered in the cold of Russia.

Fat and Felt in Beuys's Artistic Performances

Beuys related his own body to the materials fat and felt in his artistic performances. In the description of his depressive crisis quoted above,

Beuys explained his being affected by war as the burden of a body: 'I had for too long a time dragged a body around with me', which had to be put down: 'something also had to die'. Then 'an orderly phase of renewal, (...) a physical change' could take place. That was how the artist suggested that he had already physically gone through the transformation he wanted to be fulfilled in his *Theory of Sculpture*. Thus Beuys, according to his own thinking, seemed to be predestined to work therapeutically as an artist-shaman: 'My intention is (...) to stress the idea of transformation and of substance. That is precisely what the shaman does in order to bring about change and development: his nature is therapeutic' (Tisdall, *Joseph Beuys*, 23). Beuys stage-managed himself in this role, especially in his artistic performances; I will point out two of them as examples.

In *The Chief*, performed in Copenhagen and in a gallery in Berlin in 1964, the artist spent eight hours wrapped in felt. From time to time he made noises through a microphone which were described as 'breathing, breathing out, rattling in the throat, coughing, groaning, grumbling, whispering, whistling tones' (Vostell in Tisdall, *Joseph Beuys*, 94). Two dead hares lay on the ground, at both ends of the wrapped artist. There was also a second felt roll wrapped around a copper rod. Another copper rod leant against the wall.

Beuys and his commentators interpreted this performance as the representation of a development through suffering and symbolic death. Remaining in the darkness of the warming, isolating felt seemed to represent a kind of pupation which transformed the artist. Beuys commented:

It was a parallel to the old initiation of the coffin, a form of mock death. It takes a lot of discipline to avoid panicking in such a condition, floating empty and devoid of emotion and without specific feelings of claustrophobia or pain (...) Such an action (...) changes me radically. In a way it's a death, a real action and not an interpretation. (Tisdall, *Joseph Beuys*, 95)

Following his own interpretation Beuys not only represented this transformation symbolically but underwent it with his own body. This idea refers to the figure of the shaman who anticipates the healing of the community by healing his own body. In *Mainstream*, performed in Darmstadt in 1967, the material fat was crucial. Ten different performances were repeated within ten hours in different combinations. Beuys had prepared the room with a *Fatwall* before. That was how the corners, according to Beuys the symbol of fixed thinking, were turned into curves towards the performing space.

This preparation of the performing space made it comparable to 'shamanistic places of worship'.[9] The performance *Fatbed* was one element of *Mainstream*: Beuys lay motionlessly with bent legs wide open between five wedges of fat, for about half an hour while loud music was playing. Contemporary reports suggest the loudness as well as the motionlessness of the artist were perceived as unbearable, as 'a nerve of provoking monotony' (Huber, *Joseph Beuys*, 21). From time to time he was afflicted with cramp-like spasms. This sequence in particular is interpreted as a shamanistic initiation, reflecting Beuys's own words (cf. Schneede, *Joseph Beuys*, 172–3; Tisdall, *Joseph Beuys*, 146). Beuys is said to have used shamanistic practices 'to show that conscience which passed through pain and suffering can have a revolutionary effect' (Schneede, *Joseph Beuys*, 173). His technique of 'rapt absorption' (Huber, *Joseph Beuys*, 101) is understood in a shamanistic context, too. Spectators of the performance outlined the 'priest-like seriousness of his conduct' (Huber, *Joseph Beuys*, 13). Beuys, posing like a woman giving birth to a child in *Fatbed*, alludes to a rebirth, a resurrection of the artist.

Mastering the Substance, Performing Masculinity

These two examples, others could be added, show at first glance two different ways in which the artist related himself to matter. On the one hand, he appears as master of the substance, the alchemist who transforms the substance and steers this process. On the other hand, Beuys exposed his own body to the influences of the substances which are said to have transforming powers as, for instance, in the performance *Fatbed*. But the emphasis on the physical discipline in his artistic performances made this difference a relative one.

Referring to the performance *Mainstream* one commentator outlined Beuys's 'ability to self- and body-mastery' (Huber, *Joseph Beuys*, 101). From this point of view, the artist put himself in an analogical relation to the artistic materials as well as to his body: both were mastered as matter. Both functioned as a substance to which Beuys acted as a forming, shaping creator. Thus Beuys followed the classic figure of the sculptor who moulds his material. This figure is not sexless but traditionally male. On top of the traditional hierarchy of the genres, sculpture has the strongest male connotations. Creating a form is the traditional goal of artistic creation and has always been gendered in Western art theory and history. The formation of a supposedly female material was regarded as an expression of male creativity.[10]

Beuys uses this gendering in his *Theory of Sculpture*, characterizing the solidified form which had to be overcome as 'the male, (...) the cold, hard, crystallized, burnt-out clinker that I would call the male intellect, the cause of much of our suffering' (Tisdall, *Joseph Beuys*, 50). Although the solidified male is supposed to be liquefied again by the influence of the female chaos, the actual driving force of the artistic process, the motion reshaping the substance, however, is still supposed to be male. Quoting Beuys: 'the real meaning of Materia with its root on MATER (mother — as in "mother earth"), as one pole of spirituality while *the other* encompasses the whole process of development' (Tisdall, *Joseph Beuys*, 105, emphasis mine). The opposite pole of the female as the real driving force — implicitly Beuys was still talking about male creativity.

An out-of-date form of masculinity is to be transformed and renewed with the help of a supposedly female force. Beuys performed a comparable alignment and appropriation of the female in another element of *Mainstream*. In *Gauze Filter: Woman*, the artist stood erect wearing a triangular filter of gauze over his genitals, which according to his statement means 'a change of character, a vagina as a balance to the heavy lead balls in the action' (Tisdall, *Joseph Beuys*, 146). Beuys also referred to the meaning of the filter as 'a membrane that has to be broken through or penetrated' (Tisdall, *Joseph Beuys*, 74) and he frequently associates gauze and wounds in his work. In Beuys's *Theory of Sculpture* something permeable, wounded, is supposed to be female too. Gendering the wound made it possible to leave it symbolically behind by passing through the female. Looking at Beuys's *Theory of Sculpture* from this point of view, dissolving a solidified form by chaotic energy in order to finally transfer it into a new order, can be interpreted as a symbolic healing of a damaged manliness. At the same time it can be considered as an up-to-date version of male artistship, because the breakdown of fascism also required a redefinition of the role and function of the male artist-as-creator.

Redefining the Male Creator

The figure of the sculptor shaping and renewing society in Beuys's *Theory of Sculpture* refers to a myth of masculinity and creativity which has its models in Pygmalion and Prometheus. Both are said to have established a new race by moulding female human figures. Historically more concrete and closer predecessors can certainly be found in the role of the artist under German fascism. The fascistic idea of building a healthy 'body of the people', the German 'Volkskörper', assigned to art the task of outlining and visualizing visions of this new, ideal body.[11] The body that was supposed to be shaped represented at the same time society, and vice versa. The sculptor as the creator of art in the public sphere in particular was assigned an outstanding role in this process; the best known example is Arno Breker.

Along with the breakdown of fascism the idea of the artist shaping society was discredited, the idea of the artist as 'creator of the new and the future'[12], however, still remained relevant. Male artists in postwar Germany had to claim a clear break with the fascistic past to be able to take up the traditional concept of the artist connecting creativity, formation and masculinity.

Abstraction was supposed to affirm this break by representing freedom and democracy in opposition to the representational art of national-socialism. The *Informal* postulated a changed relation to matter in postwar art. Outlining the autonomy of matter, the idea of 'independent substance'[13] was crucial in this artistic trend. If one considers the history of modern art, as the art-historian Monika Wagner does, as a 'continuous threat of the traditional bastion of art, the form, through the material', postwar art represents a situation in which 'the mastery of matter (...) and with it the model of the gendered hierarchy itself was in danger of getting lost' (191). This meant that the traditional power of the male artist-as-creator was questioned, too. Representations of a rampant, devouring substance as well as artistic performances 'injuring' the substance in the *Informal* can be understood as the search for a new positioning of the male artist-as-creator in this relation.

Mastering the Body, Shaping Society

In this artistic context Beuys began to develop his *Theory of Sculpture* at the end of the 1950s. Instead of the prevalent relation to the material in the *Informal* that was considered as aggressive, Beuys emphasized the therapeutic, healing character of his relation to, and his work with, the material. His artistic work was not restricted to a relation to matter, but was explicitly related to a society that according to Beuys needed to be healed. At the same time, the artist performed the healing in ritual-like treatments of his own body; thus the latter functioned as a kind of promise of salvation. His body, mythically cured by the Tartars, had demonstrated the healing Beuys wanted to hand over to society in his artistic work.

The idea of an individual body overlapping with a collective one, particularly in combination with the metaphors sick and healthy, healing, purification and formation refers insistently to the fascistic idea of a 'body of the people', the 'Volkskörper'. The physical 'purity' and 'health' of the individual were considered as preconditions for the convalescence of a supposedly threatened collective body and vice versa. The fascistic concept of the male body unified two body-concepts, a 'body of capacity' and a 'body of sacrifice'.[14] This body-concept propagated both the conquest of the own physical weakness as well as the willingness to sacrifice oneself for the community as desirable qualities of the ideal male 'Aryan' body. In my opinion it served as a specific ideological orientation to war and thus to the production of soldierly masculinity.

'I had for too long a time dragged a body around with me.' The body undergoing transformation in Beuys's work shows parallels to the weak, sick body that should be defeated according to the fascistic ideology. Beuys's artistic performances deal with a weak, injured body represented by the body of the male artist. It is the war-injured body of a soldier, that had admittedly been ennobled by wounding — Beuys, wounded five times during the Second World War, got the *Golden Casualty-Insignia*. However, he did not succeed in making the greatest sacrifice of soldierly masculinity, which would have meant to die for the victory of the fatherland. From this perspective the 'body of sacrifice' had failed in a double sense. In the artistic work of Joseph Beuys this injured body symbolically died and was renewed by being transcended and thus overcome by a disciplined 'body of capacity', with the help of a female chaotic energy.

'Show your wound, because one has to reveal the wound which one wants to heal.' 'A wound which is shown can be healed.' Show your wound — whose wound is exhibited here? Who or what has to be healed? And from what? As the American art-historian Donald Kuspit comments: 'Beuys embodied both the ruined, defeated old Germany and the hopeful new Germany determined to heal its wounds'.[15] 'Beuys's own wounded body', Kuspit continues, 'was a cold, torpid form from the Nazi past, and the fat and felt the nomadic Tartars wrapped his body in, warming it to new life, were the healthy chaos, the healthy amorphousness' (195). Whereas Kuspit takes up Beuys's way of stylizing himself very affirmatively, the focus on gender — as I have pointed out — opens up a more critical perspective. The metaphors of wounding and healing in Beuys's work can now be understood as a gendered promise of salvation. A synopsis of the different aspects I have discussed brings up three addressees for this promise:

— the war-injured male body that is supposed to be symbolically healed and renewed through female chaotic energy;
— the defeated German 'body of the people' and with it the defeated German nation which are supposed to be healed respectively redeemed by the artist as a creator of the new, that is by a revised model of the male hero;
— the narcissistically offended male artist of the postwar era. The mythical figure of the healing artist Beuys raised for the first time in postwar Germany the claim that the male artist-as-creator could also shape society.

Historicizing and Gendering the Work of Joseph Beuys

In other words, Beuys's artistic work can be understood as an individual way the artist got over his war experience which questioned the way he formerly had seen himself as a man, soldier, German. However, this process of getting over his war experience is not limited to an individual dimension. Beuys's destabilization resulted from a social event, it refers to social concepts of masculinity and national identity and as an artist Beuys was a public person. Thus Beuys at the same time offered a public model of how to deal symbolically with social uncertainties.

I have made the point that Beuys fell back to proved models of male mastery and heroism finally reaffirming the gendered symbolic order. In my opinion the function of the wounded male body in this context was to guarantee the status of a victim. Without this status it would not have been possible in Germany at that time to reaffirm heroic masculinity as Beuys did. The myth of the Tartarian legend transferred the former soldier Beuys into an imaginary no man's land and resolved questions on his participation in military actions. At first glance one may identify Beuys as the subject of this process, but the indispensable contribution of the critiques in establishing him as an artist makes clear that there are numerous participants. Of course, there have been some different voices: The American art-historian Benjamin Buchloh was the first to criticize 'the twilight of the idol' and suggested that 'the repressed returns with ever-increasing strength'[16] in the work of Joseph Beuys. An extended Beuys-biography has reconstructed the historical context of Beuys's military service that was generally left out in the narratives on the artist and pointed out his political affinity to right-wing groups.[17] However, the presence and effectiveness of the repressed fascistic past in the artistic work of Joseph Beuys is still to be analysed systematically.

Finally, I want to point out the *making* of an artist, that is, the significance which is assigned to an artist and his work, as a paradigmatic object of interest for studying the construction of identities in modern Western societies, in particular constructions of gender. The artist as an 'individual' in the public sphere, whose 'identity' is deeply gendered, can serve as an example for the fundamental overlapping of individual and social concepts of identity. His — or her — celebrity indicate that he — or she — is performing a model of masculinity — or femininity — and other identifying categories which is not necessarily dominant but surely up to date.

CORINNA TOMBERGER
Carl von Ossietzky-Universität Oldenburg

NOTES

1 Beuys in *Süddeutsche Zeitung*, 26–27 January 1980, quoted in *Joseph Beuys, Zeige deine Wunde*, II, *Reaktionen* (Munich, 1980), no page numbers.
2 Beuys in *Die Abendzeitung*, 13 February 1973, in *Joseph Beuys, Zeige deine Wunde*, II, *Reaktionen*.
3 Caroline Tisdall, *Joseph Beuys* (New York, Thames and Hudson, 1979), 8.
4 This is not an autobiography but contains extensive quotes from the artist, see Götz Adriani, Winfried Konnertz and Karin Thomas, *Joseph Beuys: Life and Works* (New York, 1979), another example containing 'Life Course/Work Course' is Tisdall.
5 *Franz Joseph van der Grinten zu Joseph Beuys*, edited by Friedhelm Mennekes (Cologne 1993), 158.
6 Mircea Eliade, *Schamanismus und archaische Extasetechnik*, translated by Inge Köck (Frankfurt, Suhrkamp, 1989; first publ. 1951).
7 Götz Adriani, Winfried Konnertz and Karin Thomas, *Joseph Beuys: Leben und Werk* (Cologne, DuMont, 1994).
8 Uwe M. Schneede, *Joseph Beuys: Die Aktionen* (Ostfildern, Hatje Cantz Verlag, 1994).
9 Eva Huber, *Joseph Beuys: Hauptstrom und Fettraum* (Darmstadt, J. Häusser, 1993), 15.
10 Monika Wagner, 'Form und Material im Geschlechterkampf oder: Aktionismus auf dem Flickenteppich' in *Das Geschlecht der Künste*, edited by Corinna Caduff and Sigrid Weigel (Cologne, Weimar, Vienna, Böhlau Verlag, 1996), 175–96.

11 Cf. Barbara Schrödl, 'Pygmalions Geschöpf und Gefährtin. Die Repräsentation von Künstlerpaaren im Spielfilm des NS' in *Mythen von Autorschaft und Weiblichkeit im 20. Jahrhundert*, edited by Kathrin Hoffmann-Curtius and Silke Wenk (Marburg, Jonas Verlag, 1997), 254–5.
12 Silke Wenk, 'Pygmalions moderne Wahlverwandtschaften. Die Rekonstruktion des Schöpfer-Mythos im nachfaschistischen Deutschland', in *Blick-Wechsel. Konstruktionen von Männlichkeit und Weiblichkeit in Kunst und Kunstgeschichte*, edited by Ines Lindner et al. (Berlin, Dietrich Reimer Verlag, 1989), 73.
13 Antje Oltmann, *'Der Weltstoff letztendlich ist . . . neu zu bilden'. Joseph Beuys für und wider die Moderne* (Ostfildern, edition tertium, 1994), 129.
14 Cf. Daniel Wildmann, *Begehrte Körper. Konstruktion und Inszenierung des 'arischen' Männerkörpers im 'Dritten Reich'* (Würzburg, Königshausen & Neumann, 1998), 110.
15 Donald Kuspit, *The Cult of the Avant-Garde Artist* (Cambridge, Cambridge University Press 1995), 90.
16 Benjamin H.D. Buchloh, 'Beuys: The Twilight of the Idol, Preliminary notes for a Critique', *Artforum*, XVIII:5 (1980), 40.
17 Frank Gieseke and Albrecht Markert, *Flieger, Filz und Vaterland. Eine erweiterte Beuys Biographie* (Berlin, Elefanten Press Verlag, 1996).

Tom's Men: The Masculinization of Homosexuality and the Homosexualization of Masculinity at the end of the Twentieth Century

For most of his life the artist we know as Tom of Finland lived a double life. By day he was Touko Laaksonen, successful Helsinki advertising executive, retiring from this post only in 1973 at fifty-three years of age. By night, at home, dressed in leather gear, Touko became Tom of Finland, working well into the night on what he called his 'dirty drawings'. Throughout the body of his work, a legacy of some five thousand drawings, Tom created a gay utopia full of horny lumberjacks, sailors, policemen and construction workers, all bursting out of their uniforms or their jeans and T-shirts. Tomland is a fantasy world in which masculinity is held up as the highest ideal, in which it is the most natural thing in the world for virile men to be attracted to other virile men in public. His drawings idealize the male body, even exaggerating physical features to the point of caricature. As he himself said: 'I'm not trying for realism. I want to express our fantasies'.[1] Through his fantasy of total maleness, Tom sought to eliminate gay guilt, to correct injustices, to validate gay men, their desires and their experience, to destroy the stereotype which equated homosexuality with effeminacy. In the introduction to the first published collection of his work, *Retrospective*, he wrote: 'I started drawing fantasies of free and happy gay men. Soon I began to exaggerate their maleness on purpose to point out that all gays don't necessarily need to be just "those damn queers", that they could be as handsome, strong, and masculine as any other men' (Ramakers, *Dirty Pictures*, 65). He called his technique 'photorealist'. Working from photographs of live models, his favourite medium, a graphite pencil, allowed him to achieve a clarity of line, a sharpness of focus, a crispness of detail and a high level of finish which leaves no sign of the artist's hand. Hyper-realistic, his images have an immediacy which surpasses the 'reality' of a photograph. Ideal too for photographic reproduction and photocopying, for many years his images were pirated, with Tom receiving scant recompense for his work.

Tom's ideal male is square-jawed, snub-nosed, clean-cut, with short hair, immaculate sideburns and sometimes a moustache. He is always well-built: broad shouldered, slim-waisted, with massive upper body muscularity: 'big pecs, tight abs, bubble butt', as the saying goes. Tom's men are icons of masculinity. As with any icon there are conventions: his men have a certain look but a limited number of facial expressions, a range of stances, postures, attitudes, a kind of instantly recognizable 'Tom' specificity about them.

Testimonies to the power of Tom's iconography can be found in the film *Daddy and the Muscle Academy*, where a series of American men talk about Tom's influence on their lives.[2] One such declares: 'It wasn't until I saw Tom of Finland's work that I realized it was possible to be gay and positive'. Tom's first drawings of the 1940s and early 50s were evocations of sexual encounters he had actually had, or reminiscences of men he had met or admired: Finnish lumberjacks and loggers, farm labourers or truckers. And throughout his career he continued to iconize proletarian masculinity. In *Daddy* one of the interviewees confirms the importance of such images: 'Seeing two blue-collar men together enjoying each other made it more acceptable to me. From a blue-collar background, up to this point all associations had been negative with it. It made me more comfortable with the fact that I am gay'. Tom put paid to the notion of the gay man as a sissy. He likewise banished the spectre of gay men as the third sex, not quite men, not quite women. He established the look of the gay man as masculine and virile, and this proved emancipatory. In 1980 Robert Pierce, reviewing Tom's show at New York's Robert Samuel Gallery, mentioned what such images had meant to him as a young man: 'Tom's work wasn't pornography. It was salvation.'[3]

Tom had broken into the American market in 1957, sending drawings to Bob Mizer's *Physique Pictorial*. And it has to be admitted that the publication of Tom's work coincided with the changing ethos of the 1960s. At the same time as Tom was working away at his advertising firm during the day, drawing his 'dirty pictures' at night, Andy Warhol was bringing muscleman Joe Dallessandro out of the world of the porn flick and into his art films, Kenneth Anger was celebrating the biker in *Scorpio Rising*, and by 1969, at the Stonewall bar in New York, gay men were asserting themselves, becoming more visible, and starting to reinterpret themselves. Tom's masculinization of gay male self image can thus be seen as coinciding with a general shift in perceptions, for example, the shift from gender-based identities to sexuality-based identities. Nevertheless, voices in the gay community itself testify to Tom's importance and influence. In the *Daddy* film, Nayland Blake states that Tom provided 'a blueprint for the appearance of gay men in the latter part of the twentieth century', and Tom's fellow erotic artist Etienne adds, referring to gay American men: 'They started to dress and comb their hair and take stances and attitudes that are in his drawings'.

What Tom is particularly credited with is the 'clone' look at its height in the 1970s, surviving into the 1980s, and not even totally dead today. The constituents of the look are: jeans, preferably Levi's 501s, preferably tight, button fly often with the bottom button left undone, a broad leather belt better to cinch the waist and emphasize the V shape of the torso, boots, tight T-shirt and/or plaid workshirt. Further additions to the theme run to: keys dangling from the belt, the jeans being ripped, a coloured handkerchief in a back pocket, a black leather jacket. As Shaun Cole writes: 'All these clothes had a clear meaning in the wider American culture: toughness, virility, aggression, strength, potency'.[4] Obviously one must find a place in the genealogy of this look for Marlon Brando, both in *A Streetcar Named Desire* (1951) and in *The Wild One* (1954). As Stanley Kowalski in the former film, in his preshrunk T-shirt and his specially tightened jeans, both deliberately devised by the costume designer to show off the sculpted body he had been honing daily in the gym, Brando created an image of male beauty, power, and sexuality which immediately took root in western culture. The eroticism of the look would be further enhanced by the addition of the black leather jacket worn by Brando as Johnny, leader of the biker gang, in *The Wild One*. James Dean would pick up the look, and rebel virility would become popular among teenage males and gay men. Graham McCann comments that, by the early 1960s, 'the rebels had become role models'.[5] Tom had bought his first black leather jacket in London in 1957 and his drawings would celebrate this look, pushing it into the realms of all time gay favourites.

The macho clone look had the advantage of not being a difficult look to achieve, or even an expensive one before designers got their hands on it. Tom was providing gay men with an aspirational vision, which they, at first in the United States but eventually everywhere, started turning into a reality. Robert Pierce in his review of Tom's 1980 show in New York wrote:

I see the much-maligned Christopher Street clone look — work boots, Levi's, plaid shirts, leather jackets — as a kind of realization of Tom's fantasy world. Gay men, through the symbolic power of clothing, are asserting their image of themselves as men. Tom's fantasy is being realized on Christopher Street and this is one of the reasons that it's possible to show his work at Robert Samuel. ('Tom of Finland', 13)

A new masculine identity in the image of Tom's hypermasculine fantasies was being forged. The recurring refrain between the sections of the film *Daddy* is 'I'm a Tom's Man/I'm one of Tom's Men'. In the film a member of a gay rock band confesses: 'Since I found this [look] attractive, I thought it would be hot if I made myself look as close to that as I could'. Tom himself called his men 'prototypes', and by the mid 1970s was witnessing gay men turning his original visions from fantasy into reality.

Divested of their clothes too, the massive bodies of Tom's men were moving out of the realm of the unattainable. Washboard stomachs, bulging biceps and firm pectorals were all now within every man's reach through bodybuilding and steroids. What Tom had not thought possible to imitate was happening before his eyes: Tom's readers could actually transform themselves physically into Tom's Men. Again, Tom needs to be put into the context of a general phenomenon. The first Gold's Gym opened in 1965, *Playgirl* magazine started in 1973, the *Chippendales* were created in 1978, the first issues of *Men's Health* and *Men's Fitness* date from 1987. Although the authors of the recent book *The Adonis Complex: The Secret Crisis of Male Body Obsession* do not mention Tom of Finland at all, concentrating instead on the influence of the Hollywood action heroes as represented by Arnold Schwarzenegger and Sylvester Stallone,[6] for gay men it is Tom of Finland who had the greatest influence on their body image. Thanks to him, 'muscles, especially the pectorals, have replaced the sweater and swish as predominant gay signs'.[7]

Tom certainly saw himself as partially responsible for the phenomenon amongst gay men. In 1981 he said in an interview:

The macho style is very fashionable, you see. These days you see many guys who are almost a spitting image of the type I draw. Bodybuilding can take you some way in that direction. I sometimes wonder whether it is good for me to encourage that. It's difficult to say what is natural and what isn't. But in this way it's all becoming a bit over the top. These men are a prototype. They wear the same clothes, have the same haircut, the same mustache. I give that macho fashion another five years. Then everyone will be so used to it that it won't be exciting anymore. (Ramakers, *Dirty Pictures*, 12)

For Tom, being gay is a public act; by far the greatest number of his pictures show men out in the open, indeed having sex in public or semi-public spaces. The higher visibility of gay men with good bodies during the last few decades has contributed to the higher profile of the pumped-up body and to the desirability of such for both gay and straight men. Without realizing it, straight men have been influenced by Tom. Even if they think they can trace the roots of the phenomenon to the action hero, in analysing the Schwarzenegger film *Commando*, Mark Simpson points out that Arnie is really decked out in what Simpson styles 'foppish muscle drag'.[8]

Tom's men have been accused of all looking alike; icons do tend to resemble each other; a look described as a 'clone' look is bound to produce identikit specimens. In the 1970s, this was actually quite useful for gay men. Their gaydar could pick out at a hundred paces whether a man was gay or straight just by external signs. As Richard Dyer attests: 'Visibility, and hence typicality, means that it is easier for gay people to meet others like themselves'.[9] But gradually, as heterosexual men started buying into the clone look, it became more and more difficult to tell who was gay. 'The appropriation of gay macho drag by heterosexual men' (Simpson, *Male Impersonators*, 25) meant that a subcultural look was entering the mainstream. Cole remarks: 'Anyone could be mistaken for a "poofter" now that sartorial pointers had gone' (*Don We Now*, 101). Indeed Lynne Segal comments that ironically 'gay men could be distinguished from straight by their *more* "masculine" appearance'.[10] Attributes of working class masculinity may have been hijacked by Tom for his macho project, but a spin-off of the success of that project was that even straight men found the masculinity of the look attractive. As Simpson states: 'According to heterosexuality, that which is masculine is not queer' (*Male Impersonators*, 107), so it never entered straight heads that the clone look might be a gay look.

Michael Bronski writes: 'The eroticization of the male body over the past half century is a direct result of the influence of gay culture'.[11] Consider the following example. In the early seventies a new phenomenon was reported in New York's gay clubland: after hours of dancing, sweating men were taking off their shirts and dancing bare-chested, stuffing their T shirts into back pockets, or tying shirts around their waist. It was just such a night in the gay club, the Flamingo Bar, that proved an epiphany for Calvin Klein, according to one biography. It was 1974:

As Calvin wandered through the crowd at the Flamingo, the body heat rushed through him like a revelation; this was the cutting edge (...) [The] men! The men at the Flamingo had less to do about sex for him than the notion of portraying men as gods. He realized that what he was watching was the freedom of a new generation, unashamed, in-the-flesh embodiments of Calvin's ideals: straight-looking, masculine men, with chiseled bodies, young Greek gods come to life. The vision of shirtless young men with hardened torsos, all in blue jeans, top button opened, a whisper of hair from the belly button disappearing into the denim pants, would inspire and inform the next ten years of Calvin Klein's print and television advertisements.[12]

'Unashamed, (...) straight-looking, masculine men' in a gay club: the 'embodiments of Calvin's ideals', the triumph of Tom of Finland's fantasies. Gay, as traditionally conceived, would not sell to straight men, but Klein saw the potential in this new gay look. Bordo comments that the gays Klein was so taken with 'embodied a highly masculine aesthetic that — although definitely exciting for gay men — would scream "heterosexual" to (clueless) straights'. She calls the advertising campaigns that resulted 'the mainstream commercialization of the aesthetic legacy of Stanley Kowalski', and I would add that the link between Kowalski and Klein was the work of an advertising man in his own right, Tom of Finland. Once out of the closet, the fit, toned male body has made leaps and bounds in the hands of gay designers, gay photographers, gay consumers. The ubiquity of such images has turned a subcultural phenomenon into 'an aesthetic norm, for straights as well as gays' (Bordo, *The Male Body*, 181, 185). As Peter York declares: 'American capitalism can co-opt almost anything no matter how ostensibly subversive'.[13]

What straight men who bought into the clone look never saw was the conscious eroticization of blue collar workclothes, the fetishization of symbols of masculinity. The exaggeration, the irony, the parody, the subversion at work in Tom's images of masculinity all passed them by. In bodybuilding, gay men play with the boundaries of masculinity pushing male gender characteristics to the nth degree. Such physical ostentation is wasteful, extravagant, excessive; it offers up the male body as spectacle; it is also ambiguous. It is telling that in bodybuilding circles 'pecs' are called 'tits'. Ultimately, it is all show: it is 'muscles as a masquerade of proletarian masculinity'[14], for such muscles are not the result of hard manual labour on farms, or in construction, or out in the woods.[15] Such bodies have no use in our sophisticated urban culture; the only purpose they serve for gay men is to attract other men, a perversion of what the male body is meant for according to compulsory heterosexuality.

Nor have gay men actually changed inside their new armour. This is the body as fancy dress, as drag, as melodrama. Not without reason, Mark Simpson entitled his book *Male Impersonators*, the subtitle being *Men Performing Masculinity*. Far more care and time is taken by gay men to get the look right than men are ever expected to spend on their appearance. In *Daddy* one of the leathermen says over an image of him lovingly polishing his black leather boots: 'We pride ourselves on the way we dress'. One doesn't want the reality of the real bikers' scuffed leathers and muddy boots; one strives instead for the perfect image of everything shiny and just so, as one turns oneself into a hot erotic spectacle to be gazed upon. On admiring a particularly striking example of a male body in an American gay bar, one might hear whispered: 'LLT, TLJ': 'Looks like Tarzan, talks like Jane'. No matter how hypermasculine these men look, the topics of conversation will still be *Changing Rooms* and *Home Front in the Garden* or *Sing-along-a Sound of Music*. As Pronger states: the 'fundamental irony of gay experience (...) is that of seeming to be what one is not' (*The Arena of Masculinity*, 150). In fact, gay men would not want it otherwise: heady with the eroticization of all that is fetishistically masculine, one nevertheless shies away from the full implications of hegemonic masculinity. Some gay men do not know when to stop, and can pile on the gloves, and chains, and studded armbands and wristbands until they are as decorated as Christmas trees. Another of the leathermen in *Daddy* comments: 'The more these guys have on of these things ... the more I like them'. Such reification turns masculinity into decor. But at least for gay men 'it is possible to separate this fantasy image from the reality of that fantasy' (Blachford, 'Male Dominance', 201). And again one can look to Tom's men as the prototype. Ramakers writes of the post Stonewall era: 'A great appropriation was begun of the symbols of hegemonic masculinity in its most corporeal expressions. Gay men creatively and extensively "perverted" masculinity and all its idiosyncrasies to elaborate a hybrid new identity. Tom's work served these men as a highly outspoken and quasi-omnipresent primer for their project' (*Dirty Pictures*, xii). The 1976 picture of the hitchhiker can serve as an example of Tom taking his men over the threshold into hybridization (fig. 1). No longer a real biker, the young man is not even sporting a coherent biker look. It is rather a hybrid: an accumulation of masculine symbols rearranged, adapted and transformed until given a new erotic and sexual meaning, that of a macho gay man: earring in the right ear, tattoo, studded leather cuff, handcuffs, amyl nitrate sniffer around his neck, riding crop

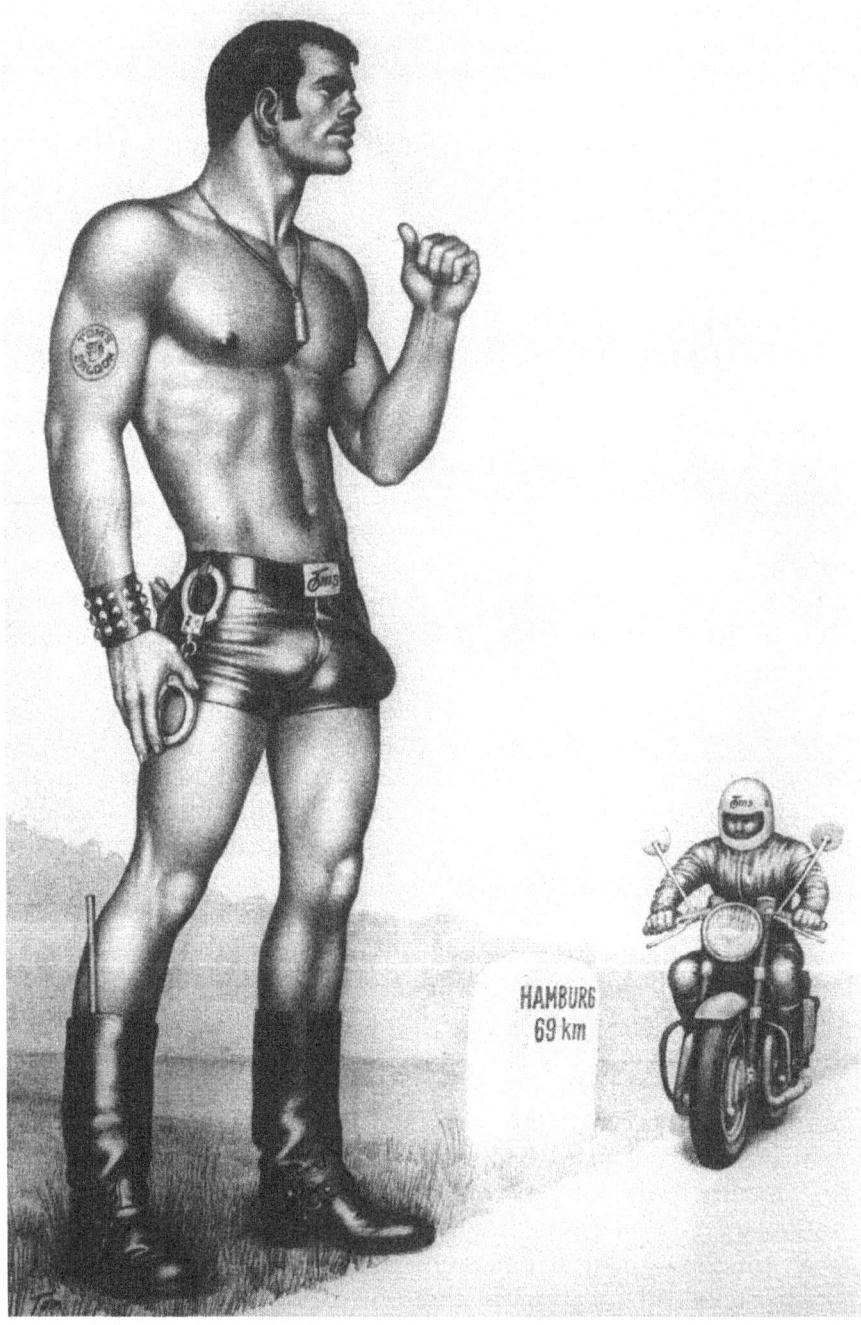

Figure 1. Tom of Finland, *Hitchhiker*, 1976. Courtesy, Tom of Finland Foundation, © 2003.

in boots, handkerchief in a back pocket. In writing of the macho type, and discussing another image, Dyer talks of 'the conscious deployment of *signs* of masculinity' and concludes: 'In marking off the macho man from the simply straight man, this gay type retains the idea of (male) homosexuality implying something different in relation to gender, but here there is no notion of a biological in-betweenism but an excess of masculinity' (*The Matter of Images*, 42). Bordo declares that Tom's hitchhiker's look is one that 'cannot be taken seriously'. She compares Tom's drawing with an advertisement for Versace underwear, jointly captioned 'Ironic phalluses', commenting: 'the symbols of masculinity are so overabundant they become playful parodies of themselves' (*The Male Body*, 98, 99).

A review of Tom's 1989 show at New York's Feature gallery appreciated some of the complexity of Tom's images:

Tom's depiction of power relationships also makes for a more complicated discourse than those that are the concern of standard smut. Tom conjures up images of authority not to worship at their feet, but to subvert them (...). Tom is well versed in the vocabulary of mythology. On the surface, he fosters the iconography of an ideal body type, a gay *übermensch* (...). Tom's work, however, is ultimately about deconstructing that mythology. His icons, while physical representations of what we've been groomed to believe is perfection are, in the end, rendered harmless and vulnerable. See Dick run, indeed. (Quoted in Ramakers, *Dirty Pictures*, 15.)

Had they realized the ultimate source of the macho look they were adopting, had they realized that it was gay men they were imitating, straight men would not have been amused. The hypermasculine images seen in Tom's art, especially of those men in uniform like policemen or soldiers, immediately conjure up images of authority and power. And yet in his eroticization of masculinity, Tom actually undermined such traditional patriarchal images. He says himself in the *Daddy* film: 'This concept has always fascinated me. To realize that an unyielding user of power — not necessarily an abuser — is a soft and humane person. Unleashing the fantasies reverses the roles.'

Pronger states: 'Because it both embraces and violates masculinity, homoeroticism is paradoxical eroticism' (*The Arena of Masculinity*, 71). There is nothing immutable about masculine roles in Tom's work. Because he also drew comic strips as well as individual drawings, one can see from one frame to the next that any one of his men is capable of being top in one encounter and bottom in the next, of penetrating and being penetrated, enjoying either role. Herein lies

Tom's violation of orthodox masculinity, for which the real taboo is violation of the male body. Tom's masculine utopia is phallocentric, but the possession of a penis does not bestow any intrinsic rights or privileges on one or other of the partners.

A violation of orthodox masculinity which could be seen as even more subversive is that of tenderness between men. It was important for Tom that his men were friendly, and he vowed that 'every story would end happily'.[16] As someone comments in *Daddy*: 'Maybe there's a lot of brute force (...) but it always ends up with people having a sense of camaraderie and laughter'. And Etienne adds that in Tom's drawings the 'sense of fun is very important'. Nor are affection, friendship, fidelity and companionship absent from Tomland. Tom himself had a loving and fulfilling partnership of 28 years. And Ramakers can claim: 'Perhaps Tom of Finland's single most significant contribution to the development of a counterdiscourse on male sexuality lies in the integration that his work offers among sex, tenderness, and oddly, community' (*Dirty Pictures*, 236).

Touko Laaksonen died in 1991. Finland now honours Tom of Finland sending exhibitions of his work around the world. There is a Foundation in his name which carefully preserves his drawings and markets Tom of Finland merchandise and clothing. Every gay man recognizes a Tom of Finland drawing. His spirit is present in every gay bar, and a fetish night or leather event invariably has recourse to one of his images for its advertising.

Cole closes his chapter on the macho man by saying: 'What the clone did leave was the legacy of the masculinization of homosexuality and an emphasis on overtly masculine images and physiques' (*Don We Now*, 101).[17] In 1980 Tom gave the macho look another five years. Twenty years on, there are starting to be signs that things might be changing. In the April 2001 issue of the gay magazine *Now UK*, a young Czech porn star was hailed as having a 'wonderful un-pumped body'.[18] And an article in the January 2001 issue of the British gay lifestyle magazine *Attitude* addressed the question: 'Can you still spot a fairy before he opens his mouth?'[19] In reply, the fashion designer Julien McDonald commented:

Gay men have adopted uniforms that have made them look butch: leather, cowboy, military. These are looks that are all identifiably gay. The trend now is to look like the boy next door or a football player. Nobody wants to look gay or camp. I think that the older generation of gay men still hang on to this overtly gay look, but younger gay guys just want to blend in. (...) It signals a need for conformity, not for standing out. ('The Usual Suspects', 56)

In the twenty-first century, with no guidance from gay men, what are straight men going to do?

GUY SNAITH
University of Liverpool

NOTES

1. Quoted in Micha Ramakers, *Dirty Pictures: Tom of Finland, Homosexuality and Masculinity* (New York, St Martin's Press, 2000), 73.
2. *Daddy and the Muscle Academy*, written and directed by Ilppo Pohjola (Filmitakomo Oy, 1991).
3. Robert J. Pierce, 'Tom of Finland: The Case for Gay Art', *The Soho Weekly News* (6 February 1980), 12–13 (12).
4. *Don We Now Our Gay Apparel: Gay Men's Dress in the Twentieth Century* (Oxford, Berg, 2000), 94. Nevertheless, the look did not escape criticism even in gay circles. John Marshall, for example, wrote as early as 1981: 'However, the emergence of "macho men" within the contemporary gay world illustrates, in an ironic way, the extent to which definitions of male homosexuality continue to be pervaded by the tyranny of gender divisions' ('Pansies, perverts and macho men: changing conceptions of male homosexuality', in *The Making of the Modern Homosexual*, edited by Keith Plummer (London, Hutchison, 1981), 133–54, 154).
5. *Rebel Males: Clift, Brando and Dean* (London, Hamish Hamilton, 1991), 168. He relates: 'The moment the young Robert Zimmerman (Bob Dylan) saw *Rebel Without a Cause*, he adopted James Dean's blue jeans and boots, his slouch and smirk; a black leather jacket was added in imitation of Marlon Brando in *The Wild One*' (7). McCann also points out the sexual ambivalence of all three of his rebel males, 'playing at being masculine' (27–8).
6. Harrison G. Pope, Katharine A. Phillips, Robert Olivardia, *The Adonis Complex: The Secret Crisis of Male Body Obsession* (New York, Free Press, 2000).
7. Brian Pronger, *The Arena of Masculinity: Sports, Homosexuality, and the Meaning of Sex* (London, GMP Publishers, 1990), 273. One is reminded of the gay quip: 'No pecs, no sex'.
8. *Male Impersonators: Men Performing Masculinity* (London, Cassell, 1994), 25.
9. *The Matter of Images: Essays on Representations* (London, Routledge, 1993), 21.
10. *Slow Motion: Changing Masculinities, Changing Men* (London, Virago, 1990), 149.
11. *The Pleasure Principle: Sex, Backlash, and the Struggle for Gay Freedom* (New York, St Martin's Press, 2000), 81.

12 Quoted in Susan Bordo, *The Male Body: A New Look at Men in Public and in Private* (New York, Farrar, Straus and Giroux, 1999), 180.
13 Quoted in Gregg Blachford, 'Male dominance and the gay world' in *The Making of the Modern Homosexual*, 184–210 (185).
14 Chris Holmlund, 'Masculinity as Multiple Masquerade; The "mature" Stallone and the Stallone clone' in *Screening the Male: Exploring Masculinities in Hollywood Cinema*, edited by Steven Cohen and Ina Rae Hark (London, Routledge, 1993), 213–29 (214).
15 Compare Yvonne Tasker's comment on the 1980s Hollywood action hero: 'If muscles are signifiers of both struggle and traditional forms of male labor, then for many critics the muscles of male stars seem repulsive and ridiculous precisely because they seem to be dysfunctional, "nothing more" than decoration, a distinctly unmanly designation' ('Dumb Movies for Dumb People: Masculinity, the body, and the voice in contemporary action cinema' in *Screening the Male*, 230–44, 239).
16 F. Valentine Hooven III, 'Drawn and Now Quartered; The Tom of Finland Foundation Finds a Home', *Advocate California* (14 March 1989), 8–9 (8).
17 Despite the positive values gay men have found in Tom's work, he has also been blamed as the source of various negative aspects of the contemporary gay world such as body fascism, narcissism, objectification, conformism, misogyny, and 'attitude'.
18 'Czech Mate', *Now UK*, 28 (April 2001), 25.
19 'The Usual Suspects', *Attitude*, 81 (January 2001), 56–60. The question is posed thus in the table of contents (7).

Freak Flag: Humour and the Photography of George Dureau

When I wrote *The Male Nude in Contemporary Photography* twelve years ago, I downplayed theories of humour.[1] I acknowledged the humour in a few of the works I discussed, but I did not examine its larger theoretical implications for the topic at hand. There were several reasons for this. First of all, I was in my twenties, a little unsure of myself and very unsure my subject would not be dismissed — by the academy as well as the public at large. I was a graduate student in the conservative world of art history, where photography itself seems to demand an apology, and all the more photographed men, unidealized genitals in plain view. It was a bit of a gamble to bring my feminist scrutiny to photography of the male body, to speak in plain terms not of the Lacanian phallus but of the real penis, to say more than most want to hear about the homophobic censure that surrounds the subject and how it unites with misogyny in a sterile prophylactic marriage. In short, I was very serious, and, with the unwieldy adhesive of French post-structuralist and psychoanalytic theory, I put that signifier right back onto the pelvis, and lo and behold, my enlightened department actually let me get away with it.

I took pains to allow none of that derisive joking, which serves to protect us from our discomfort with nudity. I wanted to break through that defensiveness. Jokes are aggressive; they often serve to protect power by identifying and dismissing 'outsiders'. One of my central arguments was a bid for photography which turned the traditional objectification of art into a field of interaction, an alternate subjecthood. So, humour did not serve the task at hand: just getting these questionable pictures into the academy in the first place and, with luck, getting whatever public could manage to plough through my text not to dismiss them nor feel outraged by them. A man with his pants down is in an uncertain position. He submits himself, through photography, to having himself, genitals and all, 'shot'. I decided therefore to protect these men from further 'exposure'. As best as I could I shielded them from jokes.

Perhaps, too, I was afraid of humour. I had so far strayed from the polite lady I was brought up to be, that humour would really be going over the top, you know, a little too masculine (being a feminist was bad enough). Well, I have strayed even farther from that polite lady in training, and now what has become essential to me is not a confrontation with fear but a neat side-step, and that is humour. After a while, taboo becomes familiar, courage once summoned relaxes, a human face appears — and whaddya know, it's the guy around the corner, known him forever. The taboo, once silent and intimidating, becomes a story, and humour helps us tell it. In fact, humour tells it best, because only humour, in Freud's definition, can substitute for the distress of fear and anger — wit, cleverness, control — pleasure.[2]

Freud offers the most precise distinctions between jokes and humour. Jokes are aggressive, always a bit tendentious, riding the edge of hostility. By the means of wit, they offer a substitute for the sexual act, thereby freeing libido. The release of inhibition, stemming from the preconscious, and rising — in its partially sublimated state — to consciousness, creates an economic preservation of energy, which would normally be damming up the libido and its urges. Jokes find a way to satisfy the demands of libido in a socially acceptable manner. We laugh as though at an act of sexual aggression, and the laugh of the joke is a hard, convulsive laugh. Freud does not make the comparison to orgasm, but it fits. The doubling over of the body and release of the intense laugh can best be compared to the orgasmic state and is a surrogate for it.

Humour, on the other hand, often does not produce a laugh. It produces pleasure, a smile, perhaps a chuckle. Humour substitutes for distressing emotion, cleverness, control, mastery, a witty alternative. As the intense and perhaps distressing emotion is circumvented, humour provides another sort of economy, for it is taxing to deal with emotional extremes. Humour is the vehicle for the super-ego, sensing the nascent distress of the ego, to perform a neat side step, an act of narcissistic self-preservation in rising above the situation. By not taking it so seriously, one triumphantly out-smarts the capacity for pathos. Humour is clever and rebellious, and very much a tactic for survival. According to Freud: 'The ego refuses to be distressed by the provocations of reality, to let itself be compelled to suffer. It insists that it cannot be affected by the traumas of the external world; it shows, in fact, that such traumas are no more than occasions for it to gain pleasure'.[3] Freud makes a third distinction: that of the comic, which is an emphasis on the incongruous, where for the effect of release, the ideal is dismantled, thereby saving the person the costly effort of maintaining it. I believe, however, that the comic as so defined by

Freud is really a method, rather than a separate genre. That is, the comic, incongruous play, is a tool for both joking and humour.

The distinction between joking and humour is a necessary one in this paper. I will argue for both in the photography of George Dureau. First, I will deal with humour, and by that I don't mean that something is laugh-out-loud funny. What I mean is it that takes a situation of distress and substitutes — at least for part of the distress — pleasure. It can produce a smile, connectiveness, a delightful uncanny, that strange comparison that opens a window in the head. Anton Ehrenzweig likens the experience of the underlying symbols of art to the joyous release from the unconscious that occurs with jokes.[4] Underlying signs are the key in this essay, too, for I am arguing for a current of humour that unexpectedly complements the fear and confrontation which is instantly apparent in the photography of George Dureau. His work consistently defeats expectations, but, first, the expectations are granted a recognition — in order that they may fall, comically and/or with great import. What I would like to do here is to telescope my criticism of Dureau's work, beginning with my initial fear and defensiveness, touching upon the idealism of my book and ending with my more recently developed sense of humour toward this work. In addition to exhibiting humour, the photographs also embody the process of joking — but not the static objectification of the joke. To be more specific, the men in the photographs are not jokes; they are making them — perhaps at our expense.

When I first encountered Dureau's work I wanted to run away. I was maybe all of twenty three, and I saw his imposing, large prints of nude, male, black and handicapped men while living in New Orleans, his native city.[5] Some of the most powerful photography I had ever seen, they overwhelmed me, and I could not look at them for long. As I became acquainted with George, and swapped prints with him, it was hard for me to believe that such a friendly, effusive man could make such hard-hitting work. Since then, George Dureau's work has kept intersecting with my life at certain critical moments, and each stage has been fraught with terror, but each has forced me to think my way out, and the outside where they have journeyed with me has been every time profoundly pleasurable, a place with humour. The humorous economy at the expense of distress has been working on a meta-level in my life. So, today I have shed the academic mantle that forbids a certain pronoun, you know the one, that overblown singular letter. I am not pretending that humour is not personal. It is very much first person singular, narcissistic skills firmly intact.

Humour coaxes us to adopt the point of view of a protagonist surmounting difficulties, not with heroics but with wit. Likewise, the male nude of history, covered in mantles of codes for ideals, heroics, strength, aggression, dominance, or, when all else fails, a delivering agony, death, or at minimum the insanity/addiction brought on by genius, this male hardly requires the protection of dignity or distance. Patriarchy clothes the man all too well with those. What more serves the purpose is humour, singular, personable, and certainly gentle.

As we after thirty years of critical debate come once again to regard images of men, I propose that it is time to begin with the first person singular, a little conviviality, a bit of kitchen-table banter. Of course, I will up the ante, for I will show not just male nudes but minority men — handicapped men, African-American men, gay men, and straight men who enjoy unclothing before the camera. With regard to minorities, I am suggesting that humour itself is the riskiest business. To see the humour within the aggression that marks the Dureau photograph is to accept the men he shows, not simply as objects of art, but as men in a more complete light, with the full scope of human emotions — aggressive, coy, angry, calm, desiring, desirous, ironic, delivering their jokes, insider ones that may take many viewings, even years to 'get'.

Craig Blanchette (1992), by George Dureau, represents a world-class wheelchair racer (fig. 1). His coy, over-the-shoulder, beauty queen pose is truncated by the space where the rest of the 'ideal' form should be. Beautiful form and absence manifest the same physique. His athletic fingers curl, the natural reflex of his wheel chair racing, in a tense, almost simian pose, the most animated part of his body. Is this unconventional posing of a man in a female poise a confusion and neutralization of signs, or a commentary on the absence implied by conventional beauty as dictated by patriarchy, or is this the unconventional beauty of an athletics predicated, in seeming opposition to athleticism itself, on loss? Likewise, Dureau's *Wilbert Hines* (1983) makes the incongruous comparison of an uplifted boxing glove to the arm which it covers — one too short to box with anything. There is a calm, frontal and iconic seriousness to this image of Hines as a fighter, as if this sport were his entitlement and expectation.

I wish to pause at this juncture to speak a little about George and his working methods. First of all, George would like us to know that he is not, as the first edition of the catalogue *Typical Men!* has described him, an African-American.[6] George Dureau is a white guy, a native and resident of New Orleans, Louisiana. In his seventy-first

Humour and the Photography of George Dureau 93

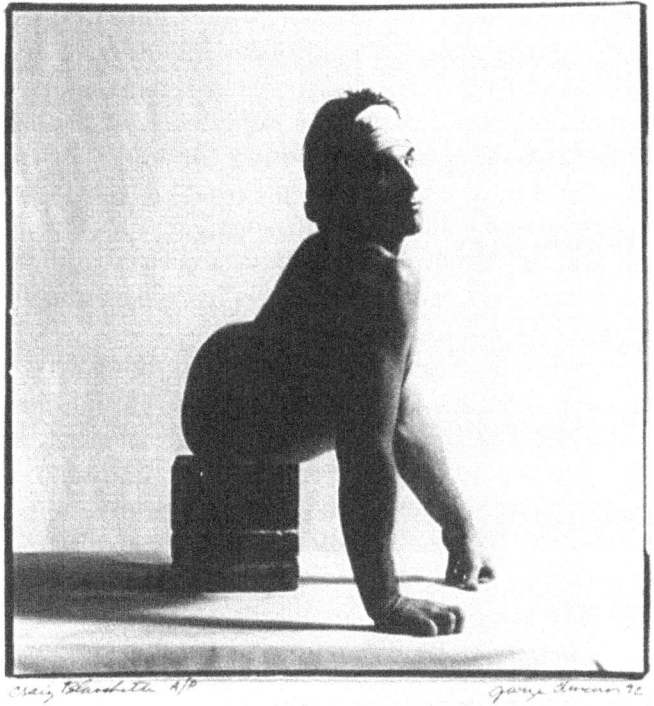

Figure 1. George Dureau, *Craig Blanchette*, 1992.

year, Dureau has achieved the status of an icon in his hometown. His paintings, drawings, and to a lesser extent, his photographs are seen everywhere, and known by everyone. To the world outside that world-unto-itself, New Orleans, George Dureau is known as a photographer. Some regard him as the greatest influence on Robert Mapplethorpe, who was his friend and who had visited him often. It is Mapplethorpe's notoriety that has had great influence on the recognition of Dureau's work, but not on the style of Dureau's photography. Yes, they both in silver halide photographed black men, some of them body builders. The resemblance ends there.

Their methods, style, interests, and the import of their work could not be more different. George photographs his friends, whom he befriends with a gentle acceptance, and an eye towards the long-term. Some are his lovers, most not. All of these men come into and out of his life, not just his camera lens, and he cooks for them, converses for hours with them, employs them when they need a job, strolls about the city with them, gives them money or a place to stay, and he has even taught one friend, Earl Leavell, how to drive. These biographical details would be neither here nor there if they didn't somehow work into the pictures themselves. Many of his friends have been models over the course of many years, decades even. They choose when they want to visit George, and they come repeatedly, obviously enjoying his friendship and the process of posing for him. For each 20 by 24 inch print, and most of his work takes that imposing size or larger, there are hundreds and hundreds of negatives, and dozens of prints from many sessions. Each photograph is, essentially, a slice of a long conversation that has been going on for years and threatens never to end.

It helps to know at this juncture something of New Orleans and its people. New Orleans is sub-tropical, hot, humid, and dreamy. The air most of the year is so thick you could cut it. Nobody does anything fast. People do their best to hide their aggression and to be, on the surface at least, congenial, hospitable, gracious, and everybody is upper-crust and everybody is black or somehow related or relating to somebody black. New Orleans is the stoop-sitter town of towns. A house is just an excuse for a porch, or a stoop, and this is where the populous sits, and observes, and dreams, and talks, and drinks; even the anti-social person here is more sociable than your average New Yorker. New Orleans is a town where secrets seem to exist for the sake of making stories, stories that go on for centuries, the more macabre or appalling, the better. Its history, like those of many urban areas, is brutal, vicious, disease-ridden, in short, god-awful, but New Orleanians cherish their history of malarial swamps, prostitutes, octoroon balls, and the bitterness of slavery. A lot of the city sits on top of cemeteries. They make good foundations in the swamp. Here, evil takes the strangely gentle face of the story teller, and here it is transformed, cherished, and protected, as though the best one could do in life is to retell the suffering and get the leg up on it.

Dureau is part of that society of New Orleanian story-tellers, and the men whose stories he's telling are willing contributors to the tale. As an artist with a classicizing eye, Dureau is moulding his models to his sense of form, and in that way they 'speak' art, but there are all those messy details that do not conform, stories within the story, small giggles at the edges.

Joshua Troy Brown (1979) is certainly handsome, but he's cross-eyed. His hair is unkempt, arms akimbo, no piece of marble is he. His look is arrogant, and contraposto sway-hipped, he stands, a little like David, but with all idealism dropped. He lets us know he's an object, maybe, for this second, but the next one will have to have a new negotiation.

Similarly, *Jonas Williams's* (1979) body is self-contained in its gesture, his eyes somewhere else entirely. His genitals are a locus, but they seem almost tacked-on, objects of desire but unfitting the dreamy-boy look of Williams. The seam of the cloth on which he sits is distracting, included as a counter-point, a bit of reality that does not jive with the beautiful boy in contemplation pose.

Dureau is a classicist, or, rather I believe, a classicizing mannerist at heart. His interest in line and balance and the body as isolated sculptural form is apparent, but, consistently, he messes up the classicism. After all, classicism is not about humour, nor much about stories or anecdotes. As Sir Kenneth Clark reminds us, the classical nude is about ideals. It is never the guy around the block.

A comparison with two types of classicizing send-ups is apt. In Robert Mapplethorpe's *Bob Love* (1979), the classical allusions are there, but they are pure sarcasm, at Love's (pun intended) expense (fig. 2). The swirled, studio-set drapery, the pedestal, the high-keyed studio light, the sculptural firmness to the body all point to versions of antiquity, but Love, here, is slouched, dull-eyed, legs splayed, his

Figure 2. *Bob Love*, 1979 copyright© Robert Mapplethorpe Foundation.

penis a locus on its white, white plate. The drapery, setting and light are contrived. We know, and Love knows what he is intended for, to hell with the classicizing package.

Dureau's *Glen Thompson* (1982) holds the same pose, with classicizing references to the isolation of body as form (fig. 3). Here, too, the classical references are undercut, but to a wholly different effect. Thompson's dead-centre stare, head tilt, straight spine, and crossed arms speak of resistance, a little coy, a little angry, a complex of desire and defensiveness. The blankness of the studio, its self-reflexivity as studio, borders on the comical — it is incongruous, defeating our expectations of the perfection of the studio shoot. The rug and tablecloth call attention to themselves. His feet are suspended, dangling like those of a kid in a too-big chair. He is perched — somewhere between a come-on and a back-off, dark shining muscles against a white-out space, as though dangling by an invisible wire. Behind the tough confrontational front, there is irony and absurdity, a collapse of meaning into non-meaning.

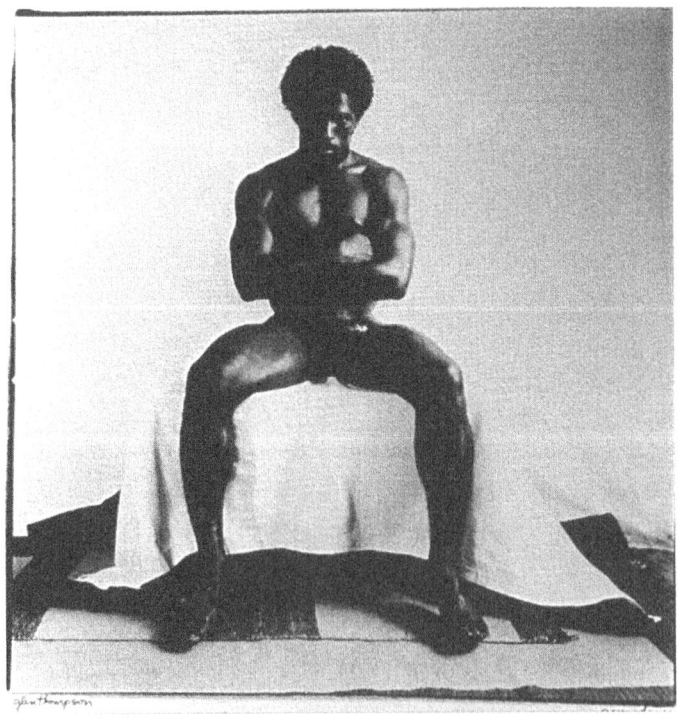

Figure 3. George Dureau, *Glen Thompson*, 1982.

Both Mapplethorpe and Dureau loved pedestals, but for Mapplethorpe the pedestal and the form of the body equate — they are props, both perfect, and both reduced to objects, form (Robert Mapplethorpe, *Tom*, 1986).[7] Dureau, however, marshals the classical signs to make them absurd. In his *Glen Thompson* (1981), the pedestal is a rough splintery box, with visible nails, a little tipsy to the left, and looking like a bit of refuse from a house demolition. The floorboards are equally marred, with a mysterious painted line — a ball court? Mr. Thompson stands, toed-in and arrogant, impatient, as though to say — and when George is this session gonna be done? I got places to go. The seam of the seamless cuts through Thompson's ankles. Sure, Dureau could have rolled the seamless out so that Thompson would have an isolated space of pure white on which to stand. But he didn't, for that is not the story. The sharp outline of Thompson's fine physique marks the contours of desire, but the story is in the lowered head drop-dead-why-don't-you look, and all the pieces gone awry. Desire's not gonna be easy. His body is sculpted by weightlifting, but he's no piece of sculpture for sale.

Dureau uses natural light, with some studio fill, resulting in an illumination that complements the subject. In no manner do we feel that his men are material to be sculpted into objects. The high-keyed, isolating studio lamps of other photographers' work, such as Mapplethorpe's and George Platt Lynes's, are absent. The camera distance is always discrete, and the body is usually full-figure or at least half-figure, never cropped to a detail or part. In short, the light and the cropping are personable, imparting dignity and respect to his subjects.

Dureau loves the pedestal, but for him it becomes a symbol emptied of meaning, its classical signifiers of perfection, idealism, and cool concentration of form turned into their opposites. With *Windell Platt* (1982) and *Stanley Hurd*, the pedestal is a counterpoint to the idiosyncrasies of their forms. Dwarves, or 'little people' as they themselves prefer to be called, balance their own idealism atop their perches, like Hellenistic anomalies come alive. Many little people came to Dureau as they passed through town with circuses or freak shows. The strong and athletic bodies of Hurd and Platt reference the gymnasiums of antiquity, especially with Hurd's prop of a rod, but there is little doubt that the audience for which they perform is expecting something wholly unlike the gymnastic ideal. The dead-on stares of these men reveal nothing of that or of their lives as performers. Isolated from their customary props and environments, they ask us to regard them as ideal forms in their own right.

Can Dureau be serious about this, or is he tongue-in-cheek? I believe the answer is both. Dureau's photographs of little people command our regard, and one of the means by which they do so is by allowing the classical symbols to impart dignity, while they simultaneously collapse under the weight of the ulterior significations transferred to them. Such significations imply the absurdity of classical ideals, the comedy of dysfunction to perfect form. According to Nancy Walker, 'the humorous vision requires the ability to hold two contradictory realities in suspension simultaneously — to perform a mental balancing act that superimposes a comic version of life on the observable facts'.[8] Mahadev Apte cites incongruity, exaggeration and distortion as methods by which the familiar code becomes humorous.[9] Certainly, we have seen these in the photographs of Dureau. If we are not laughing, or even smiling, it is because a repressive factor is at work.

Mary Douglas helps us to understand what that may be. In her by now classic essay, 'Jokes', she argues that jokes rely upon the total social situation.[10] If humour fails, it may be because of social censorship against taking lightly what is 'judged too close to the bone, improper, in bad taste, or irrelevant, on behalf of the hierarchy as such or on behalf of values which are judged too precious and too precarious to be exposed to challenge' (152).

As a society, we have just recently gotten used to imparting dignity and rights to handicapped persons. Persons who consider themselves label-free are not sufficiently close to those whom we label to permit joking. We have formal acceptance but no ease. Dureau is asking us to get the humour in situations where we are counselled to betray no familiarity. Mary Douglas warns us that jokes remain within their social group, mirroring its patterns, mocking it, subverting meaning. The joke is in the social structure, and the joker allows us 'the opportunity for realizing that an accepted pattern has no necessity' and 'that it may be arbitrary and subjective' (150). In order for this to happen, the joke cannot go too far, cannot disrupt the social equilibrium too greatly. When it does, a reactionary response can be expected.

I can attest to witnessing this response with regard to Dureau's *Wilbert Hines* (1977) affectionately termed by the artist, 'Wing Ding at the Mantle' (fig. 4). I have lived with this photograph for a decade now. First, Wing Ding scared me, then he allured me, and then I found in him a perfect example for my ideas about the male nude,

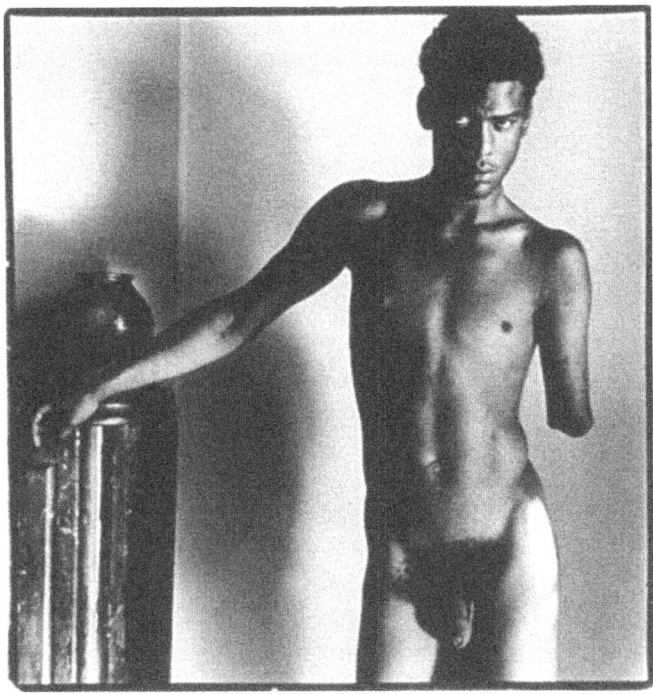

Figure 4. George Dureau, *Wilbert Hines*, 1977.

and featured his image him on the cover of my book. This print hung proudly in my study, a gift from the artist. I used to salute him, his stare was so commanding. Just recently he has started amusing me. But there's more. Wing Ding has featured in a custody battle. Because I hung this photograph in my private study, in a home with children, I was an unfit mother, went my ex-husband's argument. I exhibited extreme cruelty, because I refused to take him off my wall. We had a little war, my then husband and I — he would take down Wing Ding on the sly, and, on the sly, I would hang him back up again. Down and up, down and up, down and up. It was like the advance of armies on a battlefield map. No arguments, mind you. It was just the image of Wing Ding's body that became a symbol for a power struggle between conflicting proprieties and properties. Even before the custody battle collapsed, and I won, I found this darkly comic.

The male nude in my home became freighted with so much unspoken language that the images could no longer bear their significations. Wing Ding had become like a family member, and I couldn't imagine denying him his place of honour. But, of course, Wing Ding himself was never the problem. The real issue was not him, his body or even the male body. The meta-language was/is always about power, and images of male bodies threaten. They threaten most those who feel already threatened in their hold on status.

Interestingly, I have never noticed any child paying the slightest bit of attention to Wing Ding. Just another dude, another picture on the wall, black and white, bor-ring. Now, Disney they like. Nudes have no meaning for them. It is only the adults who react. And, yes, Wing Ding's a teen bearing what teens are best at — trouble. Is it because he's black, one-armed, nude, dangerous-looking, or because he has a penis? Or is it all of them? Wilbert stands at the mantle, a classicizing youthful torso that puts one in mind of the Kritios boy or the lithe limbs of Praxiteles. Like the Kritios boy, Wing Ding has one arm, and it bears self-inflicted scars that resemble graffiti. And that's the frisson, here, scars or graffiti, body or sculpture, private or public. Wilbert Hines is both sides and neither. In this image he is somewhere in between — undeniably human, dangerous, angry, coy, sway-hipped, back-arched, nipples erect, a sexual agent, and he is an ancient sculpture, beautiful as they are, better incomplete. This incompletion, carrying for the viewer our implied completion, or our complementary pathos in the lost thing, is a request. Wing Ding's asking too much of us. It's legitimate to emote before the broken thing that places history in our midst. Is it legitimate to respond, in similar fashion, to the clipped-wing boy who places his own history in our face? Perhaps we do not want to be included in the story. It undoes social expectations to imagine the Kritios boy as flesh-and-blood model, with a penetrating look-back, to puncture form with sexual availability, to make the wry claim that the ideal is — pardon me, I use the word for effect — the ideal is a cripple.

I propose that Wing Ding and Dureau are playing with signifiers, funny and serious at once, in a theatrical send-up. Nancy Walker, whom I have already cited, claims that humour is a weapon and means for survival of a minority group. In her study on women's humour, she claims that women are more story tellers than joke tellers, more anecdotal and conversational. That is, women see humour more as a means of communication than a demonstration of cleverness. For Patricia Spacks 'humor grew out of play and banter, joking and good times — often the domain of women'.[11] A similar structure is occurring, here, between the gay photographer and his model-friends, about whom he endlessly relates histories and anecdotes. In fact, Dureau calls himself a raconteur, a great story teller in the

Figure 5. George Dureau, *Earl Leavell*, 1980.

Southern tradition, a point also made frequently by Edward Lucie Smith in his writing on Dureau (see note 5). The humour in Dureau's photography is on the inside, the story of relationships, given to the public in glimpses, posed shots, little classicizing packages that kick the stuffing out of their form. Earl Leavell, born with radial club arms, was a frequent model of Dureau's, and the photographer enjoys relating that he taught Leavell how to drive, and now he is a professional trucker. From his prints of Leavell, the profile image is the most subtle — *Earl Leavell* (1980) (fig. 5). The witty play on perspectival foreshortening and Leavell's shortened forearm is something we think about upon reflection, after the initial poise of the figure settles on us. He appears with the pensive dignity of a thinker-figure, or a work of African sculpture. The viewer does a double-take, noticing the arm, curved as driftwood is, echoing the material of the pole he holds. Dignity and abnormal shape marry, and once again typical signification is broken. The frontal view version of Leavell is unambiguous, confrontational, yet also pensive and dignified in Leavell's expression. Compare this with the torqued pose of body-builder, *Lann Sawyer* (1985), and suddenly there is a register of twisted 'perfect' form and the perfect variations of handicapped form, so that the two relate on another level. The ideal becomes a contortion of its own law, akin to the handicap of circumstance or birth. Forms conflate, boundaries begin to break down in a way we may not be wholly comfortable with, but which is, visually, witty. Nancy Walker reminds us that 'humour (. . .) tests the boundaries between groups of people' (114).

Another story informs the following two images of B.J. Robinson, the first dating from 1986, and the second, from 1992. My first impression of *B.J. Robinson* (1986), wrapped in a flag, was that this was a Vietnam War Veteran swaddled in the US stars and stripes (fig. 6). No, Dureau corrected: Robinson was a Thalidomide victim, born legless with feet attached directly to the torso. Subsequently, his feet were amputated. The flag is not the US flag but a signal flag, meant for ships. When Dureau wrapped him in this signal flag and asked him to pose on his hands, Robinson remarked that, wrapped in stars, he would seem as though he were flying. The idea of 'hoisting up' Robinson as a 'freak flag' crossed Dureau's mind. This notion of 'freak' derives from counter-cultural slang of the sixties for any extreme individualism that might seem abnormal, attractive, or both.

Figure 6. George Dureau, *B.J. Robinson*, 1980.

It is also street slang for unusual sex and gay sex. His hands poised together and body twisted to provide both frontal and side views, Robinson is a freak flag—whether wrapped in a signal flag or the stars and stripes, the signifier is the same: here I am world, proud as a patriot, and whaddya think of that? Robinson is our soldier—the visual symbolics permit him to trespass boundaries, and Dureau makes a witty play on their collapse. Robinson signifies gay desire, the Vietnam Vet, the proud handicapped man, the patriot, the long-haired freak, the freak show freak (he once was employed to pose in a wax museum), the muscular man who, according to masculine code is self-sufficient, independence itself, home of the free and the brave. His quizzical right eyebrow seems to query us: which one of these write-ins will you inscribe on me? B.J. and Dureau are teasing us, egging us on, inviting us to play with the signs.

In the second image of B.J. dating from 1992, he is poised atop a hollow cylinder—an image, as are many of Dureau's, both frightening and sly (fig. 7). It is impossible to tell where his body ends or begins atop the dominant cylindrical form, which reads in several ways. The first reading is absence or loss—that which signifies the missing part of the man. The second is femininity—the interior space, a circle,

Figure 7. George Dureau, *B.J. Robinson*, 1992.

or room, suggesting penetration and gestation. Gays, women, and handicapped persons conflate, and the signs are those of absence, loss, containment, penetration, and also that of a protected space, interior and mysterious, generation, and plurality. These lead to a third set of signs: the mysterious circle, or globe upon which the man balances, an Atlas in reverse, or a Fortuna atop her wheel, the cycle of life, and the gift of beginning and creating human beings, as well as oneself. Now, when I add the information that the hollow cylinder is a cast of a classical column, we have upon the classical sign, which is hollow, empty, a large amount of anti-classical freight. B.J. stares us down, confrontational, arms akimbo, a stern-creator look on his face, his balance in contradistinction to the dizzy play of signs he sets into motion.

For the freak of 'freak flag' and the 'cripple' which preceded handicapped, both of which linger stubbornly in the social consciousness, Dureau has substituted a wealth of signs. Those who are thought to receive less, who ought to receive our pity, or at least the dignity of formal distancing that labelling implies, are in this photographer's hands a totality of signification, a world unto themselves of meaning.

We are taught that it is in bad taste to laugh or smile at the handicapped person, for their signifier is that of 'loss' or 'misfortune', as though the whole person were subsumed into this one sign. Alright, the image of B.J. seems to say, if you want to make of me a sign for 'loss', then here it is, a loss made manifest, a loss made present. Like the jokes that choose a stereotype and explode it by taking it to the extreme, Robinson and Dureau are making fun of us, this world and its teachings about handling the 'disadvantaged' with kid gloves and discrete, polite distance, and all those odious notions of charity. In rushes a world of meaning, and I, for one, hear within it the sound of laughter.

Mary Douglas, whom I have also frequently cited in this essay, asserts that all jokes are potentially subversive, an anti-rite: 'Laughter and jokes, since they attack classification and hierarchy, are obviously apt symbols for expressing community in this sense of unhierarchized, undifferentiated social relations' (156). The breakdown of symbolics in the Dureau photograph is this sort of insider joke, from the outsiders labelled, well, take your pick: gay, black, handicapped, Hispanic, lower class white. There is a sort of community in this covert joking, an in-your-face with the stigmata. Conventional standards for loss or disadvantage can become absurd when pictured; cameras, after all, only record presence.

Not only humorous, Dureau's photographs are joking, but the aggression and sexual charge of the joke is on us. We are the objects of the intense stares, confrontations, and sexual energies of these men. Barry Sanders claims that laughter decentralizes power, situating it in the individual, against the face of authority. He draws on ideas from the Russian critic, Mikhail Bakhtin:

> Laughter is a vital factor in laying down that prerequisite for fearlessness without which it would be impossible to approach the world realistically. As it draws an object to itself and makes it familiar, laughter delivers the object into the fearless hands of investigative experiment — both scientific and artistic — and into the hands of free experimental fantasy.[12]

Dureau is similarly fearless. Like a storyteller, illustrating his tale with pointed moments, Dureau is asking us to stop and 'hear' the stories — histories a little scary but full of flippant, courageous humour, the triumph of mental work. As with the economy of the process of humour, his subjects refuse to be distressed or affected by their traumas or limitations. Misfortune becomes only a means to gain pleasure. In this elegant economy, Dureau by-passes the customary attitudes of pity or reserve by sending them back, undercut with incongruous meanings, distortions, exaggerations, impossible associations, and an absurd treatment of traditional codes. He also is not afraid of the joke, but the reason we may not be laughing is that the joke is on us; as objects of it we are disadvantaged in perceiving it. Dureau takes disadvantage and sends it back to its source — those who think in such terms, in other words, all of rest of us confident of body and privileged.

In a world that until very recently and perhaps still may make of these men a joke, Dureau takes the joke and makes him a joker. His photographs can be unsettling, for they impart power and dignity to those we often feel superior to. They frighten, but they also allure, inviting us in. They're telling the joke of the limitations the social script sees them as embodying, and they're telling it both with gentle humour and with aggressive, sexual looks. Sometimes we're smiling with them, and sometimes they're laughing at us. The extent that we feel comfortable enough to hear the laughter may be the extent to which we are able to accept the very difficult things this work asks of us — to see these men in a relational light, as full persons, to get close enough for humour.

MELODY D. DAVIS

NOTES

1. Melody D. Davis, *The Male Nude in Contemporary Photography* (Philadelphia, PA, Temple University Press, 1991).
2. *Jokes and their Relation to the Unconscious* (1905), *The Standard Edition of the Complete Psychological Works of Sigmund Freud* (hereafter *S.E.*), XIII.
3. Freud, *Humour*, *S.E.* XXI (1927) 162.
4. Anton Ehrenzweig, *The Psychoanalysis of Artistic Vision and Hearing: A Theory of Unconscious Perception* (London, Routledge and Kegan Paul, 1953).
5. See George Dureau, *George Dureau, New Orleans: Fifty Photographs*, Introduction by Edward Lucie-Smith (London, GMP Publishers, 1985).
6. Michael Worton and Judith Still, *Typical Men !* Exhibition Catalogue (University of Nottingham, Djanogly Art Gallery, 2001).
7. Melody Davis, *The Male Nude*, plate 23.
8. Nancy Walker, *A Very Serious Thing: Women's Humor in American Culture* (Minneapolis, University of Minnesota Press, 1988), 82.
9. Mahadev Apte, *Humor and Laughter: An Anthropological Approach* (Ithaca, NY, Cornell University Press, 1985), 16–17.
10. Mary Douglas, 'Jokes', in *Selected Essays in Anthropology* (London and New York, Routledge, 1999), 148–64.
11. Patricia Meyer Spacks, *Gossip* (New York, Alfred A. Knopf, 1985), 27.
12. Mikhail Bakhtin, *The Dialogic Imagination: Four Essays*, edited by Michael Holquist and translated by Caryl Emerson and Michael Holquist (Austin, University of Texas Press, 1981), 23.

In Conversation: Photographer Ajamu and Cultural Critic Anita Naoko Pilgrim

We developed this article in two parts. The first part is based on a discussion we held about Ajamu's work as part of the Men's Bodies conference. At that time, Ajamu was working in the medium of black and white still photography. The second part we wrote in January 2003, discussing more recent developments in Ajamu's work. In the intervening time, Ajamu has been a Theory Researcher at the Jan van Eyck Akademie, a post-academic institution in Maastricht, the Netherlands, and has changed media from still photography to video installations. In terms of philosophy, we found that in this new medium it had been possible for him to develop further many of the ideas we had been interested in exploring in our discussion at the conference.

I. Men's Bodies

Anita — I've worked with Ajamu for about four years now, I wrote a chapter about his photography in my PhD thesis.[1] In my PhD work, I was developing a model of a more collaborative way of working. Ajamu does a lot of thinking and writing about his work, and it would be stupid to ignore that. I much prefer to work with people in developing thinking on their work. So I was delighted when he offered me the chance to join him in conversation about his photography, and for us to talk together about his work at the *Men's Bodies* conference.

In our conversation, we decided to cover three themes:

1. Ajamu's personal history, leading to an exploration of ideas of the body and black subjectivity.
2. The body and blackness/queerness.
3. Playfulness. (We mean by this, serious pleasures and the politics of queer.)

In talking about Ajamu's personal history, we didn't mean to deny the Barthesian idea of the 'death of the author'. We both think the viewer can have their own idea of a picture. However, we also think that setting the work in the context of the experience from which it was developed can offer the viewer another layer of understanding.

(This is particularly the case with Ajamu's work which is explicitly concerned with concepts of identity he has been forced to come to terms with through his own lived experience.)

Personal History

Anita — Ajamu grew up in Huddersfield, West Yorkshire, which is a small town of which he once said to me, 'it might as well be a village'. The black and the gay communities were strictly segregated here, and crossing over between the two was a physical as well as a mental challenge. Ajamu has described one episode that occurred while he had a job collecting glasses in the (white) gay club *The Gemini* (since closed down) in Huddersfield.

> The black club was just around the corner. I used to stand across the road, wait for the road to be clear of black people, run across the road. When I was leaving I would ask someone to look [out for me]. This was like 1983. (Quoted in Pilgrim, *Feeling for Politics*, 259)

Ajamu — There were particular unsaid codes (or when it was said, it was usually in terms of abuse), of how black men were supposed to act and behave. I was at this point dressing in leathers, white T shirt, in what can be described as a predominantly white gay clone look in Huddersfield at that time. For some black gay men, who were in the closet, wearing the particular dominant look in the black community, which was very different, was a means of protecting one's self, of surviving in a small town, not just surviving verbal abuse but also physical abuse. Masculinity was embodied in a hard-edged kind of way, so there was no room for any looks/behaviour that were perceived to be different or feminine. Being different from the acceptable 'norm' was equated with being a battyman/sodomite.

This was where I began to ask questions about what is 'this black', that is different from 'that black'. The representations of gay men (white) in the media were not only limited but downright offensive (John Inman, Larry Grayson, Frankie Howerd), so I was caught dwelling in this strange place, around my own identity. My way out of it was to begin to create alternative images to what I saw, and to capture on film my own desires and fantasies. I started off by photographing black men I was attracted to, without them being aware of my sexual desires or identity. At that point I was thinking about images more critically, and not just in terms of technique.

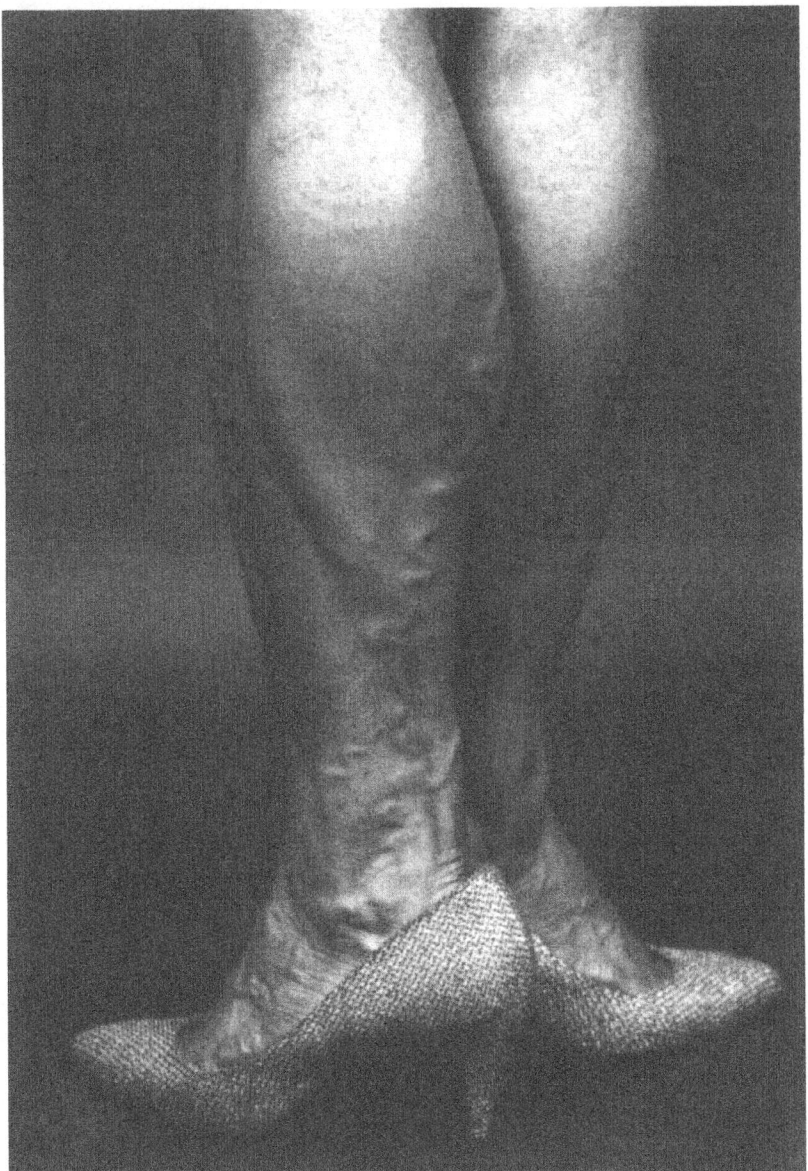

Figure 1. Ajamu, *Silver Heels*, 1993.

My increasing frustrations led me to playfully challenge ideas around what could be termed the 'identity politics' put forward by artists, cultural activists/critics, philosophers. My view was that I should attempt to move beyond the binary position, adopted by these people, that did not go far enough — to move beyond the either/or

110 *Paragraph*

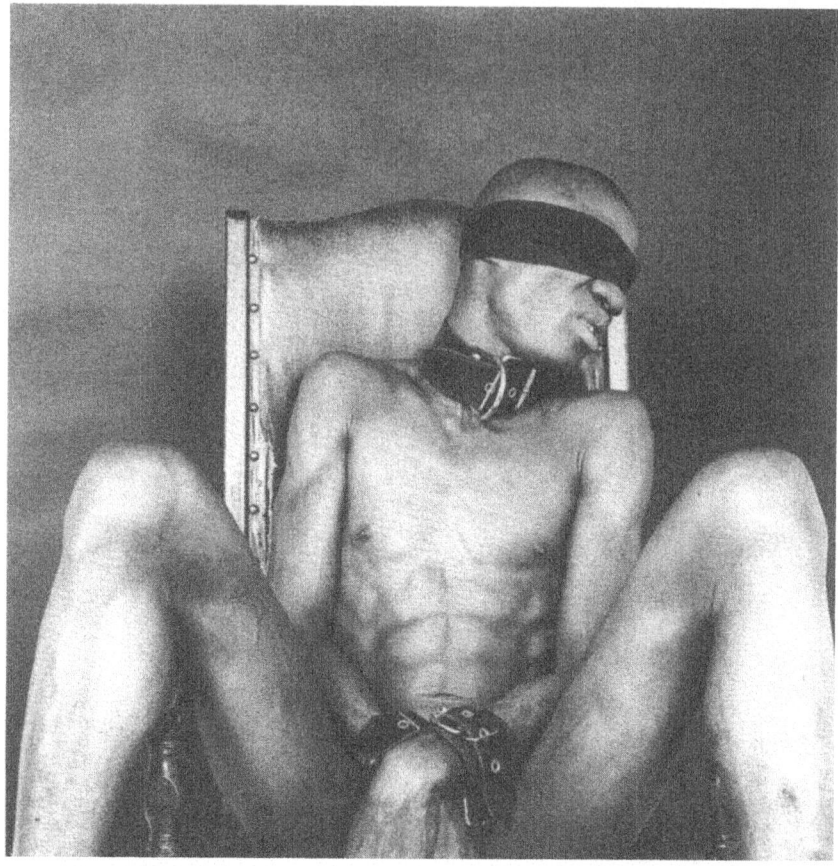

Figure 2. Ajamu, *Untitled (from Black Circus Master Series)*, 1997.

boundaries, the ideas put forward that always appeared to fold back in on themselves. My aim was to side-step some of these discourses, and to re-think the space in between, the multiplicity of the inbetweenness; to play with and against the 'either/or' boundaries, within the space, the 'and' space (as in black *and* gay), the slice of the binaries. More importantly, to ask what were the consequences of such a re-thinking.

The Body and Blackness

Anita—I particularly like the way your work transcends the essentialism/anti-essentialism debate which has been a problem for sociological thinking on issues like those of 'race' politics. Although we want to move beyond fixed ideas of the body and say 'race' isn't

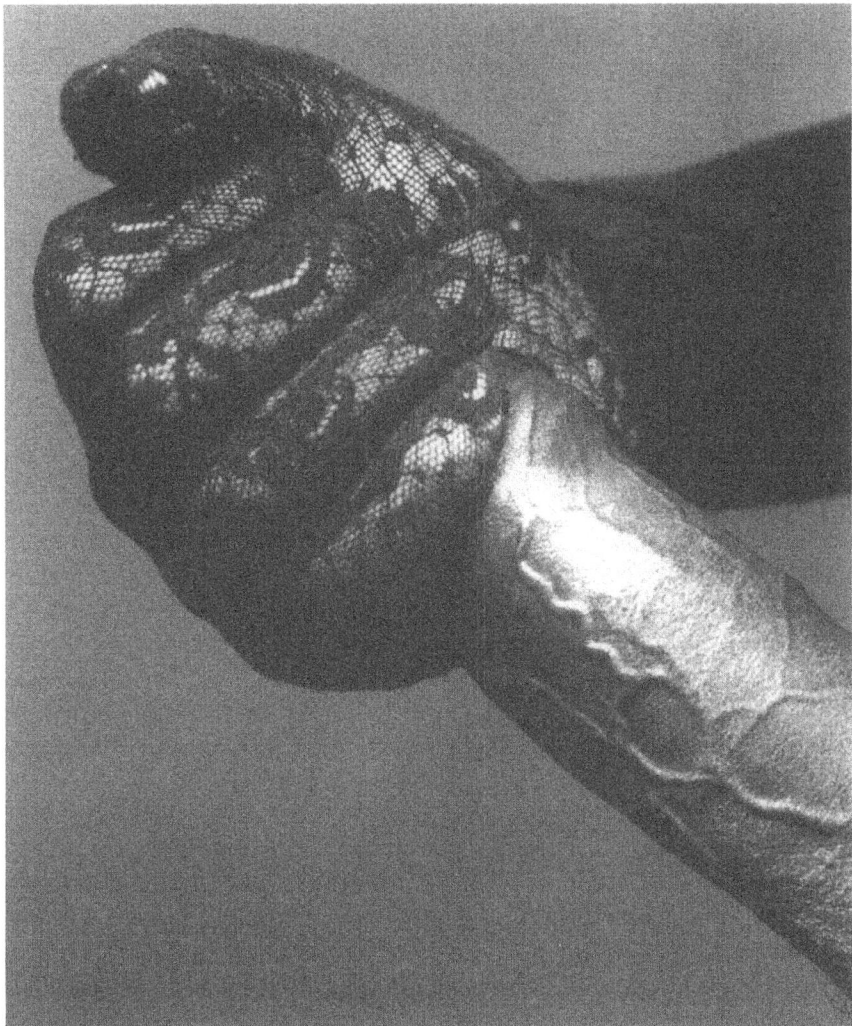

Figure 3. Ajamu, *Cock and Glove*, 1993.

about essentialist things like skin colour, we also have to acknowledge that many people still read 'race' as about these things. In your photographs, the bodies are there, they can be read in these ways, but there's also an undermining of these fixed binaries. For example, the blonde feminine wig on the black male body heightens our awareness of that body's masculinity and blackness, but simultaneously makes fun of that awareness. Hair is no longer a fixed marker of identity when a wig signifying desirable white femininity fits the head of a black man. By extension, other essentialist markers through which we are reading the person as black and male (skin, build of body) become questionable too. You achieve that undermining through queering what's there.

But before we talk more about the playfulness of queer, perhaps you could say something which is more on the serious side of 'gay politics' rather than 'queer politics'. I know that the *Black Gay Men's Conference* was a very important event in your life.

Ajamu — The first and only national *Black Gay Men's Conference*, October 1987, was a milestone with regards to the Black UK queer experience. I was living in Chapeltown, Leeds (a large Afro-Caribbean area) at the time, and I was extremely alienated and lonely. I came across an advert in *The Caribbean Times*, contacted the organisers and came to London for the event.

There were over 60 Brothers/Bristers at the event, the workshops covered issues from safer sex, to Black lesbian and gay history. Black Berri, a musician from the States, performed many songs from his album. This was the first time I felt I was coming into a place I could call home and belong. By January 1988, I had moved to London.

Anita — Bodybuilding was a theme of the conference, and I know it had a significance for you too.

Ajamu — Bodybuilding for me was one of those areas that I have always been interested in, especially as it's become an archetypal image of the male body, and most photographers are still obsessed by this so-called ideal body type.

My practice has been a consistent attempt to subvert, re-think, play with these limited modes of representations around particular bodies in a multi-dimensional way, since most men, myself included, do not look like this or fall into these categories, what do these images do to men in regards to self-esteem, etc. I am aware that since the advent of AIDS as an example, there was a strong desire on the part of many gay men not to fall into the stereotypical notion of the 'sick Homo' yet on the other hand this obsession with the body beautiful is not only tired but marginalizes many men from within our own queer communities.

Playfulness (or Serious Pleasures)

Anita — There is a tension between binaries about which you feel a certain ambiguity. Kobena Mercer describes this kind of ambiguity in writing about Mapplethorpe's photographs of black men.[2] He recognizes their racism, but also finds them very beautiful and sexy. I think some of your most exciting work comes, as you were saying earlier, out of your exploring the 'and' space, or the slice between binaries. The binaries set up can be on the one hand offensive, on the other hand they can contain beauties and challenges. Could we enjoy feelings of desire without the dynamic tension of binaries? I don't believe we could, and I think this is the reason why we are unable to simply discard concrete markers of identity in spite of the problems of racism, sexism, homophobia to which they are also attached.

You get a lot of fun out of playing with ambiguous material. For example, your work has relationships with pornography and Sado-Masochism, as well as with bodybuilding.

Ajamu — The issue of Sado-Masochism, in my view the most intellectual of the sexual practices, has always fascinated me, on a physical and political/philosophical level. These so-called 'Dangerous Games' or 'forbidden desires' raise many problematic and uncomfortable issues for many black people in my view. In particular, this is in regards to what some of the 'toys' signify (the whips, collars, chains, handcuffs) or let's say master and slave scenarios. I have wondered is there such a thing as a black collective memory around Slavery? (N.B. SM is based on consent, slavery was not.) Can SM offer or create a peculiar kind of radical black subjectivity? Can a black person or anyone perceived to be 'other' embrace SM as purely pleasure without it being seen as a pathology?

I am curious to know whether play, humour, jokes, can be used as some kind of technique to re-think ideas round 'identity politics', the body, genders, race/isms, pleasures and sexualities. My interest (apart from finding vanilla sex — suck and fuck — boring) in the 'Theatre of SM' is because of the chance to play out a wide variety of roles, that will not be tolerated or accepted in wider society or even in lesbian, gay, bisexual and transgender communities. SM play was never meant to be politically correct, that's why I enjoy it, pushing and exploring my own 'me-selves', limits and boundaries.

Anita — Maybe if, as Foucault says, we can't step outside of the relations of power, we can play inside them.

Ajamu — That's what the Fooky says, then I agree, she gets amen to that!

II. New Work

To our way of thinking, play is the direct opposite of seriousness. At first sight this opposition seems as irreducible to other categories as the play-concept itself. Examined more closely, however, the contrast between play and seriousness proves to be neither conclusive nor fixed. We can say: play is non-serious. But apart from the fact that this proposition tells us nothing about the positive qualities of play, it is extraordinarily easy to refute. As soon as we proceed from 'play is non-serious' to 'play is not serious' the contrast leaves us in the lurch for some play can be very serious indeed.[3]

'The voice may well be the key to the presence of the present'.[4]

Ajamu — My current work in progress involves extending the traditional definitions of fine art photography, and exploring physical performance by moving away from Black and White photographic imagery into working with video.

Poetics of Provocation is an investigation into how the seriousness of play can be used as a strategy to re-think notions of identities, the body, race, genders, sexualities and pleasures. It can be argued that we have all played, at some moment in our lives, and recognize play and know what it feels like. Yet to define what play 'is', and more importantly how play 'works' has been a difficult concept to grasp, across many disciplines. General notions of play include fun, wit, jokes, humour. The kind of play I am proposing has a peculiar property to it altogether: on the one hand it frames something, and on the other hand, it has no life of its own. It installs fun, humour, harmlessness yet at the same time it does include risk, provocation, mischief, misunderstanding and danger. It has a strange technique to it, it moves in many directions simultaneously, the 'nature of it' is paradoxical and ambiguous.

Working with over three hundred words, some of which I chose myself, with a larger proportion given to me by family members, close friends and fellow artists, I am exploring these words and their attachments in relation to the various names and personas I have worked with/created over the years. These words are simultaneously about me, and not me, and the peculiar 'in-between-ness' which they represent raises a host of questions with regards to identity as something containable/'rigid'. In fact this space created by these words points to an 'elsewhere' and perhaps a different kind of politics. (The completed project will include three additional short pieces, working with three large monitors and one floor projection.)

Anita — the work in progress *Poetics of Provocation* currently consists of a six-minute video in which two heads, both Ajamu's, face each other. The heads wear a heavy collar, bringing images of slavery to mind. The two heads hold a conversation composed of descriptive words, such as: photographer, vulnerable, battyboy, hairy, ignorant, uncle, nipple, cock, lips, assertive. The various facets of Ajamu's identities are being constructed and deconstructed simultaneously here in a conversation with 'himself'. Then, just as other people form and re-form their idea of who oneself/Ajamu is, the viewer listens and reacts: Yes, that confirms my idea of the Ajamu I know; oh, that's a side to him I didn't realize was there. Ajamu has taken words describing several persona he has formed, including 'Carlton Cockburn' (his birth name) and 'Miss Tissue' (the character in the blonde wig who is in some of his still photography). This is no mistaken attempt to get at an 'authentic self'. There are several 'selves' being described, male and female / blonde and black, not only by Ajamu but also by his family, ex-lover, friends and fellow artists. In an affirmation of that concept 'the death of the author' (which we briefly mentioned above), the voices of viewers/family and community members have already been incorporated into this work.

Can you say a bit about your work at the Jan Van Eyck Akademie and the shift from still photography to video?

Ajamu — I applied to do a research project at the Jan Van Eyck Akademie, and was accepted as a Theory Researcher. The Jan Van Eyck is a very small academy, almost monastic in character, with three departments (Fine Art, Theory and Design), and about ten participants in each. You are there for two years. There are seminars, lectures, studio visits by lecturers, and by the advising researchers. Participants come from all over the world. One of the best things about the Jan Van Eyck is that you are not just attached to your chosen department, but are able to move between all three of them.

The Jan Van Eyck Akademie allowed me to re-think the work I was doing, and where I wanted to go with my work. I've been constantly producing work, but there came a point where I just felt stuck in the work I was doing and the medium I was working in. The Jan Van Eyck allowed me the freedom; it was a place to experiment, play and explore — mediums and ideas. Who am I, and where am I now? I was the only black person at the Jan Van Eyck, and one of the few openly queer practitioners there. There was no black community around Maastricht and the gay community was extremely small. Here am I, removed from Brixton, where I had been living for twelve years and where the black and the gay communities are very strong. That then raises other sorts of questions about who I am and where I am now.

This was my chance to explore video and work with various computer programmes in terms of pulling the video together. We had access to the building and equipment 24 hours, access to technicians, a stipend to keep us and funding to develop ideas as well. The financial and technical freedom was central. It freed up stresses I had in London applying for grants. For two years I could just play and experiment without having to justify my ideas. And there was a cross-dialogue between people from all over the world.

Anita — Can you say a bit about the leap this enabled you to make from still photography to video?

Ajamu — It was a leap and an extension. The point I got to in photography was that the medium could no longer work how I wanted it to, or answer the questions I was posing. I was working with questions of identity, let's say the voice: tone, timbre, timing, rhythms. I wanted notions of time and speed in my images. With video I was able to move away from the visual voice into exploring those questions on how identities could be produced, through tone and rhythm, time and space.

When we discuss 'race', gender, etc, it's a dialogue with the public/monologue with ourselves establishing the idea of the 'authentic self'. Maybe there's no core.

Anita — Maybe it's all periphery.

Ajamu — Calling you 'dirty queer', what happens when you inhabit that space. That offers a different way of being, possibly.

Anita — Foucault would call that 'reverse discourse', taking over a negative definition such as 'nigger' or 'queer' and owning it with pride instead of shame. But your work seems to develop on from that. You don't only have your voice re-occupying the negative definitions, the voices of others who may have called out such words trying to put you down (and thereby raise their own sense of identity) are also there.

Ajamu — The point where you can't hear what's going on [where the voices of the two Ajamus merge together in the video installation], I think that is the space I'm trying to articulate around identity questions. I think what we're trying to articulate is the 'unsayable something', to borrow a term or phrase from johnny dethilo, around these questions. The space I'm trying to articulate resides elsewhere. When we talk about 'race', sexuality, gender we are used to using attachments, to attach them to something, but I think this space cannot necessarily be spoken. I think that's one of the frustrations, or limitations actually, around how identity questions are being posed or explained.

Anita — Can you say a bit more about your description of the 'play' that happens in that 'space' as having 'no life of its own'?

In Conversation: Photographer Ajamu and Cultural Critic Anita Naoko Pilgrim 117

Ajamu — On one level, this thing I'm trying to articulate, it's something, and it's nothing at the same time. If I tap out at this speed, 1, 2, 3, 4; then if I tap out at this speed, 1, 2, *pause*, 4 — there's still something there, but there's nothing there.

Anita — It's implicit. I think I understand, although it's not a concept easy to put into words: the space which has nothing except our implicit assumptions in it. But that is where our identities are formed, in a space of implicit and inarticulate assumption.

What I like about the space your new work provides is that it seems to corrupt the binaries which so much of identity depends on. In our discussion at the *Men's Bodies* conference, we were already concerned with those binaries: black/white, male/female. So much of identity seems to be formed by rejecting something in order to be something. That dynamic between binaries, the frustration which leads people to reject you as 'battyboy' in order to identify as heterosexual, is present in this new work (in the voices of those who describe you in this way) in a way in which it wasn't present in the still photography which sought to re-occupy denigrated identities such as 'queer'. I think that the presentation of that dynamic moves us a stage closer to the collapse of those binaries, the acknowledgement that our 'identity' is not a fixed sole existent subject defined against some Other object, but is a dynamic, fragmented set of 'faces', some of which might appear to contradict others (as Miss Tissue seems to contradict Carlton Cockburn). It's as if there are pieces of identity all over the floor like bits of toys to be played with.

Ajamu — Or bits of dirty laundry!

Anita — Yeuch! Sometimes we might put them in the wash, but we don't have to get them whiter than white.

Over the last year, I've been waiting to understand the new work Ajamu was developing, unsure about how successful his change of medium might be. I was puzzled by the shift to video, feeling that his previous work had depended so much on the technicalities of still portraiture to convey what Ajamu wanted us as viewers to think about: bodybuilder in a bra, a man's foot in a woman's high-heeled shoe. Now I understand what it was he couldn't get from still photography and needed in order to continue to provoke us in our ideas about ourselves: rhythm, words, voice. These give that sense of the present that Dolar describes, the present in which our identity is formed. Our identities in the past have been fixed by the passage of time. In the future, we have no way of knowing who we will become. The dynamic 'conversation' with ourselves and others, power-laden and playful, through which we constantly describe/inscribe ourselves, happens in the here and now, a space which is both something and nothing, with no life of its own yet full of energies we and those about us create, some of which comes from the tension between binaries.

AJAMU X
Jan Van Eyck Akademie

ANITA NAOKO PILGRIM
London Metropolitan University

NOTES

1 Anita Naoko Pilgrim, *Feeling for Politics: the Translation of Suffering and Desire in Black and Queer Performativity* (Unpublished PhD thesis, Goldsmiths College, University of London, 2000).
2 Kobena Mercer, *Welcome to the Jungle: New Positions in Black Cultural Studies.* (New York and London, Routledge, 1994).
3 Johan Huizinga, *Homo ludens: a Study of the Play-Element in Culture* (London, Routledge and Kegan Paul, 1980).
4 Mladen Dolar, 'The Object Voice', in *The Gaze and Voice as Love Objects*, edited by Renata Saleci and Slavoj Žižek (Duke University Press, New York, 1996). (Ajamu found the quote in the catalogue to an exhibition called *The Bastard*, held in Antwerp, November 2002).

What is a Man? Looking at the Traces of Men's Sexuality, Race and Class in the Work of Some Contemporary Photographers

This article focuses on selected works from an exhibition (*Typical Men! Recent Photography of the Male Body by Men*, Djanogly Art Gallery, Nottingham, March–April, 2001, curated by Michael Worton and myself) that was an attempt to explore the representation of the male body in one particular medium in the last two decades of the twentieth century.[1] Photography evokes the question, not just of realism but, of the real for many viewers even though some contemporary photographers, such as David Newman, explicitly manipulate images to a considerable degree.[2] Our close relationship to photography in everyday life, creating memories for ourselves, arguably makes our relationship to art photography a particularly acute or intimate one. This intimacy, and sense of the real, aroused by photographs makes particularly sharp the question of what must be *covered* (made apparent *and* hidden) in our image of man. In the historical period in which photography has developed it is the penis which has above all been covered, the penis that might not measure up to the mighty phallus, the signifier of masculine power and of desire. Men can (be shown to) *have* emblems of the phallus (other parts of their body, instruments). But the penis itself, not presented in an idealization, might seem too frail, too fleshy, in a context where it might unwittingly be the object of desire.[3] Moreover the whole body as phallus (*being* the phallus) can be a kind of feminization.

The decision to use only male photographers in the exhibition was partly a pragmatic one relating to the size of the space available, and the desire not to invite generalizations about how each sex approaches the male body from a necessarily small sample. It was also in part an invitation to a particular kind of speculation/specularization/self-reflexivity, asking the questions: how do men look at themselves (relating to the question of narcissism and of homoeroticism) and how can men present men as objects of desire? This objectification can of course be of interest to women too. The generalization 'men' (and 'women') was importantly and deliberately fractured by the evocation of specific histories — with their implication of race, class, generation, sexuality and so on. The constellation of attributes conjured up in response to the question 'What is a (real) man?' is self-evidently historically and culturally specific. Even what may at first appear to be a biological lowest common denominator is more slippery than it seems. If even sex is culturally determined, gender (masculine or feminine) is even harder to pin down. One key issue is that of the boundaries between public and private, and what is permitted to be shown in either domain.

Pictures in the Exhibition

Typical Men! included about 100 images, featuring around 20 artists from a range of countries (Canada, The Czech Republic, Finland, India, The Netherlands, Nigeria, the UK, the USA, Venezuela) — although the 'from' disguises other, sometimes multiple, nationalities or choices of places to live. Some were well established: notorious such as Robert Mapplethorpe or Joel-Peter Witkin, or achieving marks of distinction such as exhibition in the Tate (John Coplans). Some were very new on the scene: Lee Wagstaff is only in his early 30s and graduated from the Royal College of Art in 2000. Some are now dead. Some are gay, some are not. There was considerable heterogeneity of styles. Many others could of course have been included. Some work which we were eager to include (such as that of Dieter Appelt, Hervé Guibert and Yasumasa Morimura) was not available for loan.

In this article, I shall focus on only a small number of images in order to try to pull out some of the dense network of explicit references the artists have put into their work. And, just as importantly, I shall focus on the readings that we as viewers might want to construct ourselves, and, in particular, some of the questions that the images might make us ask ourselves. The exhibition was, above all, supposed to pose questions about typicality, rather than posit conclusions. Many pictures here could be looked at as purely aesthetic objects. A photographic (or painted, sculpted) portrait can show us a figure stripped of any social or historical context. However, in this article, I shall be looking (sometimes with, sometimes against, the grain of the images) for social and political meanings particularly around race, sexuality and class. Other significations, such as age, health or mortality will inevitably be of some relevance. I shall begin by analysing the work of three American photographers (Mapplethorpe,

Dureau and Harris), and would make no apology for this bias since the United States has special power and significance in our world of globalized imagery.

Robert Mapplethorpe

Mapplethorpe is perhaps the best known and most influential of male photographers of the male body.[4] His work, and its reception, has made an important contribution to the shift from the margins (gay erotica or other specialized purposes, for a select market) to the high art mainstream which photographs of the male nude have undergone. Certain images are still of course vulnerable to censorship by those who regard them as pornographic, and still highly controversial. In terms of sexuality (and for women) his role in promoting the male body as a desirable object is highly significant.

Critique

As a wealthy white man, who often photographed poor African-Americans, and who had sex with many of his models, Mapplethorpe is vulnerable to charges of exploitation. Thus far he stands in a long tradition of male artists, whatever their sexual predilections. However, the critique of Mapplethorpe goes beyond the biographical. Setting aside opposition to his more explicit images from, say, the religious right, there is another debate that raises the question whether Mapplethorpe aestheticizes in a way which objectifies. His models are already selected for their stunning muscular physiques, and he represents them as beautiful objects, collector's pieces, via his insistent references to classical sculpture (the fleshly bodies of his models made to look as if made from marble) and via fragmentation, or details of pose and camera angle. He is renowned for his depiction of perfect bodies (as perfectly desirable commodities) with no wrinkles or sags — his images are the opposite of the Coplans self-portraits, which feature the ageing male body in enormous close-up. Melody Davis has asked whether race substitutes for sex in photographs which, beautiful as they are, do no more than glamourize the excluded.[5] In other words, whether the strategies commonly used to objectify women are here deployed in the objectification of black men. Kobena Mercer has commented that African-Americans in Mapplethorpe's pictures are all nude, always decontextualized, and that 'according to Mapplethorpe's line of sight: Black + Male = Erotic/Aesthetic Object'.[6] These men are not *doing* but *being* — they are feminized in a way that disempowers men who, by virtue of class and race (and indeed sexuality), are already disempowered.

Typical Men! included five Mapplethorpe images of African-American men. In *Thomas* (1987) the model's pose makes a deliberate reference to the classical discus thrower. It could be argued that this is the classical sculptural take on the familiar image of the black man as sports hero, which is the media's tamed and domesticated version of the frightening physically-powerful black man as criminal.[7] *Phillip Prioleau* (1979) shows the model perched on pedestal like St Simeon. This could be seen, as Davis suggests, as Mapplethorpe (the powerful) exalting the powerless — a tactic frequently deployed with women, made into goddesses — because of their (physical) perfection. This elevation ignores realities of racism and poverty. *Leigh Lee* shows a model with bleached blonde hair, and *Dennis Speight* is bent over with his penis visible below his chin. The whole (or part) body can be seen here as emblematic of the phallus — the phallic ideal — a kind of fetish. The other fetish object is the perfect maternal breast, perhaps represented in Mapplethorpe by perfect available buttocks as in *Ajitto*. Like women, these men are interchangeable objects, but have no collectivity.[8] Mark A. Reid makes an additional point: Mapplethorpe has been treated by the white art establishment as having had the first and last word on the black male nude. Meanwhile a number of interesting black artists who work on the male nude have been relatively ignored.[9]

Recuperation

One key question is that of the context of viewing — Mercer's first reading of Mapplethorpe was fairly hostile, but later he published a 're-vision' in terms of undecidability — analysing contradictory elements in the work. Earlier I commented that Mapplethorpe had sex with many of his models (sometimes sado-masochistic, as reflected in the imagery). Yet if we turn the sentence around, and remark that Mapplethorpe often photographed his lovers, the implication is slightly different. Mapplethorpe is known to have died of AIDS, and the Mapplethorpe Foundation has a significant charitable role raising money for research into HIV. Many of the men he photographed died of AIDS. In the U.S.A., even more than in the U.K., you die more quickly if you are poor (which has direct relevance to the issue of race) since you have no money for health insurance, and therefore restricted access to AZT and other treatment. The photographs can thus function as *memento mori*. Mapplethorpe's relationship to his models/lovers was not necessarily *only* as exploitative as is often assumed. Mercer quotes Ken Moody from a BBC TV interview: 'he is actually very giving' (197).

And to finish finally with the biographical, which appears to haunt photography even more than other art forms (perhaps unsurprisingly) — in the face of a social marginalization of gay vision (and continuing threat from censors), Mapplethorpe could be said to set up a certain reversibility of the gay gaze. Equally Mapplethorpe was fully aware of the lack of beautiful images of (urban) black men in Art. Some of the more contentious images (featuring the paraphernalia of sado-masochism or setting a black man's penis against his formal suit) can also be seen in Art-Historical terms of Modernist shock value. They bring together high art and pornography, the aesthetic ideal and our racist stereotypes. There is perhaps a difference between a white woman on a pedestal and a black man?

George Dureau

Dureau is, like Mapplethorpe, a white gay American, more affluent than most of his models.[10] Like Mapplethorpe, many of his models, pictured in black and white, are African-American men, and many are poor, surviving through different kinds of hustling, some are also his lovers. *Contra* Mapplethorpe, Dureau's images of street people are not pictures of conventional perfection; they include little people and amputees. He does not fetishize the perfect body — but presents instead the realities of bodies.[11] This invites political readings in terms of class and race, and the realities of life in New Orleans, which has a higher than average rate of genetic abnormalities, and accidents which lead to amputation, combined with inadequate medical care — in particular for those on very low incomes (which includes a preponderance of people of colour). The viewer of these images may be particularly struck by the contrast with the hyperreal Hollywood male; Jeff Hearn and Antonio Melechi claim that the British see American men as 'different to us, they are shown to be bigger, stronger, fitter, younger, healthier, better-looking, sexier, more tanned, more famous, and they are usually white'.[12] This is clearly not the case in the photographs of George Dureau, and yet neither does he present us with a set of victims who stir up our pity as sometimes happens in the rather different tradition of photo-journalism for instance.

124 *Paragraph*

Davis argues, both in *The Male Nude* and in 'Freak Flag' that Dureau's models, unlike Mapplethorpe's, are presented as *subjects*: they gaze out at the spectator, they show some rebellion, some wit. The subject's head is always included — unlike much of Mapplethorpe's work. Davis also refers to the condition of production of the work — while Mapplethorpe (like many artists) was known for pushing models into holding uncomfortable poses, Dureau is a famed story-teller/interlocutor who sees his models as friends, if not family, with whom he can catch up during or around relaxed posing sessions. The dialogue with the model raises the issue of the (auto)biographical — particularly as some models are photographed at intervals over significant stretches of time. I shall return to the importance of autobiography below.

There were six images by Dureau in the *Typical Men!* exhibition. One witty piece (*John Slate* (1982/3)) raises the question of the black man as entertainer in American culture as it makes us pose the question: who has sure footing in American culture? Is Slate's body symbolically askew because of his missing leg or because of his rock guitarist's pose — his one crutch used as instrument instead of support? Like Mapplethorpe's photographs, Dureau's invite a return to the familiar beauty of Classical statues. We often see the whole body of the Classical (and Renaissance) tradition in the mutilated form of limb-less and more or less castrated remains, which our admiring gaze restores to their proper and original perfection. But, while Mapplethorpe's camera gives us that ideal restored in black, Dureau's image of, say, a man without legs is an even more oblique reflection of those marble part-bodies whose incompleteness we more readily forgive. Several tacitly ask the question (reprised rather differently by Ajamu): what is normal? What is it to feel like a freak? While this may be most explicit for the viewer in the shape of some of the men's bodies, of course sexuality and race are also issues. This silent interrogation can be uncomfortable for the spectator with a multiple sense of guilt. Is it a gaze of reproach that s/he faces? The viewers have to face up to their responses (or lack of them).

Lyle Ashton Harris (Photographer) and Thomas Allen Harris (Film-Maker/Performance Artist)

Typical Men! included a collaborative series of four photographs by the Harris brothers: *Brotherhood, Crossroads, Etcetera* and *Untitled (Orisha Studies)* (1993).[13] The brothers describe the first three (*Brotherhood,*

Crossroads, Etcetera) as a meditation on a famous photographic portrait of Huey Newton, the Black Panthers' minister of information. These photographs conjure up three narratives of fraternal relations, all particularly relevant to black American experience. They show one brother mourning the other, one brother killing the other, and brothers fighting together against the enemy. Love and death between men, who are literally or symbolically brothers, are here suffused with an erotic charge. Fraternal relations between men have often kept femininity (and women) at bay: here the feminine is invited back in with, say, a pose that is reminiscent of the *pietà* or, equally ambiguously, with the extravagant use of face-paint.

The Harris brothers give the images a specific political and historical location. The red, black and green velvet backdrop is a reference to black nationalism — specifically the flag of Marcus Garvey's Universal Negro Improvement Association in the 1920s, and to its use by the Black Power movement in the 60s. At the same time, they draw on a range of religious and classical myths. The Old Testament story of Cain and Abel is evoked, while Greek references include the relationship between Achilles and Patroclus, and the martial 'brotherhood' of the Spartans. The Romans and their reinscription in the French Revolution are brought together in the intertext of Jacques-Louis David's *Oath of the Horatii*. The Harris brothers do not, however, refer only to the European heritage that shaped the United States. They also use an African cosmology (in particular the Yoruba pantheon): Oshun, goddess of beauty and sexuality, is represented in both her feminine and masculine forms — sacred twins — guardian of the crossroads. Eshu, divine trickster, squats between Oshun's two gendered embodiments in *Orisha Studies* (*The Passionate Camera*, 249). Like the British-Nigerian photographer Rotimi Fani-Kayode they refuse to rid themselves of an African heritage.

Mingling with the political and mythic elements in the images, there is a strong autobiographical element for the brothers — the story of their own erotic agon. Autobiography has been seen as particularly important for African-Americans whose earliest writings were often life stories, and who felt the need to shape a public self in language, to protest, to register the existence of a black self.[14] In these photographs traditional autobiography is transformed because the Harris brothers are evoking multiple selves, and they are doing so in a way which is deliberately transgressive in relationship to African-American visual culture. In the early part of the twentieth century many in the black community believed that it was important to combat hideous images of Africans by bourgeois morality and propriety—but now, the Harrises would argue, there is a need to invoke queer nationalism as well as black nationalism.

Not all viewers will pick up on all the meanings the Harrises have so deftly inscribed in their pictures. However, there is still much for the uninitiated to reflect upon. One of the many issues these images make us reflect upon is that of the ways of embracing—how can men touch other men? Early photographers found it difficult to represent men interacting with other naked men; they therefore resorted to the evocation of healthy athleticism and classicism. These images playfully quote this earlier mode. Fighting can bring together two bodies, and, perhaps, love and hate, lust and cruelty, seriousness and comedy. A different embrace could be tender and melding so who can tell where one body ends and another begins? What are boundaries?

Luce Irigaray's work on the *caress* sees it as a means of regenerating the body—a reproduction that is not purely sexual, but a transcendental *and* carnal giving.[15] This kind of fecundity which is not only (hetero)sexual is of particular interest in this context where the touch is indeed indeterminate.

Homoeroticism is often charged with narcissism; this can be a simplistic taunt to be sent straight back or it can be an invitation to rethink what we mean by narcissism. This question is raised in a large number of images by contemporary male photographers—in self-portraits and, here, in portraits of the self with another self which are highly reflective (not only camera and subject, but also brother and brother).[16] Alongside the mirroring of self portraiture, other photographers introduce mirrors into their pictures—which brings us the question: do we know who we are when we look in the mirror?[17] Or does it blur our identity? Do we pose?

Ajamu

Ajamu X is a Black British photographer, who was born and grew up in Huddersfield, an environment significantly different from the context in which, say, Mapplethorpe (New York) was working.[18] He claims, unsurprisingly, to have felt alien within both a black[19] and a gay (and SM) context. The exhibition included five of his images, and two strong clear images (with a transvestite theme) were used in publicity for the exhibition and conference.[20] Another photograph, *Untitled (from Black Circus Master Series)* (1997), shows a young back man, naked, blindfolded, with his hands shackled in leather cuffs and a thick leather collar around his neck (see this volume, 110, fig. 2). This is at once an image of enslavement, thus suggesting a particular historical referent, and an image of sado-masochistic sex play in which a power bottom[21] can orchestrate the scenario. The effect on the viewer is likely to be a complex one, and strongly related to his or her own subject position.[22] S/he is reminded at the very least that we are posed as well as posing. Like Dureau (an acknowledged influence), Ajamu shows us 'freaks' in a number of senses including that of sexuality (queer, transvestite, S&M) and that of race. In his work too the term of abuse is reclaimed. He argues that if gay culture fetishizes the body beautiful, queer art contradicts this body fascism; and his 'freakish' work has perhaps an even clearer political message than do Dureau's or Witkin's 'freaks'. One explicit example is a computer-generated image of a man without arms or legs (from an archive of American freaks), overlaid with a black man in formal dress (*Auto Portrait as Armless and Legless*, 1988) which it is interesting to place alongside Witkin's portrait *Man without Legs, New York City* (1984) — naked but for a paper mask over his eyes.

Feminine or An-Other Masculine?

One of the questions raised persistently by the *Typical Men!* exhibition was that of (the boundaries of) masculinity and thus of femininity. Not only that of the subjects of many photographs, nor that of the artists, but also that of the spectator be s/he man or woman.[23] The viewer was perhaps forced to ask: what makes a man (or woman) masculine or feminine? Perhaps even being frozen as the passive object of the gaze, the spectacle displayed for all to see, is a feminization of the men represented — and what of any men looking at them? In 'The Way Men Look', Worton argues that men have difficulty in speaking, and in finding new ways to speak (7–8). While compelling in certain respects, of course this claim needs nuancing. In some ways men find it much easier to speak and to be seen in public (and in private) than women do. It is easier for men to speak and to be visible as *minds* or as *heroes* (in an active mode); men are more readily heard or seen as workers, whether by hand or brain, than women are — even today.[24] Posing, passive display, being captured as a spectacle has been reserved for the feminine (including feminized occupations such as entertainers) in recent history, even though there are historical periods (such as the eighteenth century) when aristocratic male display had a certain currency. The rise of the bourgeois family is associated with renewed sexual division of labour: the wife bears the burden of the domestic and also of display.

Apart from explicit references to the feminine — such as the varied trappings of drag summed up in the fetishist's favourite, the pair of stilettos — many nuances of the photographs conjured up the feminine: posture, softness, fragmentation, context, props, vulnerability, tenderness... But is it inevitable that we fall back into these gendered linguistic and social categories — we may have to start by talking of *feminization* and borrowing from sexual stereotypes, but do we need to end in those terms?

The constant reproduction of body *fragments* characteristic of the late twentieth century is associated with a masculine fetishization of certain parts of an eroticized and objectified female body. Women are reduced to a breast, a bottom, pouting lips or an item of clothing such as a high-heeled shoe standing for the fetishized foot. The parallel obsession in gay male culture with certain over-valued body parts is less well-documented, but no doubt also has its negative effects for those who might wish, but cannot attempt, to meet the demand for youthful perfection. Many of the photographs in the exhibition showed only parts of bodies: calves and feet in stilettos, an ear, fingers, a back... If fragmentation into body parts is itself a device usually associated with a masculine gaze on the female body, what further effect does it have when the image is particularly seductive — an ear whose whorls lead your thoughts to the body interior or whose metallic ring makes its fleshliness stand out (fig. 1).[25] The male body, liberated from the obligations of phallic totality, coherence and potency, is thereby released into the body sensuous. A tender fragmentation could then be seen as an empowering disempowerment. This is not to deny that the divided body can also be the body alienated and alienating, no longer the repository of passion any more than reason, but instead an object almost mineral or vegetable in its absurd distance from the familiar 'us' — thanks to the photographer's close-up or angle of vision.[26] Yet even where the partial or perfect representation of the body can make it appear inhuman, humanity can leak back into the image via the spectator's awareness of the frailty or fragility of flesh.

Stilettos, and many other elements of feminine drag, notoriously distort the body — clothing does more than cover, it can also shape. Femininity is evoked in many of the photographs by more or less contorted posturing. The masochistic suffering involved in the feminine masquerade is taken to extremes in David Newman's pain in *Logos — 7 hours. Moment from Action* (2000) and many other of

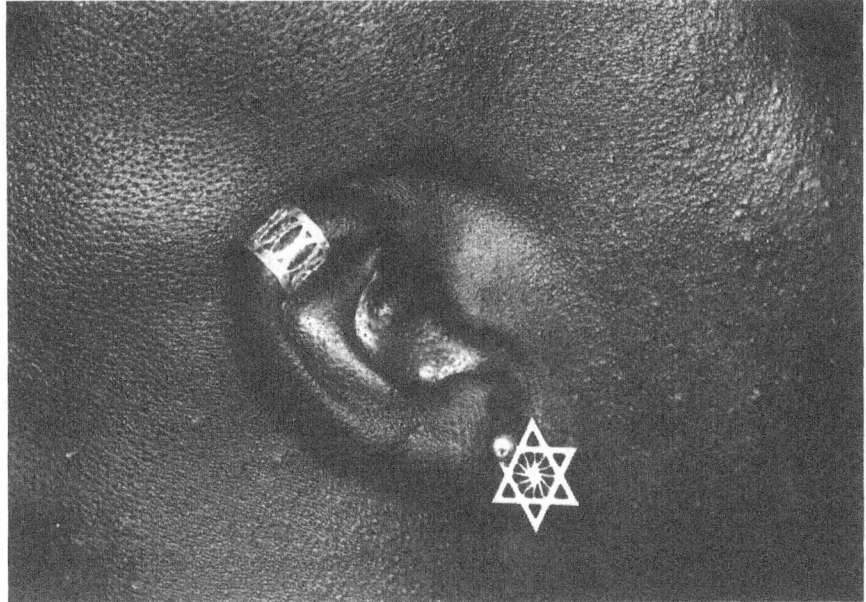

Figure 1. Ajamu, *Ear*, 1993.

his works with their images of crucifixion and their depiction of real self-induced suffering through the use of clamps or bondage. Does the masculine body have to be perfectly potent, whole and active? Is the acknowledgement of suffering culturally marked as feminine? Coplans's meticulous charting of the ageing body, softening to curves, reminds the viewer of the physical details perceived as decline — although here they could equally be seen as strangely lovely and a kind of release as well as loss. Sunil Gupta is one of several contemporary male photographers to draw attention to HIV and AIDS. *The Shroud/Pleasuredrome (from 'From Here to Eternity')* (1999) juxtaposes a man lying on a bed draped in what looks like a shroud (in fact, curtains) and what cognoscenti might know to be a South London men's sauna.[27]

Gupta also wittily draw our attention to the way the boundaries between masculine and feminine shift over time and between cultures. Two examples from the 1993 '*Trespass II*' *Series* (*Untitled 2* and *Untitled 5*) juxtapose discrete worlds of consumption, which could feed one man's complex self-identity. Gupta deploys images of quintessential Indianness, including a Mogul miniature and a Bollywood film star. Next to the miniature, there are three types of Californian beefcake for hire — above them the elements of a sumptuous (Indian?) meal, the succulent chicken already sliced, phallic vegetables just behind. Alongside the plump film star we see a naked body (Gupta's own), not the classical nude, in front of homely kitchen appliances — is that, by contrast, a typical man? Obsessions with body shape take many forms: the traditional Eastern family's desire for their son to be 'healthily' plump and well-fed is imaged in the film star poster. The toned, honed and pumped Californian gay ideal of the 1970s, by contrast, does not admit spare (or ageing) flesh. Gupta's many photographs of his own body in a range of contexts show changes over time which suggest the concerns of a man who is HIV positive, who must check for lesions and check his weight . . .

What Type of Man Are You?

Does the masculine male body have to be perfectly potent, whole and active? Would that make it the image of patriarchal power — which cannot be naked? Is the acknowledgement of suffering, of the imperfect reality of desire and being desired necessarily a 'feminization' in the sense that would leave an ideal masculinity intact? Cannot a 'masculine' body be curvaceous (or painfully thin), freakish, bare, un-ideal, a pose? Many of these questions can lead to contradictory answers. Maybe we should start with the fact that there are always already many masculinities, and that we need that fracturing by race, culture, class and so on. The important differences between men should keep us moving on in our questioning of masculinities. Treating men as aesthetic objects may be a desirable strategy for feminists (and hetero and homo-eroticism can intertwine) — and yet the critique of Mapplethorpe should make us attentive to issues of exploitation even as we derive pleasure from the images. The possibility of pleasure in beautiful male bodies should also be laced with reminders of the dangers of body fascism with which feminists should be all too familiar. Male beauty (overlapping with female beauty) needs to be an expansive context and not restricted to the muscular 'perfection' of body builders (nor boyish docility). If men do not have to be all man, do not have to bear the burden of impossible phallic potency, then they might enjoy being men, typical and exceptional, rather more. These photographic images can be funny and witty as they are erotic — while still permitting the spectator to trace material histories as s/he stares at the bodies of *different* men that saw the photographer and that the photographer saw.

JUDITH STILL
University of Nottingham

NOTES

1. I should like to thank the AHRB for their financial support of this exhibition, and also thank Keith Fairless for all the work he did on this project. Michael Worton's catalogue for the exhibition (Nottingham, 2001) contains an important essay ('The Way Men Look: Seeing, Representing and Living Masculinity Today', 6–22), which is a major intertext for this article. Worton's immense knowledge of the field (as well as his hard work in negotiating loans) was crucial in making the exhibition happen. All images mentioned in this article (except the Mapplethorpes) are reproduced in the catalogue. After Nottingham the exhibition toured to The Minories Art Gallery (Colchester) and The Gallery of Modern Art (Glasgow).
2. Roland Barthes observes: 'It is as if the Photograph always carries its referent with itself, both affected by the same amorous or funereal immobility' in *Camera Lucida: Reflections on Photography*, translated by Richard Howard (London, Fontana, 1984), 5–6.
3. Of course there are many homosocial contexts in which the display of male flesh is part of a masculine bonding between men, and desire is resolutely sublimated, displaced, expelled. There are also homosexual contexts in which there is the overt possibility of reciprocal desire, where each man is a potential *subject* as well as *object* of desire. Then exposed flesh may be welcome to initiates if not to the public at large. What has been problematic in recent centuries has been the making public of the male body, as the female body is so commonly displayed, and the making available of male genitalia for the range of reactions any casual spectator (male, female, gay, straight) might have: desire, scorn, laughter, appraisal.
4. The Mapplethorpe Foundation is a powerful body, and influences the way in which the photographer's legacy is made available. There were considerable problems in borrowing any Mapplethorpe images for the exhibition.
5. See *The Male Nude in Contemporary Photography* (Philadelphia, Temple University Press, 1991), Chapter 2.
6. *Welcome to the Jungle: New Positions in Black Cultural Studies* (London and New York, Routledge, 1994), 174.
7. Black gay video porn star Joe Simmons is referred to as Thomas in the *Black Book* (1983). This could be a wink to those in the know (a way of building community); Mercer comments on the humorous and pleasurable impact of this intertextual crossing of pornography and high art. See also Michael

Worton, 'You Know What I Mean? The Operability of Codes in Gay Men's Writing' *Paragraph* 17, 1994, 49–59.

8   They are represented in an objectifying manner; they are turned into art objects which sell for large sums of money to the profit of the artist or art dealer, while they themselves sell their bodies as models (and often as 'prostitutes') for rather smaller sums of money.

9   'Renegotiating Black Masculinity' in Mark A. Reid, *PostNegritude: Visual and Literary Culture* (Albany, SUNY Press, 1997).

10   For further exploration of Dureau's work, see Melody Davis's article 'Freak Flag: Humour and the Photography of George Dureau' in this volume.

11   Davis points out that his lighting is more naturalistic than that used by Mapplethorpe, and that the props in the photos are also natural in the sense of worn or imperfect.

12   'The Transatlantic Gaze. Masculinities, Youth and the American Imaginary' in *Men, Masculinity and the Media*, edited by Steve Craig (Newbury Park, Sage Publications, 1992), 215–32, (218).

13   *The Passionate Camera: Photography and Bodies of Desire*, edited by Deborah Bright (London and New York, Routledge, 1998) includes reproductions of these pictures and a conversation between the brothers about the images from which some of my argument is drawn (248–62, 312).

14   See Henry Louis Gates Jr., *Bearing Witness: Selections from African American Autobiography in the Twentieth Century* (New York, Pantheon Books, 1991). Thomas Harris quotes from Gates, and then makes the claim that he and his brother are transforming the notion of autobiography (*Passionate Camera*, 250).

15   'The Fecundity of the Caress: A Reading of Levinas, *Totality and Infinity*, "Phenomenology of Eros"' in *An Ethics of Sexual Difference*, translated by Carolyn Burke and Gillian C. Gill (London, The Athlone Press, 1993), 185–217. See also Irigaray's comments on Diotima's speech in the *Symposium* (25–66). Irigaray stresses the fecundity (which is more than physical procreation) between male and female lovers; however, the concept could be creatively queered.

16   David Newman's *Unnamed Action (Self Portrait)* (1985) displays touching oneself as other in a way which reopens the questions of touching the other as another oneself or of discovering otherness within oneself. Two images of the naked artist are locked in a kind of embrace, open-mouthed, hands seemingly impossibly entwined.

17   Edward Lucie-Smith's *Adam Kissing Himself* (1999) is a recent take on Narcissus, his tongue caressing the tongue in the mirror. Duane Michals's *Who Am I* (1994) shows another beautiful naked youth this time looking in a distorting mirror which gives him two faces. The photograph's meaning is doubled by handwriting below.

18 See the Conversation between Ajamu and Anita Naoko Pilgrim in this volume.
19 Ajamu has written of the hostility of many in the Black community (as well as the racism of many on the gay scene). The hostility is not of course restricted to Europe or America; Fani-Kayode would not exhibit in Nigeria.
20 In *Silver Heels* (1993), a black man's muscular calves are shot in close-up with all their imperfections (varicose veins) — the feet crammed into silver stilettos; see figure 1 to Ajamu's conversation with Pilgrim in this volume. *Body Builder in Bra* (1990) shows a wonderfully muscular upper back, whose gleaming back skin tones contrast with the rather frayed and ill-fitting bra that the man is wearing; see cover to this volume.
21 Top and bottom are no doubt self-explanatory terms in s-m sex; the power bottom is the masochist who controls the game.
22 With respect to the controversies which have raged within feminism over pornography, and particularly over BDSM, I would refer to Lynn Segal, 'The Appeal and Function of Pornography' in *Slow Motion: Changing Masculinities Changing Men* (London, Virago, 1990), 217–32.
23 This challenge provoked some extreme reactions in the Gallery Comments book. Many were highly appreciative, but some very angry — and a few simply imploring: why no naked women?
24 Of course this is still a gross generalization, and we could immediately divide up, say, the term *worker* into jobs more readily recognized as women's work or as men's work — but I would argue that those tasks most happily regarded as women's work are in a range of ways (including pay) downgraded *qua* work because of their feminization.
25 Ajamu's *Ear* (1993) or Edward Lucie-Smith's *Colin from Albuquerque* (1998) — this latter showing also a portion of shoulder squashed into the face, forming voluptuous folds.
26 Some of the work of Arno Rafael Minkkinen (as well as that of Appelt) might come into that category.
27 Other photographers who produced symbolic and paradoxical images of this kind (i.e., witty as well as sad) include Fani-Kayode who conjures up the Yoruba God of smallpox, painting the body with the spots used to decorate shrines to a divinity who must be celebrated as well as feared (*Somponnoi*, 1987). The title of Witkin's *John Herring, P.W.A., Posed as Flora with Lover and Mother, New Mexico* (1992) already suggests his bringing together of AIDS and flowers.

Fellas in Fully Frontal Frolics: Naked Men in *For Women* Magazine

The last two decades have witnessed the mainstreaming of sexually explicit materials both as entertainment and education, creating what Jane Juffer has called 'domesticated pornography'—a label which neatly indicates its main target, the female consumer.[1] But despite evidence that the production and marketing of erotic materials have been significantly influenced by women, it is still almost impossible to talk about explicit representations, especially of the male body, as genuinely arousing for women. Attempts to understand the possible relationships between female viewers and male nudes have been hampered by clinging to the following standard accounts of viewing (the caricaturing of these accounts is unfortunately unavoidable). The first standard account argues that women's emotional and psychological make-up prevent them from sexualizing the male, for example:

> Women tend to fantasize about (Heroes of the Screen ...) Yet, through nature or nurture women generally are not inclined to isolate flesh—the nude male body—from the rest of their fantasies with men, as men do with their pin-up girls. It is likely that, for emotional excitation, women do not need to see the nude or semi-nude male pin-ups. Thus, most pin-ups of Hollywood film heroes are portraits or action shots of fully-dressed leading men rather than figure studies.[2]

The second account claims that the male body cannot be rendered properly erotic. Here the difficulties of representing the male body are stressed; for example, Margaret Walters suggests that 'the male nude derives much of its power and meaning from the reverence accorded in patriarchy to the phallus'[3] therefore the male body is only capable of representing heroism or power. If it is not represented in this way, the image becomes unstable and cannot work. An image of the male can only work if it engenders the proper degree of awe in the viewer.

Processes of looking are theorized as the desire to possess the person or thing represented, such desire being the attribute of the male psyche, thus the apparatus of representation prevents women looking.[4] Richard Dyer's account of the instability of the male pin-up is apposite here: the male model appears awkward as he attempts to deny the fact of being looked at.[5] If looking is constructed as inherently male, the female spectator can only be imagined as a peculiarity and an obstruction to the proper workings of the image. As Sarah Kent asserts:

> Once a female observer is envisaged, her presence becomes a conscious element in the encoding of the image. The tensions, ambiguities and contradictions apparent in the male pin-up reflect a conflict of interests that is fundamental to this new interaction. The male model apparently puts himself at the disposal of the female viewer, while actually attempting to maintain a position of sexual dominance. And whereas the female pin-up and homo-erotic nude tend to be acquiescent or submissive — little more than a screen onto which men can project their fantasies — play-males try to assert their independence and to control the observer's responses.[6]

There is, then, little theoretical support for the proposition that women look at men's bodies and desire them. But in the course of my study into the reception of *For Women* magazine I encountered evidence that women do like looking at men's bodies and can derive sexual pleasure from their viewing. The limitations of the accounts outlined above rest primarily on their dehistoricized textual analysis. I do not have the space to offer a proper challenge to those accounts here, I simply flag their inability to explain the following response from a reader of *For Women* with whom I corresponded for almost four years:

> OK Clarissa, when I look at pictures of naked men I let my mind wander off into a world of fantasy. I have never yet found the perfect picture, so it may be his strong arms, his smooth chest, or his tight ass, that attract me. But I will always include his penis, when I am interested in sex, this little bit is very important to me. While I fantasise I concentrate on his penis, how I make him erect, touching it, stroking it, sucking it. I imagine what it feels like, smells like and tastes like, where he will put it and how it feels. I have these thoughts about his mouth and testicles too, what his body feels like pressed against me, his weight and warmth etc.[7]

Julie's claims of arousal and fantasy are difficult to understand via theorizations of women's ocular disability. I am also signalling that our models of textual investigation should be derived from the principles inherent and discernable within enthusiastic users' accounts of their reading. Thus the following analysis engages with the specificity of one magazine's nude images and their organization in order to begin to think through the conditions under which male nudes can become erotic objects for women.

For Women is the UK's only sexually explicit magazine for an exclusively female readership and is published by Northern & Shell (N & S), publishers of an array of men's magazines and currently infamous as the new owners of Express Newspapers. Launched in 1992 alongside four rival publications aimed at women readers, *For Women* proclaimed its intention to show more than *Cosmo*.[8] Certainly in its early incarnations the magazine had many similarities to *Cosmo* and other mainstream women's magazines: features on pop/film stars, gossip, relationship articles, fashion, fiction, problem pages and the defining feature: nude men. The magazine intended to bridge the gap between porn and mainstream women's publishing but *For Women* wasn't able to hide its pleasure zones sufficiently to achieve the level of respectability required by the middle shelves. The editorial team was a motley crew of 'sex radicals' and long term porn-employees whose intention was political with a small p: to arouse its female readership.[9] The magazine was not about to pull punches; it was going to give women sexual thrills through a direct address to the body. Initial sales figures required three reprints of the first issue, subsequently sales fell dramatically: stabilizing around the 50,000 per issue mark.[10]

Each issue features up to four individual photo-sets of between six and eight pages of up to thirteen photos: usually at least one double page spread and then a combination of single page images and smaller insets. The photos are usually arranged to suggest a strip-tease with a fully or partially clothed 'framing' shot at the beginning and a centrefold-esque nude at the end. Approximately half the images of each photo-set feature the model naked and full frontal, the exceptions to this being images of 'celebrity' models: a number of sports stars have stripped for the camera but have been too coy or shy to reveal all. Backgrounds vary: outdoor, studio and 'home' interiors have all featured and props, especially those which might be labelled 'sporting' and/or 'artistic' often find a place in the photographs.

A regular band of photographers are used, most are male and well-known within 'glamour' photography: Jeff Kaine, Karl Grant, Colin Clarke and Dean Keefer. Some women's work is also featured: Nicky Downey, Ruth Batten, Jeanette Jones and Mary Doyle; the styles and conventions of those photographs do not seem to be noticeably different from those produced by male photographers — there is no definable 'women's aesthetic'. Photographs are sent speculatively to the magazine and in early issues were often the by-products of work for gay men's magazines. The emphasis on the worked-out body would seem to reflect the tendency in gay porn to celebrate gym culture although the magazine did not try to cater to gay men. Indeed one of the main criteria for judging images was that they were not 'too gay'. A subjective judgement that was best outlined by one time deputy editor, Zak Jane Keir:

> Quite a few of the sets bought in in the early days had originally been shot for gay magazines and thus picture selection was a bit tricky. Basically, the male anus is not the number one focus of female sexual desire, but a lot of gay men like to see it. Therefore we used to see a lot of shots that I called 'the ring of confidence', usually a model on all fours with buttocks raised and cock hanging down like a missile. Also, check shirts and Freddie Mercury moustaches, anything smacking of the 'gay clone' we tried to get away from.[11]

Celebrity images were very sought after, early research had suggested that women would really like celebrity nudes.[12] Unfortunately the magazine found this very difficult to provide — their opportunities were limited to those men who already stripped for a living,[13] some sports stars, usually black,[14] and the occasional before-they-were-famous celebrity photos.

Despite its claims to show more, the magazine has never been able to show erections; this has less to do with the provisions of the Obscene Publications Act than with W.H. Smith's and John Menzies's interpretation of legislation. Prior to printing, the planned issue is submitted to those two companies for approval and any offending items removed.[15] For a period of six months in 1995 the models were 'covered-up': N & S's marketing and advertising departments hoped strategically placed towels and hands would get the magazine off the top shelf and thereby increase circulation and advertising revenue. The editorial team was adamant that the idea would not work and readers' letters confirmed the cost in circulation figures: if there were no full frontals then what was *For Women* offering that the *Daily Star*, calendars and pop photography were not? For a variety of reasons the penises were clearly very important to readers: as a matter of equality, as confirmation of the breaking of taboos, and in order to facilitate fantasy.

Exposing the Male Body

A convention of these photographs is the fierce colour contrast between body and background: the body is lit or flashed in order to make the edges very sharp. In studio shots, the body is lit from the side with reflectors so that it has a more three-dimensional appearance. Key lighting enhances shadows, and many of the images make use of chiaroscuro, light and shadow in order to emphasis the planes and curves of the body. By these means the body is absolutely foregrounded. In outdoor and interior shots the use of low point of view and shallow depth of field work to recede the background. These techniques borrow from modernist photography: avoiding 'painterly' or 'artistic' flourishes, no manipulation, and very sharp focus alongside a full range of tones. Modernist conventions of fragmentation and repetition are also used with alternations between torso shots and full body including the head and/or face. Some of the photo-sets mimic fashion shoots in their use of locations, accessories, poses and body styles including tanned and sculpted bodies. Settings and accessories often contribute to the possibility of story-telling referenced in the titles given to an individual photo-set, for example 'Masterpiece', 'Overall Appeal', 'Home Coming'. Titles and captions sometimes indicate the narrative possibilities of the exotic via the ethnic/cultural origins of the model, for example, 'Sittin' on the Dock of the Bay', 'Italian Job', 'Jungle Fever'.

Central to understanding these images and their appeal is their appearance as sets. In descriptions of porn's photographic imagery there is a tendency to isolate individual images from the published groups. *For Women* presents its readers with photosets structured to suggest at least a very loosely defined narrative rather than just a series of individual photographs. This is a trope of pornographic imagery; it is what distinguishes porn from the individualised pin-up and analysis must acknowledge this, thereby recognizing the intratextuality of the photosets and the relationships of the individual image to the whole. This intratextuality works on a number of levels. The grouping may facilitate a 'narrative' but this may not be so developed as to 'tell a story'. For example, 'Home Coming' is a series of ten photographs based around the theme of a G.I. returning home at Christmas — he is carrying presents — and removing his uniform. This 'story' is very obviously there; others may be less so with only a loose patterning recognizable as a strip tease, as in 'Rough, Tough and Blue' where the model in blue jeans undresses in all but one of the images. Alongside their references to other forms of popular culture, the intratextual elements allow individual images to play off each other. It is perfectly possible to find images in *For Women* illustrating the representation of male sexuality as centred on power, sexual aggression, physical strength or masculine certainty. It would also be possible to uncover illustrations of passivity, masculine fragility and emotion. The relationships between individual shots in the photo-sets offer ways of viewing the same body from different perspectives: perhaps a celebration of muscular hardness but also an invitation to imagine the sensitivity and sensuousness of the body. Each photoset includes various views of the male and masculinity as active and passive, aggressive and calm, strong and fragile. Within their own six or eight page frames the photosets proffer a display of a male body in contrasting, embellishing and/or elaborating poses which are also complemented intertextually across the rest of the magazine. It is this range of referencing which cues viewers' responses.

This 'playing off' of different images intended as a collection can be seen in the photosets reproduced here. Many of the poses make reference to classical art and more recent explorations of the male body in both art and popular culture, especially sculptural forms: the emphasis on light and shade, the muscularity of the body, the introversion, the achievement of the perfect human form. Some of the poses are very 'feminized' with hands on hip and his hair swept up behind his head. The feminine elements are counterbalanced by the musculature of the stomach, huge shoulders and almost clenched fists. The focus of the photographs changes from one to another: the muscularity of his chest, followed by a shot of the back, his pecs to the washboard stomach and his penis. The references to the exercise regime and superb shape amplify the vision before the viewer in that there is a constant reminder of the physique, as if to say 'Look at this body, it's been straining, stretching, exercising. Isn't it lovely?' His body is not an aggressively powerful one, moreover it is a body at rest: he is relaxing. Other body signs like the absence of body hair emphasize the smoothness, the musculature, the sculptural form of the body. Subdued lighting and close range shots suggest an intimacy not available in more 'public' performances of male nudity.

The first point to note is that there is a movement, a pacing of these images, large image followed by small image, by large and so on. These offer different views of the male body personalized through the use of captions and a bare-bones narrative. As with the pacing, the alternation of tensed muscle by relaxed pose helps bring the body alive — giving it a sense of movement. This is further enhanced by a use of light and shade that contributes to the invitation to enjoy the body in front of us. The tactile nature of the body is emphasized in these images, the bronzing effect of the lighting, the shine on the skin, the hairlessness of the chest, arms, legs and back add to the soft yet sculptural appearance of the body.

Early photosets used captions offering a brief introduction/explanation of the model and his striptease. For example in 'Locker Room Lust' the captions introduce Simon as a member of *Climax* strip group and invite viewers to take a particular orientation[16] to his image (fig. 1). How far viewers join in, and therefore how far the image 'works' for them, is dependent upon how much investment they have in the 'female sexual culture' on offer. In offering Simon's body, *For Women* is able to take us (viewers) where others fear to tread, sneaking us into the locker room where we are invited to enjoy Simon: 'Being the bright, bold, breezy sort of girls we are, we were all ready to volunteer our services should Simon want his back scrubbed. The mere idea was enough to get us in a bit of a lather, we have to admit.' The 'we' obviously refers to the 'girls' at the magazine but it also invites viewers to imagine how it might feel to scrub Simon's back and introduces the idea of others who might not want to look at Simon. If it takes a 'bright, bold, breezy sort of girl' to appreciate his good looks and body, those who would rather not look are obviously not *For Women* girls. When they 'admit' to getting in a bit of a lather, viewers are invited to empathize, not condemn. This idea of touching Simon's body is at odds with the images which all suggest his solitude, but it includes viewers in appreciation of his body and allows the idea of the body on display as there to be touched, as more than an image. This sets up the question, 'what would it be like to touch him? How would his skin feel?', addressing viewers' imaginations and their bodies.

The last caption invites viewers in more explicitly by posing a question: 'The necessity for exercise is the bane of many a girl's life, but we're all convinced that we'd be far more enthusiastic about our trips to the gym if we could count on finding someone like Simon to do press-ups with. Don't you agree?' Again, an invitation to imagine being with Simon, and once again the gossipy tone is used along with a double-entendre regarding press-ups to introduce the idea of a sexual interaction with Simon. The question highlights a number of assumptions: viewers are female (we girls), heterosexual and have an interest in men like Simon.

The text does two things with the issue of the display of the male body: by emphasizing Simon's role in *Climax* we are assured that it is normal for him to be seen naked and, it also suggests that we are being allowed to see something different, unique about Simon. The display is at one and the same time public and private. Simon is employed as a male performer, a strip artist, so he is used to undressing for an

Fellas in Fully Frontal Frolics: Naked Men in For Women Magazine 141

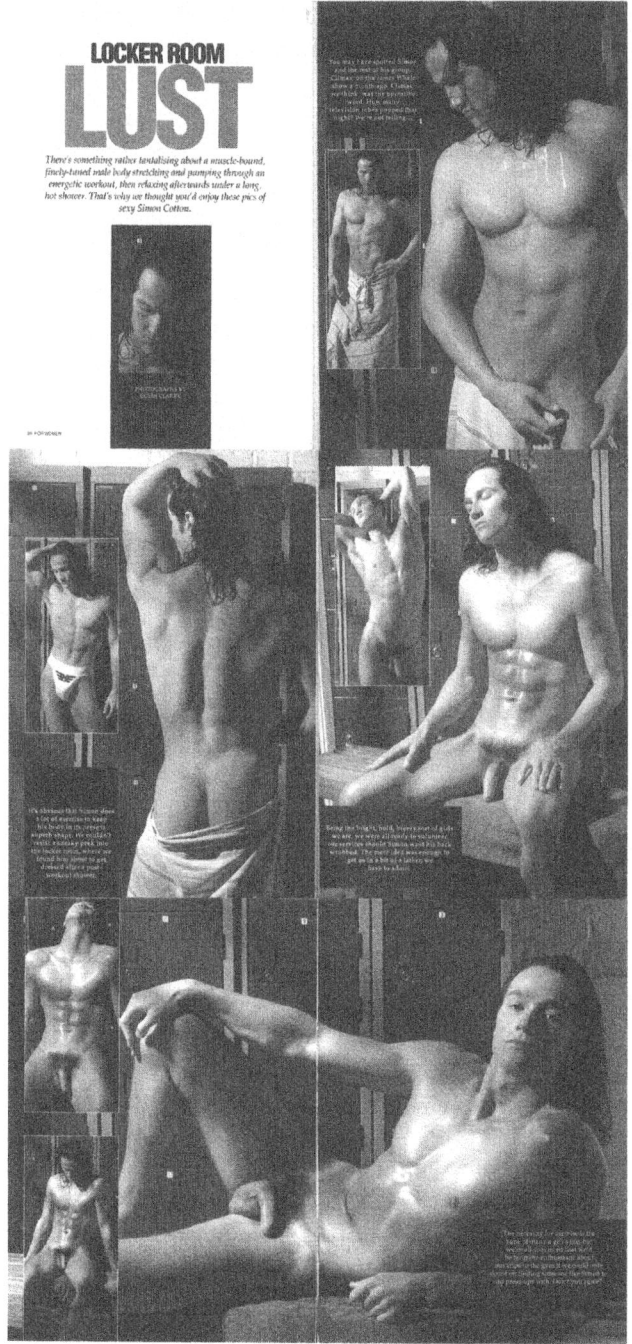

Figure 1. Reproduced by kind permission of *For Women* and Portland Publishing.

audience but by the emphasis on sneaking into the locker room we have a sense of this being entirely different from his more usual stage performance. This is a private event: within the captioned narrative of the photographs, Simon is 'unaware' of us and therefore we are seeing more than his stage persona would allow. *For Women* is able to show us the side of Simon which is not available publicly and to do so in a way which emphasizes his willingness to perform for women.

As Paul McDonald[17] has shown, that performance can best be explained by paying attention to the ways in which particular kinds of exhibitions of the male body have begun to establish conventions and a representational vocabulary of their own which viewers now expect as part of, for example, music video. One of these conventions is the eroticized male body and specifically its performance of feelings. Screen theory's 'masquerade' conceives performance as contributing exclusively to the appearance of 'possessing the phallus' and, as McDonald suggests, this 'produc[es] a rather restricted reading of the performances constructed by the male body (...) it can ultimately reduce the multiple ways in which gender is performed into the restrictive dichotomies of 'having' or 'being' the phallus, active and passive, or powerful and submissive' (283). In attempting to show how the male body in performance is not conforming to phallic power McDonald looks to the ways in which the body is presented, the modes of performance and the illustrations of moods. In *Take That*'s video for 'Pray' he draws attention to the yearning mode of presentation of the body — the body is presented in an emotional rather than a narrative situation. In other words, the body shows the mood of romantic yearning and amplifies the lyrics of the song expressing its pains and longings. This framework avoids the reductionist account of the male body as phallus and allows for the ways in which female pleasure, the pleasure of the viewer, might be understood as arising from the presentation of a specifically *erotic* male-ness which is responsive to emotion.

Where it has been shown that phallic power is not a part of the image, theorization has fallen back on the notion of the castrated or feminized male body. But as McDonald suggests, at stake is not the revelation of the male body and its phallic or feminized signification but the body's performance of being 'male' in particular ways through dance and the performance of male desire and desirability. Rather than see images of men for women as an aberration or an example of the commodified appropriation of female sexuality, they are participants in specific experiential communities. The point here is not to suggest that there are no disruptions of gendered conventions of looking, quite clearly there are, and the pleasures of those disruptions are surely amongst the possibilities explicitly offered to viewers by images of men. But the significance lies in the ways in which women experience and respond to those possibilities. Puzzled concern is a standard response to women's laughter at male strip-shows[18] — it is the only response possible unless we try to understand the ways in which those performances (whether on screen, stage or page) engage viewers, speaking to their desires, dreams and fantasies and how those make sense in women's wider experience. McDonald observes 'To concentrate on the body as an object presented in a structure of looking leads to a reading of the body as a static signifier. Reading the body as a performing body requires viewing the body as a source of action and movement', which allows us to see that the body produces 'meanings which are not contained in words but are specifically shown in physical terms'(281). This suggestion allows for a more fluid notion of the body offering imaginative experiences. Those experiences are cognitive in that viewers recognize the conventions and understand the performance of the body in terms of, for example, its music video-ness or its resemblance to, or difference from, other *Take That* videos; those experiences are also affective — the performance invites response; as *Take That* fever showed, viewers are more than capable of that!

The statement from Julie introduced earlier details a process of becoming aroused: 'There are no set rules, I just pick his best bits and let my mind wander off.' The magazine and its images are a conduit to feeling — allowing for mental activity that in turn enables the experience of bodily sensations and the use of all of Julie's senses. Those experiences can only be understood if our analyses do not start by identifying the 'phallic-ness' of the represented body or the intention to dupe. Rather we need to identify the ways in which images are presented to us, the conventions of their presentation and the modifications that occur over time giving rise to the changing expectations and involvements for viewers and producers of those images. If we take seriously the notion of intertextuality we must recognize that the photosets in *For Women* are part of a growing circuit of images of men for women, and that in that growing circuit there are dynamics which change the nature of the interactions offered. The male body is not capable of remaining true to the phallic ideal, it is not able to resist change. My analysis of the magazine and its imagery attempts to understand women's engagement with the popular male nude as an evolving and socially embedded exchange. A potted history of the complex social processes of sexual culture is beyond the remit of this paper; however, such history would acknowledge the increasing focus during the 1990s in the UK on the moral and social decay supposedly caused by women and gay men.[19] Calls for a return to family values were juxtaposed with the proliferation of sexy male bodies and aggressive female protagonists in films, novels and on television. Many popular culture forms stressed that women were taking control, demanding the rights to look at and appraise men for sexual potential and that women were enjoying that power.

In the images of 'Locker Room Lust' this power to look hardly needs to be spoken; the images seize and challenge the idea that women can't look. The photosets and pseudo-personalized talk offer an invitation to women viewers — 'look at this body — it's here for *you*'. The photographic conventions and intratextual presentation of the photosets invite readers to orient themselves to a process of viewing and becoming aroused. Julie clearly took up that invitation and was able to enjoy the pleasures of an imagined sexual interaction. Each subsequent act of looking takes with it the knowledge of prior looks. In taking up the invitation to view women make these images theirs and anticipate the statement loud and proud: Women Look!

CLARISSA SMITH
University of Sunderland
Written with the support of Falmouth College of Arts
Research Fund.

NOTES

1. Juffer, *At Home With Pornography: Women, Sex and Everyday Life* (New York, New York University Press, 1998), 1. Examples of 'domesticated pornography' might include: the *Lovers' Guide* videos, dance troupes like the Chippendales, *Desire* magazine, *The Erotic Review*, increasing sexual content in Mills & Boon and the arrival of the overtly sexual romance in the X-Libris and Black Lace imprints.
2. Mark Gabor, *The Pin-Up: A Modest History* (London, Pan Books, 1982), 162.
3. Margaret Walters, *The Nude Male: A New Perspective* (Harmondsworth, Penguin, 1979).
4. I am thinking here of Laura Mulvey's account of the male gaze based on voyeurism and fetishization of the female body; see 'Visual Pleasure and Narrative Cinema' in *The Sexual Subject: A Screen Reader in Sexuality* (London, Routledge, 1992), 22–34.

5   Dyer notes the *instability* of the male pin-up, not its *impossibility*: a distinction conveniently forgotten in the employment of his ideas to back up yet another reiteration of the proposition that women don't like looking at nude men; see 'Don't Look Now: The Male Pin-Up' in *The Sexual Subject*, 265–276.
6   Sarah Kent, 'The Erotic Male Nude' in *Women's Images of Men*, edited by S. Kent & J. Morreau (London, Pandora Press, 1990), 75–105, 87.
7   Many audience studies have been accused of focusing on spectacular readers/viewers, the fans, rather than the more 'mundane' users of a particular media form. Julie wrote me fifty letters but I would dispute the idea that she is a 'fan' of *For Women*. The collecting and cataloguing which seems an integral part of 'fandoms' was certainly missing from Julie's account of her reading although she certainly liked the magazine a great deal for at least two years. She took her part in my research project very seriously and continued to write to me long after the magazine had ceased to be of real interest to her. I am intensely grateful to her and another reader who also wrote many letters to me. They gave me invaluable insight into the ways in which a reader's investment in a magazine changes over time and that what was once right becomes wrong, perhaps inevitably. Not because the reader has 'grown up' but perhaps because no magazine is capable of keeping up with the expectations and obligations it has encouraged readers to demand.
8   Women's magazine publishing had experienced a number of major upheavals in the 1980s and 1990s: a result of changes in the marketplace had been an increase in sexual content especially in the glossy monthly publications. Angela McRobbie ('*More!*: New Sexualities in Girls' and Womens' Magazines' in *Cultural Studies and Communications*, edited by J. Curran, D. Morley and V. Walkerdine (London, Arnold), 172–94) claims that this is an effect of increased competition and an attempt to delineate differences between magazines — sexcess being a defining characteristic of particular magazines like *Cosmo*. This turn to sex was also a result of the ongoing debates in parliament and elsewhere about women's role in society. Moves in parliament sought to legislate for the family and against the rogue single and hyper-sexual female with debates and proposed legislation on contraception, abortion, single mothers, teenage pregnancy and the changing prerogatives for sex education in schools in the face of the gathering threat of AIDS.
9   Editorial team member Zak Jane Keir and regular contributor Tuppy Owens are both members of Feminists Against Censorship. Owens is also well known for her campaigning work for sexually disadvantaged groups and is one of the organisers of the Sex Maniacs Ball. Isabel Koprowski was launch editor of the magazine and had worked on *Forum* and a variety of other N & S publications; her CV includes an unfinished PhD in Latin erotic poetry.
10 In comparison with magazines like *Cosmopolitan* where success is measured at the $\frac{1}{2}$ million mark, 50,000 copies per issue may seem a very small figure. In soft-core terms this is perfectly respectable: as with most N & S publications

the budget is low (*For Women* currently operates on around £2,500 per issue), copy is set on Apple Mac, editorial has been cut back and the production team of four have responsibilities to other magazines. The low circulation figure is profitable.

11 Email to author, December 2000.
12 Zak Jane Keir: 'What we did find women were prepared to admit to was wanting celeb nudes — not very gettable in those days, though we tried. I think we did all hold to the idea that women are not homogenous and therefore we should provide as much variety as possible.'
13 Page 7 fellas, members of the Chippendales, Climax and London Knights and models from 'sexy' videos have all made appearances.
14 Black stars were apparently much easier to persuade than their white counterparts. In a set of pictures taken at Hendon Football Club, only the black players on the team were willing to show their faces *and* penises in the same shot.
15 John Menzies and W.H. Smith control as much as 80% of the UK's newspaper and periodical distribution so this submission to their scrutiny is a necessity to ensure that the magazine appears in newsagents nationwide.
16 The term 'orientation' is used here to emphasize the social nature of the relationship between the text and reader; it is borrowed from Valentin Volosinov's theory of language as dialogical and refers to the ways in which understanding an image first requires our response to it (Volosinov, *Marxism and the Philosophy of Language* (New York, Seminar Press, 1973), 45–106. Volosinov's approach emphasizes the context, form and theme of any communication, verbal or visual. The images discussed here offer a proposal to the reader to join in the narrative sequence of the strip-tease, the evaluative accent (in this case the captions) stress the fun of watching and thereby invite the reader to take up a position opposite the image; although the cheeky conversational style suggests that the response ought to be pleasurable, it cannot prevent other responses.
17 McDonald, 'Feeling & Fun: Romance, Dance and the Performing Male Body in the Take That Videos' in *Sexing the Groove: Popular Music & Gender*, edited by S. Whiteley (London, Routledge, 1997), 277–94.
18 See, for instance, Kenneth MacKinnon's descriptions of male strip shows in his *Uneasy Pleasures: the Male as Erotic Object* (London, Cygnus Arts, 1997), 147–51.
19 For example attempts to legislate against female sexuality via changes to the 1967 Abortion Bill; the introduction of the Child Support Agency; arguments over the proper solution to teenage pregnancy alongside the reiteration of 'family values' explicit in Clause 28 and complaints about 'pretend families'.

Underexposed: Spectatorship and Pleasure in Men's Underwear Advertising in the Twentieth Century

Today, advertising for men's underwear is an unavoidable, and often arresting, spectacle on street hoardings, magazines and even buses, with the most well-known of such campaigns probably being the tantalizingly voyeuristic advertisements produced for Calvin Klein. The first of these, produced by the In-House Agency, appeared as a traffic-stopping billboard in New York's Times Square in 1982, and subsequently in magazines like American GQ. By the end of the 1980s, 'Calvins' had become the generic term for sexy underwear, and the 'CK-effect' had spawned an entire industry of similarly figure-revealing, designer-label underwear by the likes of Nikos and Jean Paul Gaultier which, as Nicola Jeal attested, had made young men begin to think of underwear not just in terms of comfort but also of visual impact.[1]

As the competition heated up, Fabien Baron took over the art direction of the CK campaigns in 1992, and Steven Meisel replaced Bruce Weber as chief photographer. Since then their egregious signature style has involved the use of various film stars and supermodels including Woody Harrelson, Antonio Sabato Jnr, Kate Moss, Joel West, and, probably most notorious of all, rapper Marky Mark, who in 1992 was rumoured to have earned anywhere between 100,000 dollars and seven million dollars for the privilege of displaying his buff torso in CK advertisements. The erotic power of such publicity has simultaneously helped CK to maintain sales in the region of 100 million dollars per annum and has foregrounded the idea of men's underwear as a fetishistic object of desire; witness the sale by Sotheby's New York in May 1999 of a pair of original CK's owned and signed by Andy Warhol for 7000 dollars, and Mark Simpson's lapidary summation: 'it is not Marky's penis itself which is being sold but the confusion of it with underwear'.[2]

The sexual/sexy objectification of male bodies in advertising after CK has, moreover, led to some significant blurring of subject and object positions with regard to male and female spectatorial pleasure, and straight and gay masculinities. It can be argued that since women are still the chief purchasers of men's underwear, the eroticism of such promotions makes an unequivocal appeal to them. In an advertisement for Marks & Spencer in 1994, for example, women at a fashion show leer lasciviously as the male models posing in the latest underwear styles cavort on the catwalk. But most of these campaigns have appeared in magazines dedicated to male readers (whether straight or gay) such as *Arena*, *GQ*, and *Attitude*, and in their display of scantily clad models the ambiguities of representing the male body are not so easily or safely contained.

In addition, it would be erroneous to regard such issues as the exclusive concern of postmodern or late capitalist culture, as examples of men's underwear advertising in Britain and America earlier in the twentieth century reveal. Indeed, such promotions were ubiquitous, appearing in most daily newspapers as well as an eclectic spread of periodicals.[3] Accordingly, in this article I want to deal with the imbrication of pleasure, spectatorship and gender in advertising for men's underwear in Britain in a broader historical context. I will not, however, be elaborating a straightforward survey or narrative and nor do I wish simply to postulate a seamless suture between past and present. Rather, my intention is to uncover the mythology that only since the 1970s have developments in both men's underwear and underwear advertising become diverse or erotic. In this regard the visual and verbal rhetoric in publicity for several manufacturers in Britain during the first half of the twentieth century underscored the fetishistic nature of underwear and quite often resorted to strategies of camp and sexual ambiguity. In dealing with these issues I have drawn on visual examples from several periodical sources,[4] and not least from the monthly trade journal *MAN and his clothes*. Published in London and Paris between September 1926 and May 1959, this was one of the earliest titles devoted to male consumers interested in style and fashion, accruing an average circulation of 10,000 copies during the 1930s.[5]

On both sides of the Atlantic the interwar period in particular was crucial in the technological and stylistic development of both the men's underwear and advertising industries. On the basis of the advertisements that appeared in various magazines and newspapers between 1919 and 1939, for instance, there were at least fifty different men's underwear companies in America and Britain. Among them were several long-standing manufacturers of hosiery, who in the early twentieth century had also turned to the production of wool and cotton underwear. In America these included Fruit of the Loom, founded in 1856, BVD (1876), and Coopers (1876), who pioneered Y-front briefs and jockey shorts in the 1930s; and in Britain, I.R. Morley (1795), Allen Solly (1799), and Two Steeples (1895). As these and other companies vied with each other for trade, they not only began to produce inventive lines of underwear in different styles and fabrics but also to promote them in more novel ways. In this way, men's underwear was bound up in debates concerning a new discourse for a modern, democratic form of advertising and its importance in attracting the most suitable target audience.

These ideals were being stamped out in America by the Calkins & Holden advertising agency in New York (masterminded by design reformer Earnest Elmo Calkins), the Clarence White School of Photography (founded in 1914), and one of its most well-known graduates Edward Steichen, and in Europe by the Circle of 'New Advertising Designers', a professional alliance of avant-garde producers formed in 1927, whose members included Piet Zwart, Moholy-Nagy and Max Burchartz, and by individuals such as Ashley Havinden, art director at the British advertising agency W.S. Crawford between 1929 and 1960. Briefly, there were three chief aesthetic concerns at play here: the harmonious balance between type and image; the tension between occupied/saturated and blank/white space; and whether advertisements with illustrations or those with photographs made the most visual impact on the public.[6] Thus in the October 1927 issue of *MAN and his clothes*, Cyril H. King, advertising manager of Hope Bros., exhorted advertisers: 'to endeavour to create an atmosphere of quality by the style of layout; by well-drawn illustrations (...) and by good, legible type display'.[7]

But advertisers of men's clothing, and especially of underwear, faced another twofold challenge at this time — how to transcend the apathy or resistance of the male customer, and how to combat the idea that men don't care what underwear looks like as long as it keeps them warm. Essentially, as G.F. Curtis wrote in 1927, the overriding task was to convince the public that 'there is more in underwear than has met the eye'.[8] And, as far as Cyril King was concerned, this meant allying atmospheric advertising with 'reason why' or factual advertising. 'Men's wear advertising', he admonished manufacturers, 'must be subtle and at the same time must contain facts about the merchandise you are selling'.[9]

One of the most common ways that this double impetus was codified in advertisements for men's underwear during the first half of the twentieth century was by framing health and comfort in terms of sociability and desirability. In 1914, for example, an advertisement for the BVD one-piece union suit in *Saturday Evening Post*, depicting men and women playing quoits on the deck of a liner, allied the garment's sporting and health properties (it was modelled on an athlete's cotton shorts and vest) to the popularity of the men who wore it with the opposite sex. A similar message was still being conveyed in campaigns for Wolsey Y-fronts during the period of austerity after the Second World War. In one of these, the man who is unfortunate enough not to have access to the limited supply of such underwear stands alone in the crowd, cast as a social outsider by both those who do and their female dance partners.[10]

Hence, the rhetoric of these promotions clearly overlaps with the discourse of reform for better hygiene and living conditions that had grown apace in Britain, Europe and America since the late nineteenth century. By the 1920s and 1930s the culture of the fit and healthy body was central to such debates, and organisations such as the British Men's Dress Reform Party (1929–1937), in which J.C. Flugel was a leading figure, began to address the issue of restrictive clothing. In this respect, research was also undertaken into the efficacy of different materials for underwear, and usually centred on the relative merits of wool and cotton. *MAN and his clothes* ran a series of articles at this time supporting athletic styles of underwear in their cut and use of colour.[11] But it also noted considerable polarization in the British market for the new underwear styles in terms of age and class. Sales surveys were revealing that colourful boxer shorts, for instance, were mostly being bought by a 'younger set of men', with brands in pale blue, silver grey, pale pink and green being much in demand.[12] The association of these kinds of shorts with fashionable young males is evident in an advertisement that appeared in *Punch* (May 29, 1929). This comprised an illustration of a man wearing a button top vest with coloured stripe trunks and a tagline affirming: 'Aertex in colour adds to the gaiety of nations'.

While the word 'gay' had probably come into currency in America by the 1920s to refer to homosexuals, it is unclear whether the term was being used simultaneously in Britain in entirely the same way.[13] Nonetheless, it is interesting to note that by this time pale blue had been designated the 'trade mark' of gay men according to the recollections of several correspondents in a Mass Observation survey into sexual behaviour conducted in 1949, and to discern also the way that the male figure illustrated in the Aertex promotion crooks his wrist limply on his hips.[14] In this regard, we seem to have a more indeterminate codification of masculinity that trades on camp sensibility, a point that I shall return to in more detail below.

After 1935, the Union Suit and boxer shorts were both largely superseded by the advent of Y-fronts, pioneered by Coopers Inc. in America, with the first prototypes in knitted fabric being modelled on swimming trunks with a front pouch as worn by men on the French Riviera. From June 1939 onwards, Lyle and Scott manufactured some 60,000 of these garments per week for consumption in Britain and Europe, and by the late 1950s Y-front briefs were the favoured form of underwear with the majority of men on the grounds of style and comfort.[15] In common with earlier brands, publicity for Lyle and Scott made an overt association with sporting paradigms and masculinity, as in 'Look good..feel good', which appeared in *Picture Post* in 1954 (fig. 1). But the promotions from the period are not just instructive in the way they reveal the considerable variation that was available in cut, materials and styles, for they also connote the psychological momentum to be had in purchasing and wearing underwear. Although advertisers were still underlining practical values, the rhetoric of campaigns for Lyle and Scott Y-fronts nonetheless foregrounded the imbrication of pleasure and underwear, of not only looking good but feeling good as well (as the 1954 promotion proclaimed).

This fetishistic desire for the touch and feel of soft, contour-revealing fabric is also expressed in an article that appeared in *MAN and his clothes* in May 1927, which stated: 'Once a man has experienced the psychological stimulus of fine underwear, he will never go back to an inferior quality'.[16] It is interesting to note the editorial referring to the nexus of psychological stimulus and fine underwear, and in this respect it seems to frame sensory pleasure in the context of Freud's thinking on fetishism. Freud had alluded to fetishism in *The Three Essays on the Theory of Sexuality* (1905), and in his psychoanalytic study of Leonardo in 1911, but discussed the idea in more detail in an essay published in the autumn of 1927, which appeared in an English translation by Joan Riviere in the *International Journal of Psycho-analysis* the following year. In the *Three Essays* (65–6) Freud had postulated that fetishism is an aberration, which arises when an individual fixates on an object — a part of the body such as the foot or hair, or a piece of material or clothing — as a replacement for normal sexual behaviour.[17] By 1910, however, he had added a footnote to his original text stating that, 'The shoe or slipper is a corresponding symbol of the *female* genitals' (67), an idea that is compounded one

Figure 1. Advertisement for Y-front, *Picture Post*, 10 April 1954. Private collection.

year later in *Leonardo da Vinci and A Memory of His Childhood*,[18] and reinforced in 1927 where he maintains that the fetishized object was specifically, 'a substitute for the woman's (the mother's) penis that the little boy once believed in and (...) does not want to give up' (*On Sexuality*, 352).[19] Thus, as Freud has it, the fetish becomes a way of warding off the threat of castration.

Accordingly, underclothing has a special place in this economy of pain and pleasure since it crystallizes 'the moment of undressing, the last moment in which the woman could still be regarded as phallic' (*On Sexuality*, 354–5). By extension, men's underwear could be regarded in parallel terms, both as a way of concealing the phallic power of the male subject, and as a form of protection from his own (potential) unveiling and castration. Such a fetishistic correspondence between men and underwear seems to be intimated in the ebullient image and deictic mode of address of the 1954 Y-front promotion (fig. 1), for example, where the suggestion is made that these briefs will keep you one step ahead in the phallic game by simultaneously underscoring your savvy, viz. the pun 'Y's men wear Y-front', and doubling your sexual prowess, viz. the slogan 'be twice the man'.

At the same time, the tension between touching and looking connoted in the advertisement appears to align with the scopophilic drive and the play on concealing and revealing that is also evinced by Freud. In the *Three Essays* he maintains: 'The progressive concealment of the body which goes along with civilisation keeps sexual curiosity awake. This curiosity seeks to complete the sexual object by revealing its hidden parts' (69). That is to say, rather than being portrayed as something that should be kept out of sight, the undergarments in this advertisement (and those represented in the other figures included in this article) are implicated in an act of conspicuous consumption that positions the men represented as solipsistic narcissists, while also offering up their bodies for the spectatorial pleasure of others.

The most obvious point of attraction implied by many promotions was between men and women, and by the mid-century there was a discernible shift of emphasis in the depiction of women in such a context — away from the housewife whose investment in men's underwear was merely domestic/functional, as evidenced in the condescending reference to the 'little woman who has to wash and mend it' in an advertisement for Harvester in 1947, to the siren who could be sexually aroused by it, as configured by Eve in a more suggestive Hanes advertisement in 1950.[20] But by the 1950s gay men had also begun to appreciate the erotic charge of Y-fronts. Dennis, for example, one of the correspondents in the Brighton Ourstory project, related how exciting and outrageous Y-fronts seemed in comparison to all the other 'horrible flannel things' that were retailing after the Second World War.[21] As we have seen, a campaign for Aertex in 1929 had already connoted sexuality in more deviant terms, and during the interwar period in Britain masculine identities and sexual desire were also being queered in advertising for other underwear manufacturers such as Chilprufe, Irmo and Celanese, where men were depicted interacting ambiguously with each other (figs. 2 and 3).

Figure 2. Advertisement for Irmo lightweight underwear, *MAN and his clothes*, March 1930. Private collection.

Of course, one would not want to overdetermine the gayness of some of these texts, which could be regarded as innocently homosocial, but the camp gestures and poses in several of them do appear to nod in the direction of queer desire, and to trade on the irony that those in the know will recognize such codes while those on the outside will remain oblivious to them. Moreover, as George Chauncey Jnr's illuminating analysis of sexual practices between 1919 and 1920 among naval officers at Newport, Rhode Island reveals, these codes were not the exclusive province of gay men or 'queers'

Spectatorship and Pleasure in Men's Underwear Advertising in the 20th Century   155

Figure 3. Advertisement for Celanese Menswear, *MAN and his clothes*, April 1932. Private collection.

but had also been assimilated by straight men seeking casual sex with other males.[22]

Particularly suggestive in figures 2 and 3 is the trope of smoking. Once again, an idea from Freud's *Three Essays* (98–9) springs to mind here, inasmuch as he argues that smoking can signify a deep-seated desire to recuperate the pleasure of contact with the mother's breast, encountered as an erotogenic zone during breastfeeding. But Freud is speaking of obsessive smoking rather than the social activity that appears to take place in the advertisements. A more compelling and evidential reason for decoding these texts in terms of homosexual desire is furnished by the gay American author Edward Irenaeus Prime Stevenson, who wrote under the nom-de-plume of 'Xavier Mayne'. In *The Intersexes: A History of Similisexualism as a Problem in Social Life*, published in 1908, Mayne not only describes how the use of cigarettes was a common overture to sexual contact between men, but he also pinpoints how certain furtive or keen looks were a 'signal and challenge everywhere current and understood among homosexuals'.[23]

In a recent article entitled 'Coded Desire in 1920's advertising', David B. Boyce identifies this kind of sexual intimacy in a 1926 promotion for Chesterfield cigarettes captioned 'I can tell that taste in the dark', where two men dressed in tuxedos and top hats stare into each other's eyes as one lights the other's cigarette.[24] While it is one thing to observe such semiotic 'in-codes' in advertising for tobacco and quite another to see them mobilised in publicity for underwear, nonetheless I would proffer that this is precisely the kind of cruising that is connoted in the Irmo and Celanese campaigns (figs. 2 and 3); a point that is further compounded in the phallic symbolism of Tony Castle's illustration for the former, where we observe the seated figure glance knowingly at the man standing behind him as he holds erect his golf club/'penis'.

In fact, the 'in' codes of such advertising could have been intentional. Boyce, for example, in assessing the iconography of J.C. Leyendecker (who had been employed by Calkins & Holden and was reputed to be gay) and other advertising artists working in America during the early twentieth century, attests: 'What is clear is that a number of artists and admen of the day were homosexual, so it would not be unexpected for their affectional desires to have seeped into their ads' (26). Judging from many of the advertisements for underwear and other items of clothing that appeared in *MAN and his clothes* during the same period it is probably safe to say that there must also have been a parallel — if clandestine — gay presence in the British advertising industry. One such was painter Keith Vaughan, who between 1931 and 1939 worked as a trainee in the art department of Lintas, the ad agency of the soap manufacturer Unilever. Unlike Leyendecker, however, he was not openly gay at the time and I have not been able to identify any discernible homoerotic or homosocial tropes in publicity for their products during this period. It is not for nothing, therefore, that Jeffrey Weeks has contended: 'The Oscar Wilde débâcle and the successive controversies and scandals of the 1890s made the public avowal and defence of homosexuality a perilous project'.[25] Noel Coward's play *Semi Monde*, for example, which overtly portrays the bitchiness and unbridled sexuality of several gay characters, was censored in 1926 and not performed in public until 1977. Hence, in common with other cultural producers in Britain during the interwar period, advertising artists and agencies were made to tread a fine line in dealing with gay desire and queer identities.

Yet, even though at this time homosexuality remained illegal and was rarely spoken about or overtly represented, the visual — if not the verbal — rhetoric of advertisements such as these appeared at least to sublimate gay desire and to make an appeal to prospective gay customers, without either alienating those who weren't or incurring censorship, by mobilising camp irony and inbetweenism. Thus the strategy of camp in these promotions offered a point of identification between producer and consumer that, as Eve Kosofsky Sedgwick puts it, reveals the opportunity for projective fantasy; a way of negotiating ambiguity by asking *what if?* — not only 'what if whoever made this was gay too?' but also, 'what if the right audience for this were exactly me?'[26]

Moreover, Alan Sinfield argues that in male homosexual subcultures camp is not only a strategy for negotiating sexual identities but one that mimics 'leisure-class mannerisms and upward class mobility' as well.[27] This much is evident in the *modern* aesthetic and the haughty mien of the males represented in both the Irmo and Celanese campaigns, who seem to have much in common with the artistic and effeminate dandies described in works such as Terence Greenidge's *Degenerate Oxford?* (1930) and Caroline Ware's *Greenwich Village 1920–30* (1935).

This idea of indeterminacy brings us full circle to contemporary publicity for underwear. For even now few manufacturers would admit or desire that advertising for their goods should be regarded as unequivocally gay-oriented, a point amplified by CK spokesperson for underwear, Karen Stabiner, who has protested that their campaigns were not conceived to appeal exclusively to a gay market.[28] Thus, since the 1970s, the muscular 'statue men'[29] in the majority of underwear promotions have been represented in isolation and, accordingly, the ideal of the phallic body can be seen to make a deliberate appeal to body-conscious men, whether gay or straight, as well as to women. At the same time, campaigns for Jockey in the 1980s, featuring the American baseball player Jim Palmer, and late-1990s promotions for Versace Intensive, featuring decathlete Dan O'Brien, and Armani, featuring footballer David James, have emphasized the correlation between youth and sporting prowess by trading on the symbolically-erotic Greek *gymnos*, the athlete who still has some layers of clothing left to remove.[30]

Of course, this is not to imply that time has merely stood still. In Britain, gay men aged eighteen and above are no longer sexual outlaws, and many of the designers of men's underwear are avowedly gay (Klein, Versace, and Dolce & Gabbana), and their brands and others like them (2xist, Hom, John Crummay) have an overtly gay following, being sold in outlets such as Clone Zone. Furthermore, in comparison to examples from the first half of the twentieth century, underwear advertising since the early 1970s for brands such as Y-front and Hom has become increasingly ingenuous and transgressive in its sexual codes,[31] and since the 1990s the use of black models has also become more common.

Yet this has not been an unproblematic phenomenon. In 1997, for instance, billboards in Britain for Brass Monkeys men's pants were removed after being deemed unsuitable for public consumption by the Committee of Advertising Practice, who argued that they focused on the groin area of the male model represented and turned him into a sex object.[32] Such comments are revealing, inasmuch as they warn us to the latent patriarchal ideologies of political-correctness in the advertising industry. On one level, we are left to ponder why the Committee is not so vigilant when it comes to the objectification of women in advertising. While on another, both the campaign itself and their criticism of it appear to trade on the 'the fantasy of the big black willy', as Kobena Mercer frames it, and the popular white mythology that black men are genitally better endowed.[33]

Finally, a recent campaign for Gucci underwear that appeared in the British edition of *GQ* can be seen to represent perhaps the ultimate taboo for normative masculine identities — anality (fig. 4). As Guy Hocquenghem has propounded in his book *Homosexual Desire*, in comparison to the phallus, which is social, the anus is private. But, in keeping with Freud, he also maintains that the sublimated anus forms the bedrock of the individual's identity, that it is only through privatizing the excremental and anti-social body part that we can progress to the clean, social order. Thus he argues that the anus has liminal status, and 'only exists as something which is socially elevated and individually debased; it is torn between faeces and poetry'.[34] The Gucci ad clearly transgresses and transmutes these binary codes. Here, not only is the body part that is regarded in social terms as the

Figure 4. Advertisement for Gucci underwear, c. 1995. Courtesy of the Advertising Archives.

most private and most unclean put on show, but, bathed in seductive lighting that emphasises its pert and rounded contours, it is elevated to the status of desirability and spectatorial pleasure, for women and men, and gays and straights alike. Consequently, although this advertisement appears to be more visually economic and symbolically extreme than earlier underwear promotions, like them it does highlight the ambiguities of putting the male body on display and the way that such publicity intersects with both commodity and corporeal fetishism.

It is in this respect, then, that underwear advertising can be regarded as much more than the advertising of underwear.

PAUL JOBLING
University of Brighton

NOTES

1. Nicola Jeal, 'Back to basics', *The Observer, Living* (26 November 1989), 36.
2. Mark Simpson, *Male Impersonators* (London, Cassell, 1994), 153.
3. Advertisements for men's underwear appeared during the 1920s and 1930s in the following periodicals and newspapers, which were consulted in the preparation of this paper: *Daily Express, Daily Mail, Daily Herald, Daily Telegraph, Guardian, Evening Standard, Vogue, Home Chat, Women's Weekly, Punch, ILN, Picture Post, Lilliput, Radio Times*, and *The Listener*. In America during the same period advertisements appeared in the following periodicals: *Life, Saturday Evening Post, Autocar, Esquire* and *Penthouse*.
4. Namely, *Arena, Arena Homme Plus*, British *GQ, Picture Post, Punch* and *Saturday Evening Post*.
5. *MAN and his clothes* (July 1932) cited average ABC circulation figures of 9100 copies for the period January to June 1932; and in August 1932, it recorded sales of 10,000 copies for July.
6. For a more concentrated discussion of these issues see: D. Crowley and P. Jobling, *Graphic Design: Reproduction and Representation Since 1800* (Manchester, Manchester University Press, 1996), chapters 5 and 8; P. Johnston, *Real Fantasies: Edward Steichen's Advertising Photography* (Berkeley, University of California Press, 1997), chapters 2 and 3; B. Yochelson, 'Clarence White Reconsidered: An Alternative to the Modernist Aesthetic of Straight Photography', *Studies in Visual Communication*, 9:4 (Fall 1983), 26–44. We find these issues also being addressed on several occasions in articles in *MAN and his clothes*. See, for example, C.H. King, 'Do men *read* advertisements?' (October 1927), 28–9, and 'Style — is advertising creating it today?' (September 1930), 24–5.
7. C.H. King, 'Do men *read* advertisements?', 29. The use of suggestive or atmospheric advertising had been advocated as early as 1908 by Walter Dill Scott in The *Psychology of Advertising* (Boston, Small Maynard) in which he stated: 'The attention value of an object depends on the intensity of feeling aroused' (2). The strategies of suggestion and atmosphere were regarded as instrumental, therefore, in connoting the right association between the product and purchaser in any given advertisement, and Scott's ideas are much in evidence in advertising from the 1920s and 1930s — be it in illustrative or photographic form (although, it must be stated, it was not until the 1960s that photographic promotions for underwear became the norm).

8 G.F. Curtis, 'Little things that matter', *MAN and his clothes* (May 1927), 28.
9 Cyril King, 'Do men *read* advertisements?', 28.
10 See *MAN and his clothes* (December 1945).
11 See, for example, 'Mesh is the next-to-the-skin weave for autumn', MAN *and his clothes* (July 1937), 26: 'When we take into consideration the fact that fully half the autumn underwear sold today is cut on athletic lines, here seems to be a plain indication that men in this country are getting healthier'.
12 G. Albemarle, 'Flashes of fashion', *MAN and his clothes* (February 1931), 29.
13 See W.R. Dynes (editor), *Encyclopedia of Homosexuality*, Vol. 1 (Chicago, St James Press, 1992), 456.
14 Mass Observation 1949 Sex Survey, Sexual Behaviour (Box 4, File E, Appendix 1, 'Abnormality', 6 July 1949), housed in the University of Sussex Library, special collections.
15 'Underwear', *MAN and his clothes* (November 1957), 27.
16 'Stylus', 'Sell Better Underwear, *MAN and his clothes* (May 1927), 14.
17 Freud, 'Three Essays on the Theory of Sexuality', in *On Sexuality*, translated by J. Strachey and edited by A. Richards (Harmondsworth, Penguin, 1977).
18 Freud, 'Leonardo da Vinci and a memory of his Childhood', in *Art and Literature*, translated by J. Strachey and edited by A. Richards (Harmondsworth, Penguin, 1985).
19 Freud, 'Fetishism', in *On Sexuality*.
20 See the advertisement for Harvester captioned 'made for men who think a lot of their wives' in *MAN and his clothes* (December 1947), and the advertisement for HANES captioned 'Nothing beats a fig leaf' in *Saturday Evening Post* (24 June 1950).
21 P. Dennis, *Daring Hearts: Lesbian and Gay Lives of 50s and 60s Brighton* (Brighton, Queenspark, 1992), 52.
22 G.F. Chauncey Jnr., 'Christian Brotherhood or Sexual Perversion? Homosexual Identities and the Construction of Sexual Boundaries in the World War 1 Era', *Journal of Social History* 19, (1985), 189–212.
23 X. Mayne, *The Intersexes: A History of Similisexualism as a Problem in Social Life* (Rome, 1908), 427–8.
24 D. Boyce, 'Coded Desire in 1920's advertising', *The Gay and Lesbian Review* (Winter 2000), 26–9.
25 J. Weeks, *Coming Out: Homosexual Politics in Britain from the 19th Century to the Present* (London, Quartet, 1977), 115.
26 E. Kosofsky Sedgwick, *The Epistemology of the Closet* (Harmondsworth, Penguin, 1990), 156.
27 Sinfield quoted in M. Healy, *Gay Skins: Class, Masculinity and Queer Appropriation* (London, Cassell, 1996), 30.
28 K. Stabiner, 'Tapping the Homosexual Market', *New York Times Magazine*, (2 May 1982), 34.

29 I am basing this term on an idea of Lacan's, who in 'The Mirror Stage' argued that the erect, phallic body may be regarded as a petrified, immobile form, a 'statue in which man projects himself'. See 'The Mirror Stage as a formative function of the "I"' [1949], in *Écrits: A Selection*, translated by A. Sheridan (New York, 1977), 2.
30 See *Arena* (May 1996) for the Armani advertisement, and *Arena Homme Plus* (Spring/Summer 1997), for the Versace Intensive advertisement.
31 Two good examples of the kind of advertisement I am referring to, both of which appeared in *Penthouse* during the 1970s, are: 'Y-front, It's what a man's like underneath that counts', and 'HOM arrives in Great Britain'.
32 See 'Traffic Stoppers', *Clothes Show* (March 1997), 30.
33 K. Mercer, 'Reading Racial Fetishism: The Photographs of Robert Mapplethorpe' in *Welcome to the Jungle: New Positions in Black Cultural Studies* (London, Routledge, 1994), 190–1.
34 G. Hocquenghem, *Homosexual Desire* (Durham, Duke University Press, 1993), 100.

The Language of Bodybuilding

This paper examines the specialized language of bodybuilding. Many communities, sports, lifestyles and subcultures display this characteristic — a 'talk' which addresses their particular concerns. Such talk serves multiple functions: naming categories, distinctions and values which the wider language fails to recognize, and cementing a group identity through semantic universality. The principal contention of the present study, however, is that bodybuilding's specialized language works to normalize *its practices of bodily display and looking*. Most specifically it will be argued that bodybuilding language represents its own brand of male-on-male spectatorship as distinct from that culturally dominant and much debated 'look' — the sexually objectifying male gaze at the passive female form.

Bodybuilding is an activity with varying degrees of participation. At one end of the spectrum a small number of professional bodybuilders make a living from the competition circuit, product endorsements, publishing and appearance fees, while at the other many more individuals train in their leisure time according to bodybuilding principles without ever intending to pose or compete. This creates a problem of definition: just who exactly are bodybuilders? After all, many sportspeople — both amateur and professional — are more muscular than average, and this muscularity is often developed using methods either derived from, or at least shared with, bodybuilding. In Western society many people now have access to gymnasia, leisure centres and health clubs which offer facilities far more conducive to muscular development than those available to top bodybuilders only decades ago. For the purposes of this paper I will define bodybuilders as those who exercise according to bodybuilding principles, for whom visibly increased muscularity is a *goal in its own right* not just an outcome of training for another sport. This definition may still be inadequate in certain respects; for, on the one hand, we might intuitively seek to reserve the term bodybuilder for the comparatively few individuals who train most seriously and achieve the most dramatic results, while on the other we need to acknowledge how health and fitness culture — including a bodybuilding component — has become more mainstream in the last thirty years. So arguably anyone who has used gym equipment in conjunction with advice — either from an instructor or a wall-mounted diagram — may be said to be a bodybuilder.

It is certainly the case that fragments of bodybuilding language have entered more popular usage. Many words prevalent in bodybuilding talk derive from scientific discourses such as medicine and anatomy. Words like 'pectorals', 'abdominals' and 'quadriceps' are sometimes employed in their full form but are often truncated — ironically since it is muscle growth that is sought — into 'pecs', 'abs' and 'quads'. These better-known terms are now also used outside bodybuilding circles, popularized through the media's treatment of health and exercise — for example on the fitness pages in many Sunday supplements and the exercise routines on daytime television. Bodybuilding's use of anatomical and medical language is nonetheless distinguishable from this wider usage by the extent of its engagement. Few members of the general public will be able to locate the infraspinatus, gastrocnemius or serratus for example, but most bodybuilders do learn dozens of terms to identify the muscles they train. It is common for health clubs and leisure centres to display diagrams which indicate the correct usage of exercise equipment and highlight the muscles worked. Even a quite cursory examination of these representations will tend to add to the user's anatomical vocabulary and grasp of biomechanics. Many such venues require that new users undergo a session of instruction in the correct use of exercise equipment. Although the quality of such instruction is variable this also involves some reference to anatomy and invariably directs new users to consult the relevant diagrams on subsequent visits.

A familiar route for many bodybuilders is a graduation from leisure centres and health clubs to gymnasia specifically focused on bodybuilding. Whereas the former offer weight-training alongside other activities such as squash, swimming, aerobics and bowls the latter will simply offer a better range of bodybuilding equipment. Most specifically they will also have 'free' weights, i.e., dumbbells, barbells and a number of machines which the users load manually with barbell plates. Such equipment allows for greater muscular development but carries a greater risk of injury than the machines available in most other venues. If a gym is described as 'hardcore' or 'serious' this indicates such a difference both in the facilities available and the aspirations of the membership.

It is more rare for these bodybuilding gyms to have anatomical diagrams indicating the correct form for exercises. However, many individuals will come to such gyms with an initial grasp of anatomical language and bodybuilding technique learned from their first place of exercise, a venue which their physical ambitions have now outstripped.

The Language of Bodybuilding 165

The walls of bodybuilding gyms are more likely to feature posters and pages from the bodybuilding journals — images of past and current stars training and posing. If the gym's membership or staff includes any competitors, past or present, their pictures will tend to be prominently placed. This is also true of the signed and framed photographs from top-flight competitors which may be purchased at shows or through mail order. Such images of real individuals do not teach anatomy or bodybuilding language directly but do encourage a visual literacy in relation to the human body, priming a knowledge and appreciation of poses and bodyparts. In this way bodybuilders learn to look at others and, crucially, at themselves.

Gyms may also have representations of people from outside the world of competitive bodybuilding but who are nonetheless celebrated for their physiques and/or athletic achievements. The writer's gym (in West London) has a small area given over to cardiovascular exercise, where the representations have a particular emphasis on boxing, martial arts and film. These include photographs of Muhammad Ali, Henry Cooper, Bruce Lee and Robert DeNiro. DeNiro has often been the subject of media interest in terms of his voluntary physical transformations for particular roles, and his physique has constituted — in this respect — highly visible testimony to the efficacy of bodybuilding exercise in sculpting and altering oneself. Unsurprisingly, the images of him are those where he is at his most muscular — as boxer Jake LaMotta in *Raging Bull* and as the psychopathic rapist Max Cady in *Cape Fear*. These pictures cause an unfortunate (but presumably unintentional) rhyme with a sketch on the opposite wall of real life boxer and rapist Mike Tyson. On another wall hangs a well-known image of two more criminals — the Krays — in a boxing pose. Clearly, the relevant and connecting factor in these various representations are their masculine credentials, of physique, of violence (where the physique is tested) and also of attitude (a readiness for violence); in short, of 'hardness'. This exact combination of images is of course particular to just one time and place, a result of the owner's preferences and its users' tastes. Nevertheless, many of these representations are repeated in other gyms, and boxing/martial arts images are very common. Bodybuilders are aware that what they do may be understood as a rather passive affair where, despite their bodies' prodigious muscularity, they exist only to be looked at. Therefore, images of sport and other forms of violent activity may help to assert bodybuilding's relationship to these more obviously male arenas. It will be argued later that bodybuilding language strives to evoke exactly this impression.

Many bodybuilders also read bodybuilding journals such as *Flex* and *Muscle & Fitness* and/or books e.g., *Awesome Abs!* and *Serious Strength Training*. These are a key resource for learning bodybuilding language and facilitate the entry into bodybuilding culture. It is not uncommon for bodybuilding gyms to have a stack of back issues and other materials (often at the reception desk) which users may access before or after a workout. Books tend either to be introductory guides or to treat a single topic such as one bodypart while the monthly journals comprise articles on training and nutrition, competition reports, letters and advice pages, advertisements and photosets.

Nutrition and supplementation is probably the area of bodybuilding language most notable for its scientificity and complexity — particularly in recent years. A full page ad last year for a protein powder describes the product as 'The World's Only 100% Hydrolyzed Oligopeptide Isolated Whey Peptide Fractions'. Amongst its listed virtues are a 'Multi-spectrum Peptide Profile' and 'Ultra-High Glyco-macropeptide Fractions'.[1] Although the advertisement does include some explanatory gloss one suspects that most purchasers will still not fully understand all these terms. Rather, the language may simply conjure a sense of the product's efficacy. It is very common for advertisements for bodybuilding foods and supplements to include striking before-and-after photographs alongside the text which describes the product. In these instances the visual representations — whose intended significance is easy to grasp — exert a far greater communicative force than the difficult scientific language. Such juxtaposition would encourage any reader to regard the images of dramatic transformations *as* the essential meaning of the text, and although bodybuilders are more likely than most people to recognize and understand some of the language employed, both their physical aspirations and their skills in reading bodies make the images particularly compelling. Before-and-after photographs are potent signs for they reveal in an instant the type of physical changes desired and worked for — rarely with complete success — over many years. Despite the scepticism with which many product claims are justly regarded these images still exert a powerful draw because they simultaneously address bodybuilders' disappointments and dreams.

Discussion amongst gym-goers that is instigated by journal articles, picture pull-outs or advertisements commonly takes the form of a 'commonsense' approach to bodybuilding. Namely that most product claims are exaggerated, that the top professionals represent a level of attainment which is naturally impossible, and that there are no quick and easy routes to building a muscular body. The magazines do therefore still serve an important function by fostering communication and a sense of community amongst bodybuilders. They are often read most avidly by teenage boys and young men who have recently started training. Advice and opinions gleaned from their pages is often contextualized and mediated through dialogue with older or more experienced bodybuilders. Interestingly, some sections of the journals themselves appear to co-opt this down-to-earth language and philosophy. *Flex* currently runs an advice column, 'From the Trenches', which explicitly espouses a sceptical approach to much other training advice and information, including presumably that of its near neighbours in *Flex* itself. The column's target readers are so-called 'hardgainers', drug-free bodybuilders who train outside their working hours.

In addition to a scientific/anatomical language of the body bodybuilders also learn the aesthetic vocabulary with which physiques are evaluated and criticized in competition. Even the vast majority of bodybuilders who simply train and never compete or even spectate at shows nevertheless engage with this language. Most beginners will explain their physical ambitions as wanting to get bigger, or stronger, or 'in shape' but come to see bodies differently — both their own and others' — and will express their aims and desires through new words and concepts. For example, the expressions 'shredded', 'ripped' and 'cut' all refer to being lean which is particularly important in bodybuilding as it causes the muscles to stand out in bolder relief. Their obvious connotations of painful violence are consonant with a tendency in bodybuilding language and especially journalism to figure training and competition as somehow combative. Although their bodies suggest great potency and vigour bodybuilders are not judged through any quantifiable *activity* of strength, speed or pugilism, but on their *appearance*. The similarities with the beauty contest are considerable, with competitors parading in posing trunks (like swimming costumes), offering their bodies to the judges' gaze in order to earn a title — such as Mr World or Mr Universe. Articles on competitions labour to downplay this feminizing sense, stressing the active and martial nature of posing as if competitors literally flexed their muscles against each other; one recent report describing them as 'combatants' and 'muscle warriors'.[2]

Terms such as 'detail', 'definition' and 'separation' address whether individual muscles are distinguishable and appropriately developed; they express aesthetically the emphasis on muscle isolation learned through anatomical language and practiced through 'strict form'. A number of words relate to size, including 'mass', 'thickness', 'density' and 'fullness' but bodybuilding is not just about whether individuals have large muscles; 'symmetry' and 'proportion' are key criteria also. The term 'freaky' is sometimes used in bodybuilding to indicate that an individual has a particularly massively-developed bodypart such as calves or triceps. Although this may attract interest from fans, and lead to magazine articles, a 'freaky' feature tends not to play well with judges who look for a balanced physique with all parts in proportion. In this respect bodybuilding language and attitudes are the inheritors of classical formulations and understandings of beauty. Umberto Eco observes that 'the concept of proportion was the most widespread aesthetic concept in the whole of antiquity and the Middle ages'[3] and treatises on proportion often took the human body as the prime model. Galen's account of Polyclitus' canon of proportion runs thus:

Beauty does not consist in the elements but in the harmonious proportion of the parts, the proportion of one finger to the other, of all the fingers to the rest of the hand, of the rest of the hand to the wrist, of these to the forearm, of the forearm to the whole arm, in fine, of all parts to all others. (Eco, *The Aesthetics*, 74)

Eco also cites Cicero: 'In the body a certain symmetrical shape of the limbs combined with a certain charm of coloring is described as beauty', and St. Augustine: 'All beauty is a harmony of parts with a certain pleasing color' (72). Colour is an important consideration for bodybuilders too. Because darker skin shows off muscle definition more clearly, especially under bleaching stage lights, Caucasian competitors strive to achieve a tan through sunbathing, the use of sunbeds, and increasingly by the liberal application of fake tan prior to shows. Visible body hair is also removed for competitions, with the journals intermittently featuring articles and letters on the relative merits of shaving, waxing and electrolysis. Baby oil or similar products are the final skin treatment competitive bodybuilders use before going on-stage; this makes the skin glisten and heightens contrast. These practices with their emphasis on skin and hair suggest a similarity with the rites of female beauty, where the body is not so much trained as treated, subjected — not doing but done to.

Such cosmetic practices are merely a small facet of the sense in which bodybuilding is about illusion and appearance. For example, a key consideration for professional and leisure-time bodybuilders alike is their 'shoulder-to-waist ratio'. The ideal torso should suggest an inverted triangle, with the muscles of the lower back flaring out to broad shoulders. Hence, bodybuilders strive to keep a small waist, which includes not over-developing the 'obliques' — muscles at the sides of the waist, and paying particular attention to developing the medial head of the deltoid, a muscle at the very widest point of the shoulder. For athletes whose *strength* is actually tested e.g., weightlifters or powerlifters, this is irrelevant, their bodies may look less muscular and capable than those of bodybuilders but they are in reality significantly stronger. The appearance of muscularity resulting from having small joints is a similar phenomenon. One current competitor, 'Flex' Wheeler, is noted for having remarkably small knees, wrists, elbows etc. for his size, so the muscle above and below seems larger by 'sweeping' more noticeably into those joints, making them a genetic asset in bodybuilding. However, small joints are more liable to injury when subjected to the extreme stresses of heavy training. In competitive strength sports they would be a profound disadvantage.

Oddly, competitive bodybuilders tend to be at their weakest when they compete, making expressions such as 'in shape' or 'competition ready' radically different to their significance in other arenas. In preparation for shows bodybuilders work to shed fat and water in order that their muscles appear more hard and defined. This is achieved by dieting, by increasing cardiovascular exercise, by limiting their liquid intake, and, in some cases, by taking diuretics. Hence, when they appear on stage bodybuilders have a dangerously low level of bodyfat and are often dehydrated. Heat from the stage lights and the exertions of a posing routine — both of which encourage sweating — results in many bodybuilders feeling weak and dizzy; fainting is not uncommon. Shaping the body not towards a *real or functional perfection* but according to the demands of exhibition is another striking consonance with classical understandings of beauty. In Plato's *The Sophist* there is a dialogue on the nature of art which treats this very issue. One character argues that not all 'likeness making' is a matter of correct imitation, that those who work on *large* sculptures or paintings cannot simply produce scaled-up versions of the original:

For if they reproduced the true proportions of beautiful forms, the upper parts, you know, would seem smaller and the lower parts larger than they ought, because we see the former from a distance, the latter from near at hand (...) So the artists abandon the truth and give their figures not the actual proportions but those which seem to be beautiful, do they not? (cited in Eco, *The Aesthetics*, 75)

170 *Paragraph*

Just like the bodybuilder's physique, the form proposed here is one which deviates/exaggerates from a natural template, a structure made not to work but to be looked at.

Debates on the nature of looking have featured prominently in the fields of Film, Media and Cultural Studies. Laura Mulvey's influential essay 'Visual Pleasure and Narrative Cinema' observes that 'In a world ordered by sexual imbalance, pleasure in looking has been split between active/male and passive/female'.[4] In *Ways of Seeing* John Berger identifies the same phenomenon through the history of art and into modern advertising. Men look and women, as sexual objects, as the ocular property of men, are looked at.[5] Clearly, bodybuilding does not fit neatly into this explanatory scheme. Although there are female bodybuilders it is mainly a male domain, and therefore male bodies which are on display. As suggested earlier, one cultural form to which the bodybuilding competition approximates very closely is the beauty contest. And the beauty contest is surely the most hyperbolic realization of the problematic gendered looking demonstrable in most forms of representation and many cultural practices; hence the intermittent banishment of Miss World from our TV screens. Beauty pageants have been widely criticized for positing attractiveness as the prime female virtue, for the very literalness with which they figure competition between women, for the attention of men, in terms of looks. Amongst the cultural forms targeted by feminists, criticisms of the beauty contest have attained a significant degree of popular recognition. Whilst many would resist the notion that, for example, women's health and beauty magazines perpetuate an insidious patriarchal ideology, there is a blinding unsubtlety in the nature of Miss World and its imitators. Those evening dress and swimsuit rounds, the choreographed walks, the 360 degree twirls (so beloved of Bruce Forsyth, Miss World hanger-on and TV dinosaur in his own right), and especially the line-ups of glossy flesh seem to force an acknowledgment that such events belong to the sexual politics, the visual *droit de seigneur*, of another age. How then, may we explain the type of looking at work when male bodybuilders pose on stage for mainly male audiences?

In drawing terms from medicine, sport and aesthetics bodybuilding accesses three major fields in which the 'normal' power and sexual structures of looking—those identified by Mulvey and others and crystallized most sharply in the beauty pageant—are significantly suspended. These arenas allow men to look closely at other men, and to discuss their bodies without the necessary implication of a sexual motivation and therefore of homosexuality. This is not to argue that there are no gay aspects to the world of bodybuilding. Some gyms have a largely gay constituency, there are gay competitors, and there are clear areas of overlap between bodybuilding's physical focus and the celebration of the male physique evidenced in gay culture. This convergence can be charted in other cultural domains such as the club scene where 'Muscle Marys'—gay bodybuilders—form a highly visible grouping. Equally, many bodybuilding gyms can be the venue for the type of homophobic attitudes and banter often found in other heavily or all-male situations. Just because bodybuilding involves an awareness and language of the male body it should not be supposed that it constitutes a vanguard of enlightened or anyhow liberal sexual politics. In this respect, sadly, talk at the gym can be as casually cruel as at the rugby club bar, the football locker room, the dormitory or the barracks.

Ideas of activity and passivity are clearly at the core of understanding bodybuilding's fraught relationship with the norms of spectatorship. Sport allows men to watch other men—who are often largely unclothed—precisely because the bodies they look at are in action. Even when the body is still, as for example when boxers 'weigh in' and their physical measurements are considered, this stillness is permissible because we are contemplating the body's potential for action. Following Mulvey, we might observe that there is a narcissistic aspect to such spectatorship, whereby men identify with the protagonists. Just as with narrative fiction film, these viewed male subjects constitute ideal egos born of Lacanian misrecognition ('Visual Pleasure', 25). They are better, more capable, imbued with more determining power than the watchers who vicariously participate in their deeds. Just as central male characters play a active role 'of forwarding the story, making things happen' (28) so athletes or, sportsmen shape the outcomes of the events in which they participate.[6] Focussing on identification, however, the general reluctance of men to watch, sponsor, or broadcast women's sport suggests the extent to which they/we are unprepared to afford female participants a similar role of idealized surrogacy.

Overwhelmingly, men do not have female sporting heroes. Rather, male spectatorship of women's sport tends to revert to the sexually objectifying gaze. The tennis player Anna Kournikova is famous (and highly paid) for her prettiness more than her prowess. In the 2000 Olympics women Volleyballers were happily alluded to—in schoolboyish nudge and winking mode—by many commentators in terms of the briefness of their costumes. Many female athletes are obliged to collude with these ways of seeing, for example, through the style and poses of their photographs for advertisements, and this sexualization of the sporting body remains distinctly one-sided. By and large, men do not like it when women turn a similar gaze on male sportsmen — that is not playing the game. Not least because it threatens to shed a different light on the nature of their spectatorship.

In his article 'Don't look now: the male pin-up' Richard Dyer also considers the power-relations of looking in terms of activity and passivity:

> Even when not actually caught in an act the male image still promises activity by the way the body is posed. Even in an apparently relaxed, supine pose, the model tightens and tautens his body so that the muscles are emphasised, hence drawing attention to the body's potential for action. More often, the male pin-up is not supine anyhow, but standing taut ready for action. (*The Sexual Subject*, 270)

Just so with bodybuilding's competitions and images. The 'flexed' muscle advertises its capability for action — though we know that the real action, the training, comes earlier and this phase of display, of potential, is actually the culmination. The notion of 'flexing', from the latin *flectere* to bend, is highly revealing. One would never refer to a muscle performing real work — like digging a ditch or curling a dumbbell — as being flexed. Flexing is entirely about show, about the display of what the body *could* do. As Dyer maintains, 'muscularity is a key term in appraising men's bodies' (273) and flexing — subtle or otherwise — is the technique by which men articulate their bodies for such appraisal. Bodybuilding posing routines elevate such flexing to an art-form. There are stock poses such as 'Lat Spread', 'Most Muscular', 'Side Chest' which emphasize particular muscle groups and a well-developed physique will withstand the judges' critical gaze in each.

Interestingly, representations of female bodybuilders tend to mingle those poses used by male competitors with more traditional techniques of showing and perceiving women. As stated earlier, male bodybuilders are always liable to the charge that they do not 'do' anything, that they simply exist — in a way that prevailing cultural conventions designate as feminine — for show; a sense which bodybuilding language works to counteract. But, at least their bodies seem masculine; gross and caricatural to many, of course, but nonetheless a variation on the familiar theme of what makes a man. The posing is the 'problem', not the bodies themselves. Female bodybuilders face the opposite difficulty. Posing, preparing and arranging oneself for the gaze do not run counter to traditional versions of womanhood. Where female bodybuilders transgress norms, and in this respect they merely exaggerate the transgression of all female athletes, is with the bodies they build. When muscularity is equated with masculinity, muscular women are inevitably perceived as somehow masculine. Anxious to refute this conception, bodybuilding journals often include photographs of female competitors in poses and styles never used for the men.

The January 1994 issue of *Flex* devoted a lengthy photospread to tackling the weighty question 'who says that female body-builders are not sensual and sexy?' (124). The bodybuilder in question was shown, softly lit, in a variety of poses and states of undress; supine in a thong bikini, stretched out on a chaise longue, standing draped in gauzy fabric but otherwise naked. Offered as metonym for all female bodybuilders, the representations of this individual took refuge in those most familiar styles of seeing and understanding women and their bodies—of passivity, of sexual invitation and availability, of coyness. She did not flex, did not attempt to show the development and separation of her muscles, rather there was an effort to emphasize her breasts and hips, those parts central to the composition of women in other visual forms, from portraiture to pornography. The accompanying text made similar efforts to evoke this sense. The lubricious sibilants 'sensual' and 'sexy' reinforced the visual connotations of languor, smoothness and yielding pliability. A body understood to be 'ripped', 'hard' or 'massive' could never constitute such an invitation. Unlike the flexed body which speaks, which positively threatens, of doing or of the potential to do, her representations—just like a centrefold—ask to be done to. Needless to say, male bodybuilders are never represented or described thus in the bodybuilding press, reclining in their underpants or their boudoir, offering glimpses of those regions normally concealed. There is no discussion of whether they are 'sexy'. For the male bodybuilder it is images of bodybuilding activity, of training or at least of flexing hard, that are consistent with ideologically dominant conceptions of their gender.

In conclusion then it may be observed that the constitution and operation of bodybuilding language structures a permission (a permission normally denied) to look at the male body. Importantly, this language and look avoids many of the terms of reference and evaluation which circulate in relation to women's bodies. Within bodybuilding circles it is appropriate to observe that an individual has 'great arms', 'huge lat spread' or 'defined abs' but not 'nice legs'. Approbation is routed only through reference to muscle mass, development, and potential for strength, never through words like 'lovely', 'attractive', 'shapely' or 'beautiful'. Allusions to 'good looks' and 'beauty' for example will only appear in the Bodybuilding press when female bodybuilders are being described. The fundamental proviso extant in the permission to look that bodybuilding language affords is that the viewed male body must be seen and understood in terms of activity. Hence the flex — that quintessentially male performance — that even in stillness suggests action. Muscles contracted, teeth clenched (orifices generally tightened in fact) — the flexed body is not just hard but inviolable; a masculinity vehemently defined through difference, *not* open, *not* feminine. But should the flexing stop, the terms of looking would alter. The sense of 'straightness' which Bodybuilding language labours to create, of normalizing and de-sexualizing a male-on-male look — in a world where men do not by and large look at each other's bodies — hinges on the viewed body being understood as active.

JEREMY STRONG
London College of Music and Media

NOTES

1 Dean Brierly, 'IFBB' Report *Flex* (November 2000), 21.
2 *Flex* (November 2000), 112–13, 112.
3 Umberto Eco, *The Aesthetics of Thomas Aquinas*, translated by Hugh Bredin (Cambridge, Massachusetts, Harvard University Press, 1988), 71.
4 Laura Mulvey, 'Visual Pleasure and Narrative Cinema' in *The Sexual Subject: A Screen Reader in Sexuality*, edited by John Caughie and Annette Kuhn (London, Routledge, 1996), 22–34, 27.
5 *Ways of Seeing* (Harmondsworth, Penguin, 1972).
6 Mulvey's argument is not, of course, unchallenged; D.N. Rodowick, Steve Neale and Paul Willemen all propose that there is also an erotic or object-oriented component to the male gaze at the male hero. See Rodowick, 'The Difficulty of Difference', *Wide Angle* 5:1 (1982); Neale, 'Masculinity as Spectacle' in *The Sexual Subject*, 277–87; Willemen, 'Anthony Mann: Looking at the Male', *Framework*, Summer 1981, nos. 15–17.

'Support our boys': AIDS, Nationalism and the Male Body

This article will analyse two front covers from the tabloid newspaper *The Sun* (fig. 1). The first cover is from 16 January 1991, on the eve of the war in the Gulf, and the second is from 25 November 1991 announcing the death of Freddie Mercury from an AIDS related illness. What struck me at the time, and is the focus of the following discussion, is the startling symmetry between them. Both consist of the Union Jack as background to a male body at the centre of the image, and both are photographic constructions. I want to argue that the fact of the close publication dates is not a coincidence, but rather points to evidence of a moment of cultural anxiety over the male body and its location at a time of profound uncertainty generated by two events: AIDS and War. Whilst there might appear to be no specific connection between the body of a soldier about to go to war, and the body of a rock star who died from an AIDS related illness, both bodies are linked here through the symbolic figure of the nation. It takes the reductive, simplistic and profoundly contradictory perspective of a media text such as *The Sun* to condense these concerns down to two such images. The assertion of a singular identity attempted in each cover is undone by the rhetorical figuration of the two, very different, male bodies. What emerges is not simply a reversal of an intended meaning but an anxiety about the processes of representing these bodies.

Following the chronology of publication, I want to start with the Gulf War cover. The use of the flag in a context such as this is not in itself unusual. The culmination of a long drawn out 'phoney' war, this is the moment just prior to a rather more physical engagement with the forces of Saddam Hussein's army, with the concomitant risk to individual combatants. Its location is, again, not unusual given *The Sun*'s reputation as one of the most crudely and vociferously nationalistic of daily British newspapers with its manichean incitement to a hatred of the Other.[1] It can be viewed as an attempt to project a symbolic unity at a moment of perceived crisis or threat. The exceptional use of the flag to take up the entire front page of the newspaper, with its plea to 'support our boys and put this flag in your window', can be seen as symptomatic of a distinct uneasiness

Figure 1. *The Sun*, 16 January 1991 and 25 November 1991.

rather than the assertion of a confident identity. The attempt to cross from the private realm of reading to the public realm of display on the basis of this appeal, points to an inherent instability with regard to the figure of the nation — what Homi Bhabha calls a 'particular ambivalence that haunts the idea of the nation'.[2] As he writes in the introduction to *Nation and Narration*:

> If the ambivalent figure of the nation is a problem of its transitional history, its conceptual indeterminacy, its wavering between vocabularies, then what effect does this have on narratives and discourses that signify a sense of 'nationness': the *heimlich* pleasures of the hearth, the *unheimlich* terror of the space or race of the Other; the comfort of social belonging, the hidden injuries of class; the customs of taste, the powers of political affiliation; the sense of the social order, the sensibility of sexuality; the blindness of bureaucracy, the strait insight of institutions; the quality of justice, the common sense of injustice; the *langue* of the law, the *parole* of the people. (2)

The use of the hyper-symbol of the flag is the final attempt to fix the ambiguity of the sign in a moment of transcendence. In this way it is an authoritarian fetishism of the social and political impulse to rationalize the normalizing tendency of the, so-called, 'national interest'.

The montage of the flag and head point to a process of cultural anxiety centred, as the head is centred on the flag, on the absent body of the male soldier. The fragmented form of the representation is indicative of a sense of the loss of the secure identity of the soldier as mythical warrior. In the mythical narrative of nationhood, soldiers have traditionally occupied the symbolic centre of national identity.[3] There is also uncertainty over the question of state borders as what is effected is an ideological extension of the emotional boundaries of the nation beyond the physical boundaries. War is rarely, if ever, actually about a literal threat to the borders of the nation. What such an operation pointed to, therefore, was the tenuous nature of such categories: at the moment when they are asserted as at their most secure they are, in fact, at their most unstable.

War and the military have long been one of the key sites for forging links between hegemonic masculinities and men's bodies. The absence of the actual body of the soldier from the image points to a loss of confidence in the authority of this hegemonic ideal. This can be read through the increasing technologization of war and work where, as Harry Brod has observed, the centrality of the male body as productive or heroic has been drastically diminished and, therefore, undermined traditional male identities: the disappearing male body.[4] Indeed, one of the distinguishing features of the Gulf War was the significant increase in the involvement of women as combatants in the conflict.[5] As David H.J. Morgan observes, such a cultural shift is destabilizing, where concerns over the presence of women in combat situations are actually far more significant, expressing a: 'concern with the overall symbolic order, the apparent loosening of boundaries between men and women, and the weakening of the links between nation, the military, and gendered identities'.[6]

There are other reasons as to why the construction takes the form it does. Given its nature, photography tends to the particular as opposed to the universal, therefore the cropping of the body is an attempt to overcome this dilemma. The head can function as a metonymic representation, as the body of the soldier is displaced by its absence onto the body of the nation as a whole.[7] It is worth extending this analysis of the rhetorical figuration of the montage. The flag is mobilized by the newspaper as an attempt to present a secure and stable background to the potentially threatened body of the soldier. The flag, as sign, points to an absent or ideal meaning where there is an instantaneous shift from the vehicle of meaning to the unstated meaning. It is the flag that is intended to appeal on the basis of universalistic and generally context-free thought and in this way seeks to reinforce identity over difference, even if the identity is one that is already multiple, as is indeed the case with the Union Jack. The assumption is that the hidden meaning is known and believed even though invisible. The flag is therefore an attempt to impose a monologic order of meaning where dissent is treason.

But the synecdochic presence of the head works to *undermine* such an appeal. The symbolic appeal of the flag is interrupted by the metonymic presence of the white, male body. Because of the contiguous relationship in metonymic representation between image and meaning, the orientation is towards a lateral dissemination that is potentially endless. In this way the relation is far more unpredictable, uncertain and multiple than was intended. What such a construction as this front page points to is less an unproblematic celebration of a triumphant identity, than a confused attempt to fix a differential relationship in a state of transition. The use of a head without a body points to the difficulty of producing an ideal image that uses a photograph in an identificatory mode.

The instability inherent in this attempt can be seen in the image of Freddie Mercury published six months or so earlier. The implications of repetition are, of course, well recognized as pointing to an anxiety in the analysand.[8] However, one of the significant aspects of this image is the surprising nature of its location in *The Sun*, a publication much criticized for its unrepentant history of AIDS hate and its homophobic perspective.[9]

To see *this* image of Mercury used to announce his death from Broncho-Pneumonia brought on by AIDS was a surprise, given the previous tone of the newspaper as one where AIDS was figured as retribution for promiscuous and immoral behaviour: those with AIDS were both victims *and* guilty. As Simon Watney has pointed out, the general attitude of the press was to stress the deeply 'alien' nature of those directly affected, against the mythic and seemingly stable identity of the general public.[10] Other surveys by the Glasgow University Media Group and health sociologist Kay Wellings pointed to the relentless use of the term 'Gay Plague'.[11] Given this history, what explains the use of this image of Mercury, draped in the national flag, triumphant and seemingly healthy, on the front cover of three million or more copies of *The Sun*? Is it an example of what might be termed a slippage in hegemonic representation, or what Terry Eagleton calls the necessary recognition of the 'other' of ruling ideology, the inscription of the potentially disruptive force of otherness in dominant ideological formations?[12]

The anomaly of using a celebratory image rather than one adopting a condemnatory or shameful tone points to a structural feature of the media: perpetuating conservative attitudes whilst being compelled to recognize popular support for particular individuals. In the first instance the cover could be described as a space of discursive contestation: the discourse of AIDS struggles with the discourse of 'stardom' all of which is framed by reference to a discourse of nation. Such a discursive contest has been described by Mikhail Bakhtin:

Any concrete discourse (utterance) finds the object at which it was directed already as it were overlain with qualifications, open to dispute, charged with value, already enveloped in an obscuring mist—or, on the contrary, by the 'light' of alien words that have already been spoken about it. It is entangled, shot through with shared thoughts, points of view, alien judgements and accents.[13]

The cover fits an already established practice of the news media by positioning Mercury as fundamentally different, and therefore distant, from the public by virtue of his star status. This particular formulation of the social effect of stardom is the combination of a number of themes. Both Hollywood stars and pop stars are a staple of the tabloid press, providing a vicarious pleasure for the reader through their excesses. This also serves an ideological role in that, by continuously focussing on the lives of individuals, the narrative is never raised above this singular level of reference to a wider historical perspective. Representations such as this one of Mercury individualize AIDS and close off the public aspects of the condition. At a time when state organizations such as the Health Education Authority were arguing the dangers to everyone from HIV infection, *The Sun* perpetuated the 'exotic' nature of those with AIDS. Newspapers positioned AIDS in the way they positioned the excesses of the stars — as a source of voyeuristic fascination.

Although rock music is not a cultural sphere renowned for the visibility of gay men within it, because of Mercury's star status it is less problematic to allude to his sexuality. Mercury, as a star, by definition transcends the ordinary, occupying a separate state of being. In 1979 Richard Dyer observed that:

Stars are always the most-something-or-other in the world — the most beautiful, the most expensive, the most sexy. But because stars are 'dissolved' into the superlative, are indistinguishable from it, they become superlative, hence they seem to be of a different order of being, a different 'ontological category'. Their image becomes gradually generalised, so that from being, say, the most beautiful they become simply 'the greatest'.[14]

In this context the picture would not seem particularly unusual. Mercury is portrayed as confident, healthy and in a pose suggestive of macho nationalism. *The Sun* has a reputation as one of the most crudely nationalistic of the tabloid press, so such an image might, again, not seem out of place. Although Freddie Mercury was a star whose trademark had become a stage performance centred on a camp, 'clone' style look, coupled with a strutting sexual knowingness, this could be accommodated by the media as it rarely ever crossed the boundary from stage to public realm. Mercury was not an icon for gay men; rather his audience consisted largely of white, straight men seemingly unaware of, or unconcerned by, the gay iconography he adopted.

As a star on stage Mercury was not a person like those in the audience, he was a 'screen' onto which any number of fantasies could be projected.[15] The very distance between Mercury and the audience acted to keep him apart yet simultaneously permanently available in an imaginary form. Possibly the scale of the popularity of Mercury could be attributed to the way he acted out the subverted fantasies of the male, heterosexual audience in a way that could be read without irony and in this way posed no threat to their own identity. The realm of pop music allows young men to experiment with the terms of their own emergent identity. Popular music, although a patriarchal institution that has perpetuated many masculinist representations, has also encouraged transgression. It has provided a safe place for homoerotic and feminine fantasies to exist and provided the means for deeply submerged desires to surface. Freddie Mercury's 'stage performance' allowed the audience, briefly, to accept the reality of their own performance of sexual identity and gender roles. As Judith Butler has written of drag, it is a form of imitation and appropriation that has no originary moment other than the staging itself.[16]

In this context, the performance of Mercury on stage and even, at one point, the whole of the band cross-dressing for the video produced to accompany the song 'I Want to Break Free', allowed the audience to indulge in the fleeting fluidity of non-categorical identity, where the performativity of gender can be freely engaged in without fear of being stigmatized. Mercury was always at a safe distance and therefore non-threatening to a young, male, heterosexual audience who could enjoy the thrill of minimally participating in excessive gender performance. Mercury's performance can be extended to include nationalism given his birth overseas and the slippage evident in the fact that the flag with which he has draped himself is actually *upside down*.[17]

The photograph used by the newspaper was taken in 1986 by Denis O'Regan during one of Mercury's world tours. Mercury is standing in a triumphant pose, arms outstretched crucifix-like, but also reminiscent of a football supporter's pose of macho defiance, seen in Europe since the 1970s. The flag surrounds him but it is his hidden genitalia that are literally at the centre of it. At the top the simple epitaph 'Freddie is dead' is mirrored by the two calendar dates '1946' and '1991' at the bottom, which give a monumental feel to the announcement. The simplicity of such motifs works to position the individual as transhistorical, in a universal space of abstract temporality devoid of the attachments of life, sexuality or illness.

The contingencies of life, birth and death, beginning and end, are contrasted to the transcendental existence of the nation as represented by the flag. The flag as symbol seeks to close down on the meanings that would otherwise flood into the discursive space generated by the visual representation. The flag is mobilized to access a totality where the sign is singular in its meaning. The aestheticization of the figure of Mercury in this image privileges such a closure around the potential instabilities of the contending categories. Thomas Yingling has observed of other examples of figures presented in the media that: 'their entry into AIDS discourses has always bordered on the specular (...) making AIDS "real" by circulating images that refer not to the complex interdiscursive challenges of the disease but to other familiar images'.[18]

The choice of a photograph of Mercury unmarked by disease and adopting a pose of 'healthy' masculinity is one informed by a need to try and contain the categories of national and gendered identities. In this sense reading between the two different moments is an ironic manoeuvre, as Yingling writes:

> What allows irony to work, of course, is a traditional notion that texts are stable and expectations clear if reversible; irony sets a limit to the instability of reading by staging closure as a choice between alternatives, each of which is complete. Irony thus provides an epistemological security rather than a radical textual opening. Rather than lead to questions about the grounds of reading, the seeming undecidability of irony becomes the key to a new stability. Thus, in the name of telling us something about AIDS, the media allows us to read AIDS — the most destabilizing social question of the last decade — through a set of stable discourses. (*AIDS*, 21)

AIDS has been figured by a language obsessed with borders: the borders of the body are threatened by invasion as are, by metaphoric transfer, the borders of the nation state. Borders are deeply problematic as they are points of crossing and transgression and therefore have to be policed. Edgar Morin highlights this opposition inherent in the assertion of a border:

> The frontier is both an opening and a closing. It is at the frontier that there takes place the distinction from and liaison with the environment. All frontiers, including the membrane of living beings, including the frontier of nation, are, at the same time as they are barriers, places of communication and exchange. They are places of dissociation and association, of separation and articulation.[19]

The attempt, therefore, to articulate a response to the figure of Freddie Mercury by recourse to the symbol of the flag both asserts and simultaneously undermines an attempt to fix the problematic of representation. Compelled by popular sympathy for Mercury, *The Sun* needs to pull out the flag as the most powerful sign from its repertoire of images precisely because it needs to overcome the discursive chasm created between itself and AIDS.[20] With his death

Mercury's sexuality is no longer ambiguous for the readers of *The Sun*, as AIDS is a 'homosexual' disease. But by shifting the emphasis of the discussion through the use of this image to one prior to this moment an attempt is made to overcome the contradiction. Whilst it would be fair to say that the news coverage in the days following the announcement was typically complex and contradictory, there was a clear attempt to maintain Mercury as ambiguous in his sexuality by reference to him as bisexual and recurring reference to a female friend as the 'love of his life'.

The struggle over the representation of the body of Mercury evident in this picture manifests itself as well in relation to a notion of respectability. George Mosse has accounted for the intrinsic connection between bourgeois morality and the ideology of nationalism.[21] We can see, therefore, that an appeal to nationalism can only be staged with an aestheticized, idealized body that bears no trace of an illness such as AIDS. Mercury as a gay man has to be removed from the newspaper's discourse of homosexuality-as-disease and the flag is the ultimate vehicle for doing so. But the framing of Mercury with the flag is an attempt to *deny* diversity and difference under the weight of the abstraction of nationalism. The location of Mercury at the centre is an acceptance of difference but not on equal terms, rather terms that are defined by the actual segregation of the gay male body. Difference has always been recognized within the dominant discourse of the nation but only in terms of assimilation or demarcation. The visibility of the 'other' is, of course, what allows for the authority of the normative as 'natural'.[22]

In both images, therefore, what is visible is a profound anxiety on how to represent the male body at the two moments of war and AIDS, where the figure of an idealized masculinity is undermined. Yingling points to the repeated coincidence of stories in the print media on AIDS and patriotic coverage of the Gulf War (*AIDS*, 35, n.5). In this context it is the male body which functions as the deconstructive 'hinge' that works to point to the two incompatible readings of the newspaper covers.[23] Margins and centres are what are figured in the two constructions: the centre is the mythical nation, secure and transcendent, a space defined in relation to history (sameness); the borders are where the nation defines itself in relation to others (difference). Mercury is literally at the centre of the symbol of nation, yet as a Gay man associated with AIDS he is figuratively at its borders; the soldier is actually located at the physical borders, on the front-line, and only figuratively at its centre. In this way the anxieties of both threats to the figure of the masculine body, war and AIDS, become visible in this series of reflections and repetitions.

JOHN LYNCH
Leeds Metropolitan University

NOTES

1 Peter Chippendale and Chris Horrie write of the paper's nationalistic rhetoric: 'Mindless patriotic fervour and flag waving jingoism had always been the trademark of popular newspapers, and *The Sun*, taking over the mantle of chief John Bull tub-thumper from the *Express*, simply reflected changing circulation patterns', *Stick it up your Punter: the Rise and Fall of the Sun* (London, Heinemann, 1990), 110.
2 'Introduction: narrating the nation' in *Nation and Narration* (London and New York, Routledge, 1990), 1.
3 Graham Dawson, *Soldier Heroes: British Adventure, Empire and the Imagining of Masculinities* (London and New York, Routledge, 1994). One example of this would be the film *GI Jane* starring Demi Moore as a female soldier struggling with masculinist culture and political manipulation. This conflict is resolved by her adopting the attitudes of male aggression with the infamous retort to a violent attack by a superior: 'Suck my dick!' Thanks to Jago Morrison for this reference.
4 'Masculinity as Masquerade' in *The Masculine Masquerade: Masculinity and Representation*, edited by Andrew Perchuk and Helaine Posner (London and New York, Routledge, 1995), 19.
5 See Christine Forde '"Women warriors": Representations of Women Soldiers in British Daily Newspaper Reports of the Gulf War (January to March 1991)' in *(Hetero)Sexual Politics*, edited by Mary Maynard and June Purvis (London, Taylor and Francis, 1995), 108–22.
6 'Theatre of war: combat, the military, and masculinities' in *Theorizing Masculinities*, edited by Harry Brod and Michael Kaufman (London, Sage, 1994), 171.
7 The British artist Gavin Turk has used this image as part of his ongoing subversion of the status of the artist. He replaced the soldier's head with his own in the work *Study for a Window* (1991). Illustration in *Flash Art*, 176 (March/April 1994), 171.
8 Freud, of course, links the phenomena of doubling and repetition to the subject of the 'uncanny'. For Freud the frightening nature of the uncanny is the emergence of the repressed, where the repressed is not something new or alien but the familiar become alienated. See 'The Uncanny' in *Art*

and Literature, The Pelican Freud Library, XIV, edited by Albert Dickson (Harmondsworth, Penguin, 1985), 339–76.
9 Margaret Jay as Director of the National AIDS Trust, considered *The Sun* along with the *Daily Star* as the worst of the tabloids in their coverage of HIV/AIDS. See Raymond Snoddy, *The Good, the Bad and the Unacceptable* (London and Boston, Faber and Faber, 1992), 65.
10 *Policing Desire: Pornography, AIDS and the Media* (Minneapolis, University of Minnesota Press, second edition, 1989), 84.
11 David Miller and Kevin Williams 'Negotiating HIV/AIDS information: agendas, media strategies and the news' in *Getting the Message: News, Truth and Power*, edited by John Eldridge (London and New York, Routledge, 1993), 126–42; Kay Wellings, 'Perceptions of Risk — Media treatment of AIDS' in *Social Aspects of AIDS*, edited by Peter Aggleton and H. Homas (London, The Falmer Press, 1988), 83–105.
12 *Ideology: An Introduction* (London, Verso, 1991), 45.
13 *The Dialogic Imagination: Four Essays*, translated by Michael Holquist and Caryl Emerson (Austin, University of Texas Press, 1981), 276.
14 *Stars* (London, British Film Institute, 1979), 49.
15 Dawson writes of this process of narrative imagining: 'Being subjectively entered-into and "inhabited" through identification, the cultural forms of masculinity enable a sense of one's self as "a man" to be imagined and recognized by others. Since the imagining and recognition of identities is a process shot through with wish-fulfilling fantasies, these cultural forms often figure ideal and desirable masculinities, in which both self and others make investments. Men may wish and strive to become the man they would like to imagine themselves to be. They may also be compelled to identify with particular forms out of their need for recognition of others' (*Soldier Heroes*, 23).
16 *Gender Trouble: Feminism and the Subversion of Identity* (London and New York, Routledge, 1990), viii.
17 Freddie Mercury was born on the island of Zanzibar. There is a 'right way' up to the Union Jack where the thicker of the white diagonals goes in the top left-hand corner.
18 *AIDS and the National Body* (Durham and London, Duke University Press, 1997), 19.
19 *La Méthode, 1, La Nature de la nature* (Paris, Seuil, 1977), quoted in Geoffrey Bennington, 'Postal politics and the institution of the nation' in *Nation and Narration*, edited by Homi Bhabha, 121.
20 Richard Smith wrote of lessons learnt by *The Sun* and other newspapers from previous examples: 'After the Elton John debacle five years ago the tabloids learnt that turning a much loved celeb into a hate figure is never easy, and kicking a man when he's down — even if he's a "poof" — loses sales quicker

that you can say "Hillsborough"', 'A year in the death of Freddie Mercury' *Gay Times*, January 1993, 61.
21 *Nationalism and Sexuality: Middle-Class Morality and Sexual Norms in Modern Europe* (Wisconsin, University of Wisconsin Press, 1985).
22 Lee Edelman writes of the tropological shift of sexual desire from metonymy to metaphor where the arbitrary slippages of the former are fixed in the identities of the latter. Lee Edelman, *Homographesis: Essays in Gay Literary and Cultural Theory* (New York and London, Routledge, 1994), 3–23.
23 Paul de Man, *Allegories of Reading: Figural Language in Rousseau, Nietzsche, Rilke, and Proust* (New Haven and London, Yale University Press, 1979), 12.

A Genealogical Approach to Idealized Male Body Imagery

Introduction

Over the last two decades there has been a dramatic increase in the number of images of men in popular culture. Where once images of women dominated advertising and magazines, increasingly men's bodies are taking their place alongside women's on billboards, in fashion shoots, and large circulation magazines. However, it is not simply that there are now more images of men circulating, but that *a specific kind of representational practice has emerged for depicting the male body*: namely an idealized and eroticized aesthetic showing a toned, young body. This, we will argue, is a new phenomenon. We are not suggesting that male bodies have not been presented as desirable before; clearly they have, and heterosexual women and gay men have swooned over the years over representations of Fred Astaire, Cary Grant, James Dean and dozens of matinee idols. What is new — and culturally and historically specific — however, is the ways in which the male body is being presented: specifically, the coding of this body in ways that give permission for it to be looked at and desired. Men's bodies, it has been argued, are now coded — like women's — 'to be looked at' to use the awkward but insightful phrase current in film studies.[1] That is, the ways that men's bodies have begun to be represented over the last twenty years constitutes a disruption of conventional patterns of looking in which, in John Berger's famous phrase, 'men look at women and women watch themselves being looked at'.[2]

The aim of this paper is to explore the reasons for the emergence of this new representational practice in the UK. It is, we argue, a complex social, economic, political and cultural phenomenon, not reducible to any single cause or determinant, but the outcome of a variety of overlapping and contradictory shifts and changes. Here there is space only to begin the process of 'unpacking' and identifying those multiple determinants, with the aim of producing an outline of a genealogy of this representational practice.

There is a danger in doing this that the specificity of particular kinds of representation may be lost or glossed over — so, for example, representations of the male body that are constructed to highlight an intense vulnerability may be conflated with more muscular masculinities which owe a clear debt to gay bodybuilding culture. Clearly, more detailed and differentiated analyses are needed which will refine our understandings of the nature of the different ways in which representations idealize and eroticize the male body. However, it is worth highlighting, as others have done,[3] the extraordinary similarity of many images of the male body circulating in contemporary mainstream popular culture (for example, men's health magazines, underwear and fragrance advertising). Moreover, our own study of young men's responses to these representations suggests that only a minority make significant distinctions between the types of image, and most see them as representing a generic style.[4] Indeed, several respondents suggested (only half joking) that all the images of young, toned, muscular bodies in contemporary magazines and adverts were in fact photographs of just one man!

The characteristics of this kind of representation may be described as Edwards has done: the models are generally white (black models are still largely confined to music and sports imagery, and clear patterns of racialization are evident); they are young (under 30); they are slim, toned and muscular; they are usually clean-shaven — with perhaps the exception of a little 'designer stubble'; and they have particular facial features which connote a combination of softness and strength — strong jaw, large lips and eyes, soft-looking, clear skin.

Why, then, has this specific way of representing the male body emerged at this particular historical moment? We have identified eight different factors to be explored in this 'history of the present'.

1. Feminism and New Social Movements

Clearly, one key influence upon the way in which masculinity is regarded and presented is feminism. Feminists' interrogation of conventional assumptions about gender relations, and their problematization of 'traditional masculinity', have had a seismic effect upon popular culture and social relations. Through the influence of feminism many taken-for-granted aspects of masculinity were questioned, with forums as diverse as women's magazines and talk shows echoing feminist criticisms of traditional masculinity as distant, uninvolved, unemotional and uncommunicative. Since the 1970s, these critiques gave rise to a great appetite for a new kind of masculinity, which would encompass many traits previously thought of as feminine — emotionality, intimacy, nurturing and caring.[5]

Additionally, feminism sought to deconstruct some of the binary ways of thinking through which gender was understood — particularly the elision of women with the nature, and the ways that femininity (but not masculinity) was defined and constrained by the body. Some of feminists' energies have been concerned with overturning the binaries altogether,[6] whilst others tried to generate a recognition that we are *all* embodied subjects — echoed by a growing men's health movement that recognized the costs to men of ignoring this. At its most basic, then, feminism has helped to make men's bodies visible to themselves and others, and to begin revisioning gender relations.

The rise of a particular style of humanist psychology within the late 1970s and 1980s reinforced campaigns to 'reinvent' gender. This popular psychology took as its focus the notion of the 'whole person', and was concerned with good communication and with validating different parts of the person and different styles of interaction to those valued traditionally. Assertiveness was promoted above aggressiveness or passivity and there was an increase in interest in personal therapy, and in a range of alternative or complementary approaches to medicine or healing. Taken together, these movements put the idea of the *whole person* or the *self-actualized person* on the cultural agenda. Significantly, as Chapman and Rutherford suggested, the whole person was seen as the androgynous person, as extreme masculinity and extreme femininity came to be perceived not simply as socially restricting or damaging, but also as unhealthy.

Linked to this trend was the rise of what have been called New Social Movements. Included in this category (as well as feminism) are the peace movement, anti-racist organisations, environmental movements, movements for sexual liberation, and a variety of identity-based political organisations focusing on disability rights, post-colonial struggles, transgender identities, and so on. What this loose categorization of groups share is both a disillusion with conventional class-based party politics, and a commitment to new forms of organization and struggle, based less upon representative democracy and more upon direct action. Taken together, the New Social Movements disrupted the very understanding of what politics meant, showing that everyday life was irredeemably political. They also promoted a different model of the individual, as someone connected not simply to a family, but to wider communities and to the environment. In doing so, we would argue, they sowed the seeds for a revisioning of traditional masculinity, and helped to create a cultural milieu in which a 'new man' could emerge and flourish. The nature of that 'new man' is highly contested: he represented, for some, a shift to a more emotionally and domestically involved, pro-feminist nurturing man; for others, a more individualistic and narcissistic man whose bathroom shelves groaned under the weight of skincare and fragrance products; and, for others still, he was the 'Great Pretender', a wolf in sheep's clothing, a way for men to hold on to their power whilst appearing to have changed (see Chapman and Rutherford; Frank Mort;[7] and Nixon for discussions and comparisons with the rise of the 'new lad'). Clearly, though, his emergence is centrally connected to the growth of representations of the male body.

2. The Rise of the Style Press

A different kind of influence came from the rise of the style magazines in the 1980s. For years, people working in the fashion, magazine, advertising and retailing industries had fantasized about the creation of a magazine which could be targeted at affluent male consumers — but it was seen as an impossible dream. The main reason identified for this was that men did not define themselves *as* men, in the same way that women defined themselves as women. Men lacked self-consciousness about their sex (the 'male as norm' problem, identified by feminists), and while they bought magazines about cars or fishing or cameras there was scepticism about whether they would buy a title organized around *being a man*, rather than a specific hobby. A second problem concerned the tone such a magazine should adopt — women's magazines had long adopted the formula of treating their readers like friends, with an intimate tone, but this was seen by people within the industry as potentially threatening to heterosexual men.

In terms of understanding the emergence of new ways of representing masculinity one magazine is critical — and that is *The Face*, launched by Nick Logan in 1982. It promoted itself as a style magazine rather than a men's magazine, although the vast majority of its readers were male, and was organized around fashion and music and any kind of social commentary deemed to be chic enough to fit in its pages. Nixon argues that *The Face* developed a new aesthetic: it was not just about style, but it was emblematic of stylishness itself, creating a new vocabulary for fashion photography — a vocabulary, significantly, that extended the notion of style to include fashion spreads of menswear and advertising for body products targeted at men as well as women. The style press exercised two key kinds of influence, then — first in being the precursor of fashion/lifestyle magazines aimed at men, and, second, in pioneering radically new ways of representing male (generally clothed) bodies.

3. The Rise of Retailing: Masculinity Goes to the Mall

The rise of the style magazines can in turn be understood in terms of massive changes in the economy that were taking place in the 1980s. There was a dramatic decline in manufacturing and a rise in the service sector and retailing—itself producing a 'genderquake'.[8] The employment of increasing numbers of people within the retail sector was, however, as Mort points out, just one of a number of factors that were changing the structure and meaning of shopping and consumerism. There was a significant trend towards conglomeration within clothes retailing, with five or six companies controlling the high street by the end of the 1980s; a growth in out of town shopping; and a new sense in which shopping was promoted as a major cultural or leisure activity—with the opening of large themed shopping centres, the provision of creches and restaurants in shopping centres, and the promotion of trips to large out of town stores as a relaxing day out. Indeed, studies consistently find that shopping is the main leisure activity of the British.[9]

In the 1980s the 'new man' became a new target for fashion companies: men were the new market.[10] This was heralded as a quiet revolution in fashion companies; men had been considered a market that was difficult to crack, and shopping had always been seen as traditionally female. The move was associated with the meteoric rise of a few companies, most notably Next and the Burton group. Next, in particular, launched in 1986, traded images of the city, of share dealing and city gents: striped shirts, brogues, double breasted suits. As such it was trading on images that were circulating elsewhere through the privatization campaigns, the Big Bang, as well as in major *zeitgeist* films like *Wall Street*. Mort argues that Next allowed people to play with these images without commitment.[11] Where once clothes had been a powerful and stable signifiers of social location, increasingly they were worn in more flexible and playful ways, such that men could 'try on' new identities through their apparel. While a man might work as a labourer throughout the week, he can dress like a share-room dealer to go out in the evening, and wearing the apparel of a 'country gentlemen' (corduroy trousers and a Barbour jacket) to visit the garden centre at the weekend.

4. New Musical Trends

Mort argues further that this new playful relationship between clothes and identity was the result of a series of changes provoked by punk music and style. With its emphasis on bricolage (or on the putting together of things that are normally kept apart), for example, Doc Martens and ballet dresses, punk created a space for men and women to be able to play with different self-presentations, and broke down stable chains of signification. Thus it was no longer straightforwardly possible to read off social location from particular ways of dressing.

Surprisingly, punk is the only musical movement to have been seriously discussed in relation to questions about masculinity and identity.[12] Yet, it would seem obvious that musical styles have had a profound effect upon masculinity and upon the ways in which men live and experience what it means to be male. The kind of codification of masculinity in heavy metal, for example, is a world away from the gender meanings encoded in glam rock, which itself differs from the masculinities on offer in reggae, techno, Britpop or ska, to name just a few. Since the early 1980s music videos have facilitated the circulation of multiple images of male stars' bodies that are eroticized in markedly different ways, for example the soft romanticism of Spandau Ballet, the gender ambiguity of Boy George or Prince, the muscularity of NWA. The growing significance of dance culture, both as a live/lived club-based phenomenon, and in its classical and contemporary form, is also significant. The impact of musical cultures and subcultures upon men's experience and upon the mainstreaming of sexualized images of the male body is seriously under-researched and would repay detailed study.

5. The Rise of the Gay Movement

Another factor that is central to our understanding of the emergence of new representational practices for depicting masculinities is the growth of the gay liberation movement from the late 1960s onwards. In the UK, there has recently been a proliferation of magazines aimed at gay men, which are no longer only targeted at a gay *activist* audience. These offer new and explicitly *pleasurable* representations, not simply those deemed politically sound. This reflects the rising confidence of the gay community, at least in metropolitan areas, as well as increasing corporate recognition of the power of the 'pink pound'. These magazines, together with gay pornography, pin-ups, and particular subcultural styles within the club scene, have had a profound effect upon representations of masculinity, through a routing that has gone from gay porn through art-house photography to advertising.[13] Notably, they have served to cleave apart the association of masculinity with heterosexuality, and the elision of masculinity with activity, by showing men not simply as active sexual subjects, but also as objects of desire.[14] In other words, it is within the gay media that representations of men as erotic objects to be looked at were first produced, and, arguably, what has happened over the two last decades, is that this genre has gone mainstream.

6. The Marketing of Women's Desire

If indeed gay images of men have gone mainstream then this is partly because of the increasing confidence of gay media, but also partly a result of a realization that representations of men previously confined to gay subcultures are enormously desirable to some heterosexual women. Suzanne Moore has argued that it was precisely the growing visibility of eroticized representations of men outside the gay media that facilitated, or gave permission for, a new kind of gaze among women.[15] She suggests that this constituted a major disruption to the scopic order (the politics of looking) in which old assumptions about subject/object, active/passive were challenged. Rather than simply being objects of the gaze, women have become active subjects who can look as well as being looked at. An important literature in film and photography studies deals with the ways in which representations of masculinity are designed to disavow homoeroticism: using the 'reassuring' presence of a woman as love interest, excessive violence or humour as their main means.[16] It also details the punishment meted out to women in film whose sexuality is deemed too active or independent. Moore's argument is that this shift makes both the disavowal and the punishment redundant.

This trend in contemporary culture is evident in the new confident tone of women's magazines and models in advertisements who now look and talk back, rather than simply being passive objects.[17] It is humorously depicted in adverts like that for Diet Coke in which women queue up for an '11 o'clock appointment' in order to gaze at the toned body of the labourer outside the window as he takes his morning break to drink a coke. The choice of the labourer is interesting because it highlights the reversal that has taken place: where once building contractors ogled and whistled at women, now (it is suggested) women ogle them! (Obviously, we would not want to overstate this point, and it should be noted that the politics of looking still take their traditional form in many advertisements and many situations).

7. Reactions to HIV and AIDS

As we have already shown, the emergence of a new representational practice for depicting the male body is complexly and multiply determined. One other significant influence must be the impact of HIV and AIDS. Clearly this has had profound effects on the gay community — and many individuals — at an experiential level, but it has also been an important factor in generating *new representations of masculinity and sexuality* that have entered the mainstream. One new representation — seen best in theatre productions and in the flourishing artistic and cultural activity to which HIV and AIDS gave birth — is of masculinity as loving, caring and nurturing, exemplified by the many men who have cared for their partners while they are living or dying with HIV. The other important representational shift brought about by responses to HIV and AIDS has been the production of more explicitly sexualized and eroticized imagery. This was partly a response to the inadequacy of early government campaigns (such as Britain's 'Don't die of ignorance' promotion, dominated by large icebergs), and partly as a reaction against the sexual puritanism that HIV and AIDS seemed to threaten — captured in Billy Bragg's song *Sexuality* by the lines 'safe sex doesn't mean no sex/ it just means use your imagination'. It was also partly a libidinous, life-affirming refusal to equate sex with death, and a celebration of the pleasures of looking at and enjoying the bodies of others.

8. The New Cultural Intermediaries

Finally, the emergence of new ways of representing masculinity in the mainstream is partly attributable to the rise of the 'new cultural intermediaries', in advanced capitalist societies, devoted to discovering, measuring, interpreting and mediating a nexus of psychological and cultural questions about who we are, how we live and what we want.[18] Journalists, researchers, think tanks, marketing people, futurologists or trend spotters, and even academics, increasingly generate knowledge and discourses that come to produce — or at least become part of — the phenomenon that they are trying to explain. This can be seen very clearly in relation to contemporary debates about masculinity.

Marketing companies (working for a particular client, or attempting to produce information that will be of commercial value to a number of potential clients) produce a report about 'young men today' based — usually — upon a small number of focus groups. This is picked up by newspapers who announce the findings as a news story, and then, hungry for copy to fill their increasingly large lifestyle sections, produce detailed commentaries and think pieces on the topic. The debates are then pushed through the 'media echo chamber' and the observations about contemporary masculinity take on the status of self-evident truths.[19] In another twist, these truths may then be imported into academic research — either as 'evidence' that a project should be funded (for example, 'we are witnessing an epidemic of body dysmorphia among young men that requires examination'), or, more critically, to challenge a received wisdom. Meanwhile, more significantly, retailing companies and magazines have digested the findings and are already tailoring their products to take account of the new information about how contemporary young men are changing (softer lines appear in car designs, fragrances that pick up on the 'new sensuality' are marketed, clothes that cling to toned male bodies 'in all the right places' reach the shops, and so on).

This is a brief and oversimplified account, certainly, but it captures in essence the process by which various forms of knowledge are involved not just in describing the world, but also in producing it. While writing this paper we came across a typical example. Under the headline 'Young men reject old image' an article in *The Observer* (26 August 2001) reports on a trend survey by Informer which documents a shift away from the 'new lad' to a new form of masculinity described as 'nice bloke' (in brief: happy with equality, serious about work, juggling different commitments). This new incarnation of the young male follows many earlier shifts from 'new man' to 'new lad' to 'soft lad' and so on. In response to the new findings the editor of the 'lad mag' *Loaded* announces his intention to 'feminize' his publication. The cycle continues ...

Conclusion

This paper has pointed briefly to some of the factors that have combined over the last two decades to produce an important shift in the ways that the male body is presented in mainstream popular culture. Obviously, it only focuses on one broad genre of representational practice — centred on idealizing and eroticizing parts or the whole of male bodies. Men's bodies are presented in a whole range of other ways — in sports imagery, in music videos, in action films, in news discourse, and so on — which lie outside the scope of this discussion. The paper has also not considered how this shift may be understood — either by young men themselves (see Gill et al, 'Tyranny') or by others concerned with democratizing the scopic order (for example, to what extent does this new practice represent a transgression of normative masculinity?). What it hopes to have done, however, is to have highlighted the complexity of this cultural shift, and to have begun to outline genealogically the elements that have produced it.

ROSALIND GILL, KAREN HENWOOD
AND CARL MCLEAN
The London School of Economics and the University of East Anglia

NOTES

1 See for example, Laura Mulvey, 'Visual Pleasure and Narrative Cinema', *Screen*, 16: 3 (1975), 6–18; S. Cohan and I.R. Hark, *Screening the Male: Exploring Masculinities in Hollywood Cinema* (London, New York, Routledge, 1993); Screen, *The Screen Reader in Sexuality* (London, Routledge, 1992); S. Jeffords, *Hard Bodies: Hollywood Masculinity in the Reagan Years* (New Jersey, Rutger University Press, 1994).
2 *Ways of Seeing* (London, BBC, 1972), 47.
3 See for example, T. Edwards, *Men in the Mirror: Men's Fashion, Masculinity and Consumer Society* (London, Cassell, 1997); Sean Nixon, *Hard Looks: Masculinities, Spectatorship and Contemporary Consumption* (London, University College Press London, 1996).
4 Ros Gill, Karen Henwood and Carl McLean, 'The Tyranny of the "Sixpack": Understanding Men's Responses to Idealised Male Body Imagery' in *Culture in Psychology*, edited by C. Squire (London, Routledge, 2000), 100–18.
5 *Male Order: Unwrapping Masculinity*, edited by R. Chapman and J. Rutherford (London, Lawrence & Wishart, 1988); Vic Seidler, *Men, Sex and Relationships: Writings from Achilles Heel* (London, Routledge, 1992); R. Connell, *Masculinities* (Cambridge, Polity Press, 1995); Michael Kimmel, *Changing Men: New Direction on Research on Men and Masculinity* (Newbury Park, CA, Sage, 1987); J. Hearn and D.H. Morgan, 'Men, Masculinities and Social Theory' (London Unwin & Hyman, 1990).
6 Judith Butler, *Gender Trouble* (New York, Routledge, 1990).
7 *Cultures of Consumption: Masculinities and Social Space in Late Twentieth-Century Britain* (London, Routledge, 1996).

8 See H. Wilkinson, *No Turning Back: Generations and Genderquake* (London, Demos, 1994).
9 *Acknowledging Consumption*, edited by D. Miller (London, Routledge, 1995). S. Miles, 'The Cultural Capital of Consumption', *Culture & Psychology*, 12:3 (1996), 139–58.
10 C. Hession, 'Men's Grooming: The Next Growth Category,' *happi* (1997), 57–60.
11 'Boys Own? Masculinity, Style and Popular Culture' in *Male Order: Unwrapping Masculinities* edited by R. Chapman and J. Rutherford (London, Routledge, 1988), 193–224.
12 S. Thornton, *Club Cultures* (Cambridge, Polity, 1995); Dick Hebdige, *Subculture: The Meaning of Style* (London, Methuen, 1979).
13 N. Parsi, 'Don't Worry Sam, You're Not Alone: Bodybuilding is So Queer', *Building Bodies*, edited by P. Moore (New Brunswick, Rutgers University Press, 1997), 103–34.
14 Kobena Mercer and Isaac Julien, 'Race, Sexual Politics and Black Masculinity' in *Male Order*, 97–164; *Out in Culture: Gay, Lesbian and Queer Essays on Popular Culture*, edited by C. Creekmuir and A. Doty (London, Cassell, 1993); M. Simpson, *Male Impersonators: Men Performing Masculinity*, (London, Cassell, 1994).
15 'Here's Looking at You Kid!' in *The Female Gaze: Women as Viewers of Popular Culture*, edited by L. Gamman and M. Marshment (London, The Women's Press, 1988), 44–59.
16 See for example, S. Neale, 'Masculinity as Spectacle: Reflections on Men and Mainstream Cinema', *Screen*, 24:6 (1983), 2–16; S. Cohan and I.R. Hark, *Screening the Male: Exploring Masculinities in Hollywood Cinema*; Yvonne Tasker, *Spectacular Bodies: Gender, Genre and the Action Cinema* (London, Routledge, 1993).
17 Angela McRobbie, Feminism and Youth Culture: From *Jackie* to *Just 17* (London, Macmillan, 1991); Ros Gill, 'Mobile Positionings in Audience Responses: Not Just a Matter of Gender, "Race" and Class' (*Media, Culture & Society*, forthcoming).
18 Mike Featherstone, *Postmodernism and Consumer Culture* (London, Sage, 1995); Ros Gill *et al*, 'The Tyranny of the "Sixpack" '.
19 Susan Faludi, *Backlash: The Undeclared War Against Women* (London, Chatto & Windus, 1991).

MOVING MEN: MASCULINITY AND THE MOVING IMAGE

Reclaiming the Corporeal: The Black Male Body and the 'Racial' Mountain in *Looking for Langston*

Isaac Julien's British film *Looking for Langston* (1989) takes the American subject of the black poet Langston Hughes and the Harlem Renaissance of the 1920s. In an answer to the question what motivated him to create the film, the director stated that: 'I had to look to America because that seemed to be where most of the black gay history was located. Hughes was a perfect subject because there seemed to be so much controversy around him as a person in relationship to his sexual identity'.[1] Indeed, the film self-consciously calls into question the notion of black homosexuality that has been regarded as a 'sin against the race' that 'had to be kept secret, even if it was a widely shared one'.[2]

No doubt in part because of the film's association of Hughes with homosexuality, the film provoked an antagonistic response from the Hughes Estate which sought an injunction against showing the film in the US. In response to the Estate's legal claim, which was one of copyright infringement, Julien had to have Hughes's poetry replaced on the soundtrack. Furthermore, when the film was screened at the New York Film Festival in 1989, the audience was informed that owing to a copyright dispute the film's sound would be blocked out in two archival sequences of Langston Hughes reciting his poetry.[3] Clearly, the legal difficulties Julien experienced with the Hughes Estate themselves constitute one key to understanding black masculinity as a highly policed terrain. However, as many commentators have pointed out, the film is not a documentary that seeks to find the truth about Hughes's sexuality. The film, described by Julien as a meditation, is a 'poetic' montage of various archival materials, dramatized segments, poetry readings and music from the past and present.

In an interview with the African-American gay poet Essex Hemphill, Julien commented that he was more interested in complementing Hughes's works rather than dealing with his sexual lifestyle, and that is the reason the film is a poetic, experimental text ('Brother to Brother', 17). Elsewhere, Julien also remarked that Hughes 'is a symbol not just of the issue of sexuality within the race but for the experience of the black artist'.[4] Therefore, in order to understand the symbolic status Hughes represents in the film, I would argue that it is crucial to identify the particular position Hughes occupies within the Harlem Renaissance in relation to issues concerning the validity and appropriate nature of black literature. Equally important is the task of examining how Hughes responded to the cultural inscriptions of the black male body at the time of the Renaissance. For by conjuring up Hughes in particular, the film reclaims the corporeality of the black male body as the site of contest, while working within and against the logic of fetishism.

The 'Racial' Body and Cultural Identity

First, prior to looking specifically at the case of the black male body, I would like to start with my own sense of body consciousness, which would help illustrate the complex interplay between 'racial' stereotypes and cultural identities of gender. Whatever else I am, I know I am an 'Oriental girl' on the streets of Britain.[5] This is illustrated by an experience shared with a Chinese-American friend. Walking together, we had not noticed a bunch of homeless people sitting together at the corner, that is, not until they chanted, 'spare some "rice" please!' Initially, we were not in any state to reflect, because their shouting made us jump so much, but the further we walked away from them the more we realized the unpleasant stereotype that had been imposed on us. The fact that my friend comes from the US and I come from South Korea, and that she is almost six-feet tall and I am not, made the experience more intriguing. For the people we encountered, both of us, in all our differences, had that look which instantly conjured up 'Chinese take-away'. In other words, this was a case when our 'racial' body became the site of cultural practice — the rice-eating culture, in this case.

This is also the case when I am told how different I seem from other 'Oriental' or 'Asian' women. That is to say that I do not seem to fit the stereotypes of 'Asian' woman who is invariably submissive, subservient or shy and most of all the victim of patriarchal customs such as arranged marriages or the dowry system. People who told me this had actually met and known plenty of Asian women — at least in the movies, television programmes and advertisements. Consequently, I was expected to behave like an 'Asian' woman according to the Western popular imagination, and if not, I must be 'different'. Behind this seemingly complimentary comment there lies an ideology that imposes and reinforces the boundaries between self and other, centre and margin, the West and the rest. There also lies the pernicious assumption that 'white' is the norm against which everything else is measured.

In this sense, as Judith Butler suggests in *Gender Trouble*: 'the body is not a "being," but a variable boundary, a surface whose permeability is politically regulated'.[6] Similarly, Frantz Fanon in *Black Skin, White Masks* — still a crucial point of reference — wrote, 'not only must the black man be black; he must be black in relation to the white man'.[7] Fanon also wrote: 'when people like me, they tell me it is in spite of my colour. When they dislike me, they point out that it is not because of my colour. Either way, I am locked into the infernal circle' (*Black Skin, White Masks*, 116). However, if it is the body that structures people's perception of 'race', this is precisely why the body could be the most powerful and subversive site for deconstructing the codes and assumptions. This is why we need to turn to the 'racial' body that has historically been confined and controlled, so as to elaborate its ambivalence.

The Black Male Body and the Importance of Looking for Langston

The black male body, of course, has historically been perceived as the bearer of a bestial sexuality in Western culture. In terms of popular visual culture, it was D.W. Griffith's 1915 film *The Birth of a Nation* that introduced this archetypal figure of the black buck to the screen.[8] In the film, the animalistic black renegade Gus attempts to rape the virginal white Flora, who kills herself just in time, much as the mulatto Lynch tries to force Elsie (Lillian Gish) into a marriage from which she gets rescued just in time. As widely discussed, by explicitly personifying the buck stereotype in the characters of Gus and Lynch, Griffith perniciously played on the myth of the black man's high-powered sexuality, then articulated the great white fear (with a small element of hopeful assumption) that every black man longs for a white woman.[9]

Despite Griffith's claim that he had no political and ideological view in mind, the violent and aggressive black sexuality presented in the film was used to mobilize the Ku Klux Klan in the south, and provided a means to justify brutal attacks on black bodies. Not surprisingly, however, such a stereotype — ideologically pernicious, sociologically false — met with strong resistance and organized responses from the black community. At the film's New York premiere, for instance, the NAACP (National Association for the Advancement of Colored People) picketed the theatre, and there were renewed outcries each time the film was reissued, notably in 1921 and 1947.[10]

It is important to note that this popular film was a contemporary to the Harlem Renaissance. Inevitably, black writers and artists of the time were not only aware of this kind of visual representation, but also determined to transform the image of the black male body represented as highly and menacingly sexualized into an image that could become a culture bearer. To effect this transformation, black writers of the Harlem Renaissance sought to divest black subjectivity from the body, focusing instead on promoting 'racial uplift' through aspirations to bourgeois professional individualism and a stress on a cerebral, moral subjectivity. This was institutionally encouraged and directed by leaders of the National Civil Rights establishments and by black intellectuals. While the writers produced the literature, the black intelligentsia served as critics who helped define the movement and gave it direction, at the same time acting as liaison between the artists and their publishers, patrons, and public.

In particular, James Weldon Johnson of the NAACP, Alain Locke of Howard University, and Charles S. Johnson of the Urban League can be characterized as major boosters of the movement. But most of all, it was W.E.B. Du Bois, the best known and most influential black intellectual of the decade, who towered as a prime motivator of the younger writers of the Harlem Renaissance. Du Bois encouraged and promoted creative black talents out of his belief that 'until the art of the black folk compels recognition they will not be rated as human'. For him, 'all art is propaganda and ever must be'. He famously claimed that 'I do not care a damn for any art that is not used for propaganda'.[11] For this ultimate goal of advancing the position of black people in America, he urged black writers to choose subjects that would set examples of respectable blacks for others of their race to follow, which meant that they should avoid subjects such as black underworld characters or urban ghetto life.

The strong belief of the black intelligentsia that aesthetic issues were secondary to political ones in black literature soon came into conflict with a group of young writers who were determined to put artistic exploration before politics. Although they were emotionally attached to the Renaissance, the New Guard resented being defined, categorized or labelled. Also, they preferred the spontaneity of the black masses to the middle-class values and formality that characterized most of the black intellectuals. Equally important was the bohemian lifestyle the New Guard formed in Harlem. At the centre of Harlem's black bohemia stood Wallace Thurman and a small circle of writers, including Langston Hughes, Rudolf Fisher, and Zora Neale Hurston, who formed the essential backdrop to the black literary Renaissance.

The most significant outcome of this conflict was the publication of an arts magazine called *Fire* in 1926. Wallace Thurman edited it in association with Zora Neale Hurston, Aaron Douglas, John P. Davis, Bruce Nugent, Gwendolyn Bennett, and Langston Hughes. Hughes wrote that the idea was 'to burn up a lot of the old, dead conventional Negro-white ideas of past (...) and provide us with an outlet for publication not available in the limited pages of the small Negro magazines then existing, the *Crisis, Opportunity*, and *Messenger*'.[12] Indeed, *Fire* blended a somewhat militant and avowedly independent and bohemian outlook that emphasized freedom of expression and the quest for black identity. The cover showed a strikingly primitive black figure on red print by Aaron Douglas, and other illustrations were equally intense portrayals of nude Africans and jungle scenes. Clearly, its intention was to shock the values and conventions of the black middle class.

One of the most prominent among the New Guard was Langston Hughes. Hughes closely identified himself with the ghetto realism, not only finding his subject in the streets and cabarets of Harlem but also using black vernacular musical forms such as Blues and Jazz in his poetry. In his essay 'When the Negro was in Vogue', Hughes criticized the fallacy of promoting civil rights through the arts, pointing out, 'the ordinary Negro never heard of the Harlem Renaissance, or if he did, it hadn't raised his wages any'.[13] Significantly, Hughes's 1926 essay 'The Negro Artist and the Racial Mountain' served as a manifesto for the break away from the high culture of the New Negro Arts Movement. In the concluding sentences of the essay, Hughes wrote:

We younger Negro artists who create now intend to express our individual dark-skinned selves without fear or shame. If white people are pleased we are glad. If they are not, it doesn't matter. We know we are beautiful. And ugly too. The tom-tom cries and the tom-tom laughs. If coloured people are pleased we are glad. If they are not, their displeasure doesn't matter either. We build our temples for tomorrow, strong as we know how, and we stand on top of the mountain, free within ourselves.[14]

As such, Hughes's essay spoke for those artists who renounced 'representative' aesthetic criteria in order to capture the intrinsic conditions most men and women of African descent were experiencing. And it is this affirmation of independence that Isaac Julien found of relevance to the situation of the black artist today.[15] As the director himself puts it, Hughes is 'a symbol (...) for the experience of the black artist — the conflict between things an artist has to be and the things which are imposed upon the artist from the outside' (Gilroy, 'Climbing the Racial Mountain', 170).

Aside from the pressure from the black civil rights organizations, primitivism also turned out to be a complex issue for Hughes. As the Renaissance took root, Harlem was transformed, at least in the popular mind, into a sort of bohemia, which offered primitive and exotic pleasures. Indeed, some black artists exploited the thinly veiled desires of the white sexualization of the black body and culture, presenting new urban black forms of entertainment such as the jazz cabaret as a place of primitivistic sexual license.[16] Although Hughes was closely associated with this black bohemian lifestyle, he became uncomfortable and increasingly troubled by his white patron Charlotte Mason's fascination with the primitive nature of black life (especially when Hughes was becoming more and more political in the late 1920s and early 1930s). The problem was that Mason was looking for something in Hughes that did not really exist.

The Past and Present of the Black Atlantic: A Cinematic Analogy

Looking for Langston specifically points out this dilemma faced by black artists. Over archive footage showing black artists at work and at social events, the narrator (Stuart Hall) comments: 'it was a time when the Negro was in vogue. White patrons of the Harlem Renaissance wanted their black artists to know and feel the intuitions of the primitive. They didn't want modernism'. While explicitly criticizing the modernism that appropriated and ghettoized black art, Isaac Julien implicitly comments on the situation within which black filmmakers are working today, that is when white institutions fund black filmmakers according to their own expectations of what black films should be.[17]

As Henry Louis Gates Jr. argues, 'the film's evocations of the historical Harlem Renaissance is, among other things, a self-reflexive gesture', establishing an analogy between contemporary black creativity and an historical precursor.[18] As a black gay artist, Isaac Julien self-consciously conjures up Hughes and other figures of the Harlem Renaissance so as to connect them to his project of black gay male self-representation. Thus, as Gates points out, 'we look for Langston, but we discover Isaac' (202).

Here, of course, Gates is referring to the funeral scene at the beginning of the film where the film's director, Julien, takes the role of Hughes's corpse. Indeed, the cinematic dialogue between past and present is the key aspect of the film. For instance, Hughes's words ('Why should it be my loneliness, why should it be my song, why should it be my dream deferred overlong') overlap with those of the contemporary black gay singer Blackberri ('Whatever happened to a dream deferred? Things haven't changed much, I still find power in your words').

What follows the funeral scene is a complex montage of sound and image materials that include poems, experimental fiction, still photographs, vintage newsreels, and blues songs. We hear a radio tribute to Hughes following his death in 1967 over an archive shot taken from a train arriving at 125th Street in Harlem. We then see footage of Hughes reciting his own work ('I feel the blues a comin', wonder what the blues will bring') to the accompaniment of a jazz band. Hughes's voice is still audible, but the screen now cuts to a shot of a record on an old gramophone. Then, Blackberri's song 'Blues for Langston' starts, as we see the fictional character Alex — who could be seen as a young Langston Hughes — sitting in the bar. The shot is then intercut with a short extract of the blues singer Bessie Smith (who is known to be bisexual). Blackberri's song then continues ('things haven't changed much, we still find power in our words') over various still photographs of Hughes and others.

Throughout the sequence, the songs and words of the present are mixed with and overlaid upon the sounds and images of the past, effectively interrogating and imagining the past from the perspective of present. The fictional material, however, does not aim to reproduce period surfaces accurately. Instead, in its highly stylized black and white cinematography, the film uses settings such as the nightclub as the imaginative space where the dynamics of homoerotic gazing takes place. Indeed, the act of looking, that is, black men looking at black men as objects of desire, becomes the central aspect of the film's imaginative engagement with the Harlem Renaissance. Here, this act of 'gazing' is acutely highlighted by the camera positions, which are, in turn, determined by the exchanges of looks among men. The camera first finds Alex sitting at the bar, then reveals the object of his gaze: a black man sitting at a table with a white partner. The moment when the black man becomes the object of the erotic gaze of Alex, we see the close-up shot of the man, lit with a kick light and surrounded by shadow, that is in much the same way that classical Hollywood fetishizes its screen goddesses. The camera then elaborately shows the white man at the table noticing the gazes exchanged between two black men, consequently forming the classic love triangle, but recast here between three men.

As Alex turns around to face the bar again, there follows his fantasy scene in which he is walking in a field of lilies and poppies mapped by ponds and posts carrying white flags. Manthia Diawara argues that the scene is 'metafilmic because it thematizes the cinematic reconstruction of a dream'.[19] Alex is led, without resistance, to a destination and confronted with the object of his most profound desire, completely naked. As Alex looks at him, the camera travels along the body curves of this black man whom the voice-over calls Beauty. His lips and eyes are shown in close-ups as the voice-over comments on their plastic beauty. The following scene shows Alex and Beauty lying together, kissing and embracing. The camera lingers on their entwined black bodies, emphasizing the touch of skin upon skin, the softness of their bodies and their intimacy. As the camera holds on the still bodies of the two men, the voice-over is heard: 'he could feel Beauty's body close against his . . . hot, tense and soft . . . soft'.

Significantly, this fantasy sequence is a dramatization of Bruce Nugent's short story, 'Smoke, Lilies and Jade', which is an impressionistic celebration of androgyny, homosexuality, smoking and drugs. When first published in the controversial magazine *Fire* in 1926, perhaps not surprisingly, the piece was the scandal of the Harlem Renaissance. Du Bois had warned that the diminishing of cultural propaganda in the service of artistic beauty would 'turn the Negro renaissance into decadence', and Nugent's piece was widely regarded as the quintessential confirmation of that prediction.[20] Distinctively adapting the controversial piece from the Harlem Renaissance, the film not only claims the gay contribution to this celebrated black arts movement, but also suggests some of the impulses underlying the creative work of the Renaissance. As a voice-over (in a British accent) claims: 'We were linked by our gay desire'.

Return of the Body Beautiful

Straight after the fantasy sequence, Blackberri's song is heard on the soundtrack: 'You're such a beautiful black man who somehow has been made to feel that your beauty's not real'. Implicitly, the words manifest that the film is highly conscious of the use of the black male body in mainstream popular culture to signify hyper-sexuality. That is why it is important that the black male body in the fantasy sequence is completely divorced from any violence or animalistic traits. Indeed, what we witness in the sequence is the intimacy between the two men and the erotic dimensions of the black body. In this sense, the images de-familiarize and trouble — in Judith Butler's phrase — the dominant discourse on the black male body. By way of a critique of fetishism, the film makes black bodies fetish-objects but with new visual codings. In other words, instead of avoiding it, the film deliberately takes the black male body in order to re-position it as subject of the gaze. At the same time, the black male body is presented as the site of pleasure in order to claim gay male desire in looking at black men, and to reclaim the corporeality of the black male body that has been confined and controlled.

Equally important is the fact that the film alludes to the photography of Robert Mapplethorpe, particularly his black male nudes. Those photographs were famously campaigned against in the US on the grounds of 'obscenity and indecency', and equally denounced as 'exoticizing', 'fetishizing' and 'objectifying' the black male body. The film's project is, however, neither to denounce nor celebrate Mapplethorpe's photographs, but to re-appropriate them through a set of aesthetic conventions such as fragmentation and chiaroscuro lighting, in order to empower and address different desires. As the director himself put it, 'you have to work within and against the logic of fetishism to make your political points in the cinema'.[21]

What the film criticizes though is the white gays' unquestioning consumption of those images of black men. There is a scene in the film where a white man is seen wandering through white drapes on which are projected images of black men, some naked, which he touches and moves around. Over these images, we hear Hemphill reading his poem 'If His Name were Mandingo':

You want his pleasure, without guilt or capture. You don't notice many things about him ... He doesn't always wear a red ski cap, eat fried chicken, fuck like a jungle ... I don't suppose you ever hear him clearly? You're always too busy, seeking other things of him. His name isn't important. It would be coincidence, if he had a name, a face, a mind. If he's not hard-on, he's hard-up.

The sequence then ends with the white man lying on a bed paying a black man. What the film does here is pinpoint the racism in white gay culture and at the same time question the relationship of the white gay man to his black object of desire.

The presence of Mapplethorpe's photographs in the film has another function — that of centralizing the AIDS epidemic within the gay community.²² Thus, the film acknowledges the 'danger in love'. 'This nut might kill us', we hear Essex Hemphill saying over the gay cruising scene at night. He continues, 'This kiss could turn to stone'. As Tony Fisher puts it, 'AIDS does not only threaten the death of the body, but also the death of intimacy, of a way of life' (64). The film, then, is an act of mourning. It not only starts with the mourning of the death of Langston Hughes, but also is offered as memorium to three [black gay] men who died in 1987, Bruce Nugent, James Baldwin and Joseph Beam. Crucially, the film is dedicated to James Baldwin, who was brutally vilified by the newly (hetero-)sexualized Black Nationalism of the 1960s for his homosexuality. Perhaps more importantly, the film pays homage to the writer who wrote:

Each of us, helplessly and forever, contains the other — male in female, female in male, white in black, and black in white. We are a part of each other. Many of my countrymen appear to find this fact exceedingly inconvenient and even unfair, and so, very often do. But none of us can do anything about it.²³

Mourning, however, is never far removed from 'life' in *Looking for Langston*. As Jose E. Muñoz points out, 'the scene of mourning [of Hughes] and the bar scene (...) is [only] separated by a winding staircase'.²⁴ Indeed, there is a clear sense of celebration in the film not just for black and gay literary figures from the past but for black gay life here and now. Hence the film ends with a frenetic party scene at the club where black gay men dance to contemporary dance music ('Can You Party'). A group of 'thugs and police', as the end credits put it, break into the club but only to find out nobody is there. What the sequence illustrates is that black gay culture is very much alive, in spite of the continuing threats from racist and homophobic ideologies. Perhaps not surprisingly, this celebration takes the form of dancing, that is the bodily enactment and affirmation of living. As Langston Hughes points out at the very end of the film, 'why should I be blue? I've been blue all night long'.

CHI-YUN SHIN
Sheffield Hallam University

NOTES

1 Essex Hemphill, 'Brother to Brother', *Black Film Review* 5:3 (1990), 14–17, 14.
2 The quotes are from the narration in the film *Looking for Langston* (directed by Isaac Julien, 1989).

3 See Bad Object-Choices, 'Introduction' to *How Do I Look? Queer Film and Video*, edited by Bad Object-Choices (Seattle, Bay Press, 1991), 11–29, 17.
4 Paul Gilroy, 'Climbing the Racial Mountain: A Conversation with Isaac Julien' in *Small Acts* (London, Serpent's Tail, 1993), 166–72, 170.
5 I am echoing here Henry Louis Gates Jr who said, 'whatever else we were, we knew we were black men', in his 'Introduction' to *Thirteen Ways of Looking at a Black Man* (New York, Random House, 1997), xiii.
6 Butler's analysis of the body is concerned with the cultural politics of gender and sexuality, but it has been extended here to include the racial constitution of the body. See *Gender Trouble: Feminism and the Subversion of Identity* (New York, Routledge, 1990), 139.
7 *Black Skin, White Masks*, translated by Charles Lam Markmann (New York, Grove Weidenfeld, 1967), 110.
8 There are many traces of the black buck figure in contemporary images of black youth — for instance, the 'mugger', the 'drug-baron', the gangsta-rap singer, the 'niggas with attitude' bands. Although these images have been forced upon black men, it is also important to note that certain black men have subsequently appropriated these images with pride.
9 See, for instance, Donald Bogle's seminal book *Toms, Coons, Mulattoes, Mammies, and Bucks* (New York, Continuum, 1989), 10–18.
10 Consequently and ironically, after the controversies of *The Birth of a Nation*, Hollywood seldom touched overtly anti-black-themed films, nor would any black male characters be sexually assertive on screen, that is not until characters like Sweetback and Shaft appeared in the 1970s.
11 W.E.B. Du Bois, 'Criteria of Negro Art' originally in *Crisis*, October (1926), in *The Portable Harlem Renaissance Reader*, edited by David Levering Lewis (New York, Penguin, 1995), 100–105, 103.
12 Langston Hughes, 'Harlem Literati' in *The Portable Harlem Renaissance Reader*, 81–6, 82.
13 'When the Negro was in Vogue' in *The Portable Harlem Renaissance Reader*, 80.
14 'The Negro Artist and the Racial Mountain' in *The Portable Harlem Renaissance Reader*, 95.
15 In this sense, it is also highly ironic that the film provoked an antagonistic response from the Hughes Estate and its legal representatives when Hughes is the key rebel figure against the black middle class belief that it is important to project the 'right' image.
16 See Cary D. Wintz, *Black Culture and the Harlem Renaissance* (Houston, Rice University Press, 1988), 87.
17 Speaking of the early 1990s in Britain, Julien commented, 'Generally, Channel 4 are not very conducive to giving black workshops monies to develop fictions on 35mm. As long as we make sombre documentaries on 16mm they're interested ... Institutions just don't want to fund black

film-makers properly'. See Isaac Julien and Colin MacCabe, 'Diaries' in *Diary of a Young Soul Rebel* (London, BFI, 1991), 68.
18 'Looking for Modernism' in *Black American Cinema*, edited by Manthia Diawara (New York and London, Routledge, 1993), 200–207, 201.
19 'The Absent One: The Avant-Garde and the Black Imaginary in *Looking for Langston*', *Wide Angle* 13:3&4 (1991), 96–109, 103.
20 Quoted from David Levering Lewis's introduction to 'Smoke, Lilies and Jade' in *The Portable Harlem Renaissance Reader*, 569.
21 See Tony Fisher, 'Isaac Julien: *Looking for Langston*', *Third Text* 12 (1990), 59–70, 67. See also *Diary of a Young Soul Rebel*, 67.
22 Robert Mapplethorpe died of AIDS in March 1989. In an interview, just before his own death, Mapplethorpe commented that most of the black men who appeared in *The Black Book* are now dead due not simply to AIDS but to AIDS compounded by poverty, lack of insurance and the high price of health care and medication. See Dominick Dunne, 'Robert Mapplethorpe's Proud Finale', *Vanity Fair* (February 1989), 124–33 and 183–7.
23 James Baldwin, 'Here Be Monsters' in *The Price of the Ticket: Collected Nonfiction 1948–1985* (New York, St. Martin's Press, 1985). Quoted in Gates, *Thirteen Ways of Looking at a Black Man*, 20.
24 'Photographies of Mourning: Melancholia and Ambivalence in Van Der Zee, Mapplethorpe, and *Looking for Langston*' in *Race and the Subject of Masculinities*, edited by Harry Stecopoulos and Michael Uebel (Durham and London, Duke University Press, 1997), 337–58, 354.

Exposing Himself: Sweet Sweetback's Body

This call, this push requires a bold readiness to be 'out of order'.

Kwame Ture and Charles V. Hamilton in *Black Power*

After the assassination of Malcolm X in 1965, nonviolence as the major strategy of the Civil Rights struggle was replaced by the more militant rhetoric of 'black power'. As the epigraph above suggests, the rhetoric of the Black Power Movement called African-Americans to use their bodies as signs of radicalism and to adopt new forms of expression meant to threaten hegemonic concepts of order.[1] One new form of expression involved the creation of the Black Panther Party, a paramilitary group that carried guns and 'policed' the police. One of the party's more striking 'out of order' performances took place in 1967 when several of its members invaded the California Assembly. In his autobiography the party's co-founder Bobby Seale writes about the event in a chapter entitled 'Niggers With Guns in the State Capitol'. According to Seale the spectacle of black men carrying guns in the legislative chamber frightened white lawmakers and embarrassed 'so-called black representatives' whom Panthers referred to as 'Toms, sellouts, bootlickers'. Seale recalls someone saying, 'This is not where you're supposed to be'.[2] This performance of black male bodies with guns threatened both legislative and social order.

Though there were women in the movement—Angela Davis, Elaine Brown, Kathleen Cleaver—the term 'Black Power' was linked to media images of young black males with their fists raised and often carrying guns. These images prompted a (white) interpretation of the black man as menace who at any moment could burst from the confines of his urban neighborhood as the Black Panthers burst out of Oakland's ghetto and into the legislative chambers in Sacramento.

Cultural historian Michael Kimmel notes the historical link between notions of racial superiority and constructions of masculinity. Even after the abolition of slavery in the United States, black men were perceived as lower on the evolutionary ladder than white men—childlike, primitive, and driven by physical urges. Kimmel argues: 'Black men (...) were seen simultaneously as less manly than native-born whites and as *more* manly, especially as more sexually voracious and potent'.[3] The perceived sexual potency of black males resulted in a mythos, an eroticization, of the black penis. It was bigger, better, and absolutely forbidden to white women. In the 1970s, one popular myth circulating among my circle of white female friends was that once a white woman has experienced sex with a black man, she no longer desires white men. The popular slogan was 'Once you've gone black, you can't go back'. Black masculinity, whose prime signifier is the erect penis, became the Bacchean and Herculean Other of white masculinity, with mythical lore spinning out at cocktail parties, in bedrooms, in locker rooms, and in Hollywood movies.

The mythos was partially a Hollywood creation of an earlier period. D.W. Griffith's famous film *Birth of a Nation* (1915), which inscribes black men as predators and rapists of white women, served during the Jim Crow era to reestablish the hegemonic order of white masculinity's superiority and to shape the stereotypical 'black beast', a stereotype that conveniently enabled black men to be terrorized, with white law enforcers either terrorizing them or looking the other way. After intense criticism about the way Griffith's film depicted black masculinity, Hollywood developed less violent but no less racist black masculine stereotypes — the humble servant, the sparkling dancer, the eye-rolling fool. Then in the late 60s, Sidney Poitier became one of Hollywood's biggest stars by playing characters that were virtuous but one-dimensional and sometimes insipid. Poitier's roles prompted African-American critics such as the black dramatist Clifford Mason to accuse him of enabling whites to maintain their sense of superiority and innocence.[4]

In the early 1970s at the height of the Black Power Movement's popularity, Hollywood responded to the new black urban market by making so-called 'blaxploitation' movies.[5] In contrast to the stereotypical roles, the new black male protagonist used the inner city as a stage for performing a hypersexualized and streetsmart masculinity that called attention to white America's racist practices. Bringing to stardom such actors as Richard Roundtree as Shaft, Jim Brown as Slaughter, Ron O'Neal as Superfly, and Fred Williamson as Tommy Gibbs, blaxploitation movies featured a hero that either tried to right an injustice (Shaft and Slaughter) or attempted to prosper in the underworld of drugs and violence (Superfly and Gibbs). While these movies used white racism as a sub-theme, they tended to sidestep explicit political issues, refusing to delve into the social causes of the Black Power Movement and its resignifications of black masculinity.

Figure 1. Cover of *Sweet Sweetback's Baadasssss Song*, courtesy of Direct Cinema Limited.

In contrast to the more popular blaxploitation films where the hypersexualized hero is ghettoized within specific urban boundaries, Melvin Van Peebles's cult classic *Sweet Sweetback's Baadasssss Song* (1971) portrays an oppressed black man who becomes aware of and resists the conditions of his oppression, and then begins an odyssey of escape (Fig. 1). In *Sweet Sweetback*, Van Peebles (who both directs the film and plays Sweetback) depicts the perniciousness of social structures governing black urban street life as Sweetback is exploited by black prostitutes who in turn are used by white male enforcers of 'law and order'. When Sweetback witnesses a young black radical being beaten by white police, he retaliates by beating the police with their own handcuffs, an act that forces him to run until finally he manages to cross the border into Mexico with a vow to return and retaliate.

Van Peebles employs strategies that show Sweetback first as accepting hegemonic order and embodying the oppressive social role he has been assigned—he is in the beginning a willing participant in the white-controlled sex trade. Sexualized and racialized, the body of Sweetback operates as commodity whose use value lies in concealing and conceding to the forces of its production. During the course of the film, these forces are played out on Sweetback's body, which ultimately resists the forces that produced it. At the end of the filmic odyssey, Sweetback's body becomes the site of a militant and vengeful black masculinity. The film uses the African-American practice 'signifying' in order to make its points.

Literary critic Henry Louis Gates, Jr. theorizes about this traditional form of African-American resistance to the oppressive 'order' of the dominant culture. In *The Signifyin(g) Monkey*, Gates traces the trickster figure of the monkey from Africa through the long vernacular poem 'The Signifying Monkey' and posits 'signifyin(g)' as the master trope in African-American discourse. Gates explains that signifyin(g) enacts a double-voicedness, an intertextual relation that destabilizes the process of making meaning in dominant (white) discourse and relies instead on received meaning within the discursive black vernacular.[6] Gates's concept 'signifyin(g)' resembles Barthes's notion of 'myth', a meaning-making process by which members of a particular culture understand something as part of their collective social experience. Like signifyin(g), myth is duplicitous, a 'type of speech defined by its intention ... much more than by its literal sense'.[7] For both Barthes and Gates, meaning-making is differentiated in specific cultural contexts.[8]

In the African-American vernacular the verb 'to signify' is intransitive and followed by a preposition. That is, one typically signifies on or against something or someone. For example, the title of Bobby Seale's chapter 'Niggers With Guns in the State Capitol' signifies on the use of the term 'niggers'. Used in racist discourse as pejorative and degrading, the word when used by a black militant displaces the racist meaning as it calls attention to it.

In the United States, signifying, as theorized by Gates, is embedded within the long and complex history of black and white relations during slavery and under Jim Crow laws that attempted to keep blacks and whites separate and unequal. Under these conditions, African-Americans learned a way of talking that concealed their meaning from members of the dominant discourse community and carried meaning understood only within their own interpretive communities. Signifying may carry sexual meaning, as in the long poem Gates cites, or it may be humorous or may articulate oppression. Contemporary rap music in the United States grew from African-American signifying practices, which always have been expressions of resistance to dominant cultural and discursive practices. Van Peebles's film signifies on and against racist and oppressive practices, against the 'order' established by white masculinist practices. The film itself is uneven, at times glorifying black male sexual prowess and at other times suggesting that black masculinity's only weapon of defense is physical performance, particularly sexual performance. Though it attempts to elevate the new militant masculinity of the Black Power Movement, its portrayal of racism and oppression undermines aggressive black masculinity and, in a sense, foreshadows the eventual demise of the movement in the late 1980s.

The film begins in a whorehouse with Sweetback participating in a 'freak show' that features men dressed as women and women dressed as men.[9] The 'freak show' with its interchangeable black bodies is highlighted by the appearance of a 'Good Dyke Fairy Godmother' who waves a magic wand that transforms a female dressed as male with a strapped-on dildo into the obviously male Sweetback with an erect penis. The camera pauses on Sweetback's erect penis, then pans the show's audience, comprising both male and female, black and white, all of whom express awe at Sweetback's sexual performance. One man watches with the gargantuan eyes reminiscent of the 'coon' stereotype in minstrel shows and early movies. That Van Peebles uses this stereotype as an admirer of Sweetback's sexual prowess suggests that black male sexual performance at best lacks positive cultural capital. Reinforcing this interpretation, the film cuts to an exterior hallway where white male police are observing the performance. The white police are in a position to watch Sweetback perform and also to watch the watchers. The film cuts back and forth from Sweetback engaged in sex with an unnamed female partner to conversations between the owner of the whorehouse and the police, who want the owner to provide them with a black male — any black male — to take into custody and question about a dead body they found. One officer says, 'We want to borrow one of your boys for a couple of hours and take him downtown, to make us look good officialwise.'

This complex scene in an abstract sense signifies on the sexualizing of black bodies stemming from modernity's mind/body division — the mind associated with white masculinity and the body associated with femininity and, as Kimmel suggests, with black masculinity as well. The scene enacts the commodification of black bodies and signifies on the complicity of black participants and black audiences in this commodification. Next, Sweetback's exaggerated sexuality signifies against the historical emasculation, literal and figurative, of African American males. By having the camera pause, so that viewers have time to think about what they are seeing, Van Peebles specularizes the erect black penis, signifying on its superiority and rearticulating the old (D.W. Griffith) mythos of the hypersexual black male that historically has been so threatening to white masculinity.

Further, Sweetback, on top of his female sexual partner, engages in a heterosexual, normative sex act, affirming masculine control. Sweetback's body not only controls the female body, but also asserts the inadequacy of female homosexuality. The male on top with the 'real' erect penis overpowers both the female under him and the cross-dressing woman with the dildo. Embodying the Freudian castrated female who lacks and desires the penis, the inadequate man/woman is replaced by Sweetback, a transformation that puts to rest questions about authenticity and superiority.

Though according to dominant cultural practices Sweetback's body is 'out of order' (having sex in a whorehouse 'freak show' and placing on display the erect penis), it attempts to assume its rightful place in dominant (white) patriarchy by reestablishing the natural and inevitable order of patriarchal masculinity. Nevertheless, despite Sweetback's attempt in this scene to establish the power of black masculinity, his erect penis and his sexual performance are under the scrutiny of white keepers of 'law and order'. Even though the erect black penis asserts itself as racial and masculine spectacle, because it is under surveillance, it does not project the phallic power of white masculinity.[10]

The critic Michele Wallace and others have argued that *Sweet Sweetback* is a misogynistic film, an argument with which I agree in part. I would add, however, that Sweetback's body with the erect penis as its dominant icon does not affirm phallic, patriarchal masculinity, a power from which black masculinity historically has been excluded in the United States.[11] While Sweetback's penis overpowers some of the female characters, other women in the film exploit it for their own sexual pleasure, and its power is always circumscribed by the conditions under which it performs. In Marxist terms, Sweetback's penis has use value but no real exchange value.

After Sweetback is ordered to go with the white police as the representative black man, he appears fully dressed. His clothes compel the viewer to perceive Sweetback as a dandy, as the camera examines him from bottom to top — shoes, pants, vest, and hat. But as the camera shifts to his face, his cool stance is betrayed. Because the frame positions Sweetback's face between the backs of the two police, the viewer sees Sweetback from their perspective. As a white viewer, I am forced by the framing to assume the position of white privilege and control. But Sweetback looks back directly into the camera/at me, presenting an unexpected look that demystifies and signifies against white control. Feminist critic Gloria Anzaldua notes that the face is the 'surface of the body that is the most notably inscribed by social structures', and 'making face' has the 'added connotation of making *gestos subversivos*, political subversive gestures, that piercing look that

Exposing Himself: Sweet Sweetback's Body 219

questions or challenges ...'.¹² In this particular scene, Sweetback is clearly 'making face' with a look that issues a direct challenge to white masculinist authority. While the fancy clothes present Sweetback's body as commodity fetish, his face has a decommodifying effect that signals the end of Sweetback's acceptance of his assigned role in the social order and the beginning of his resistance.

After Sweetback beats the police with their handcuffs, (an obvious symbolic act), he becomes a fugitive on the run. As he runs, he encounters a white motorcycle gang and their president Big Sadie. In contrast to the women in the 'freak show', Big Sadie can be identified as a masculinized woman, tough and aggressive. She dresses in biker clothes and is affirmed as leader of the motorcycle gang. The subsequent contest between Big Sadie and Sweetback is about who is the most sexually potent. The two combatants are the masculinized, white Big Sadie and the vulnerable, black (and thus feminized) Sweetback who, because he is a fugitive, is at the mercy of Sadie and her gang. The sex act, however, which serves as the 'contest', enables Sweetback to 'feminize' Big Sadie's body. Sweetback's body is still under (white) surveillance, and even though he reverts to his old survival strategy of sexual performance, the strategy fails as members of the motorcycle gang subsequently inform the police of his hiding place. In this scene, Sweetback's attempts to assert phallic power are again undermined by dominant, white masculinist 'order'.

What follows in the film is a relentless chase by the police that shows their victimization of innocent people. Within the chase, several characters are profiled. Some are represented as sympathetic to Sweetback's plight — gay men who flirt with the police, Mexican labourers who give Sweetback a ride in a truck, an interracial hippie group gathered in the country. Some of those interrogated respond by denying they know Sweetback, thus signifying against and subverting the authority of the white police. In contrast, other both black and white characters betray him — white members of Big Sadie's motorcycle gang, a woman who wants only sex from Sweetback, his poker-playing pals, an Afrocentric preacher. Eventually a white vagabond trades clothes with him, allowing Sweetback to successfully evade the police and escape to Mexico. The seeming randomness of betrayal and support are signs of fragmentation within the social order over issues of Black Power and other forms of protest, and of solidarity between Black Power advocates and certain groups of outsiders, a solidarity that suggests that oppressive 'order' can be undermined by grass-roots coalitions. This sub-theme implies the dialectical relationship between and mutual dependency of the Black Power Movement and other populist movements of the 1960s and 1970s.

The end of the film circles back to the issue of black masculine physicality as survival strategy. As Sweetback runs, a chorus chants:

> Come on feet
> Cruise for me
> Trouble ain't no place to be
> Come on feet
> Do your thing
> You're on old whitey's game
> Come on legs
> Come on run
> Guilty's what he say you done
> Come on knees
> Don't be mean
> Ain't first red you ever seen
> Come on feet
> Do your thing.

By having the chorus chant about particular body parts and the camera focus on Sweetback's running body, Van Peebles again signifies on 'old whitey's game' of racist oppression and points to the difficulty of escape. But as Sweetback crosses the border, the promise of revenge flashes on the screen: 'Watch out. A badass nigger is coming back to collect some dues'.

In the character Sweetback, Van Peebles brings to the screen a black masculinity that combines an older sexualized and demonized stereotype with a new radicalized black male body. This movie's themes, more than any other of its genre, bears an intertextual relation to the radical nonfiction writing that the Black Power Movement spawned. Eldridge Cleaver's *Soul on Ice*, for example, incorporates themes of oppression, violence, and both intraracial and interracial sex. Emphasizing his own political awakening, Cleaver's collection of essays also politicizes the body of the black male — as product of oppression, as sexual performer/rapist, as political activist.[13]

Van Peebles' film suggests that under oppressive conditions, black male subjectivity resides in physical performativity, in what the body can do — in sex and in deception. The landscape becomes a theatre of potential danger where other characters may or may not be friendly or helpful. The aware black male knows that his performance may be viewed as wrong or inappropriate and that dire consequences will result. By focusing on the performing body and Sweetback's growing awareness of and resistance to the dominant social order, the movie exposes what Kobena Mercer calls the 'dialectics of white fear and fascination' with black male bodies.[14] Moreover, it examines the material effects of that fear and fascination, particularly attempts to survey, control and circumscribe the power of black masculinity and thus restore the 'order' associated with phallic white masculinity.

DOROTHY C. BROADDUS
Arizona State University

NOTES

1. The idea of order that I posit is often linked to law but is also linked to white masculinist notions of hierarchical and exclusionary order resulting from the exercise of disciplinary power.
2. Bobby Seale, *Seize the Time* (Baltimore, MD, Black Classic Press, 1991), 159.
3. Michael Kimmel, *Manhood in America* (New York, Free Press, 1996), 93.
4. Ed Guerrero, *Framing Blackness* (Philadelphia, Temple University Press, 1993), 73.
5. In *Representing* (Chicago, University of Chicago Press, 1998), S. Craig Watkins includes a detailed account of the changing demographics that led to the creation of blaxploitation films. See especially 94–5.
6. *The Signifying Monkey* (New York, Oxford University Press, 1988), 49–54.
7. Roland Barthes, *Mythologies*, translated by Annette Lavers (New York, Noonday Press, 1972), 124.
8. I use the term 'signifying' as Gates theorizes 'signifyin(g)' and as Barthes uses the term 'myth'. That is, signifying connotes a resistant practice of meaning-construction.
9. Van Peebles uses the term 'freak show' in the book that accompanied the release of the movie. See Melvin Van Peebles, *Sweet Sweetback's Baadasssss Song* (New York, Lancer, 1971), 72.
10. For discussion about the conflation of penis/phallus, see Kaja Silverman, *Male Subjectivity at the Margins* (New York, Routledge, 1992), 41–5. For discussion of 'masculinity' without the penis, see Judith Halberstam, *Female Masculinity* (Durham, NC, Duke University Press, 1998).
11. Michele Wallace, 'Race, Gender and psychoanalysis in Forties Film' in *Black American Cinema*, edited by Manthia Diawara (New York, Routledge, 1993), 260–1.
12. *Making Face, Making Soul* (San Francisco, Aunt Lute, 1990), xv.
13. *Soul On Ice* (New York, Dell, 1992).
14. *Welcome to the Jungle* (New York, Routledge, 1994), 134.

The W/hole and the Abject

The subject is constituted through the force of exclusion and abjection, one which produces a constitutive outside to the subject, an abjected outside, which is, after all, 'inside' the subject as its own founding repudiation.[1]

My wish is that every subject's encounter with the death drive might become in time more of an everyday occurrence—that the typical male subject, like his female counterpart, might learn to live with lack.[2]

Since the middle of the 1990s French cinema has seen the resurgence of a version of the realism once associated with the 1970s. These films frequently focus on life in the provinces, especially the North, rather than in Paris, and on dysfunctional male characters. Although generally praised by critics, the films have also been criticized for their mix of complacent pessimism and fashionable cinematic effects. A critic writing in *Le Monde Diplomatique*, for example, complains about 'the darkest and most despairing naturalism and the most affected mannerism and formalism'; he claims that their 'fascination for the abject and the sordid show an undeniable hatred for the people'.[3] The film heading his list is Gaspar Noé's *I Stand Alone* (*Seul contre tous*, 1998), the continuation of the biography of the protagonist of the 40-minute *Carne* (1990).[4] Such films, which explore the male's essential confrontation with abjection, are inescapable, however, because they are a necessary part of subject-positioning (as Butler implies in the first epigraph), and they can be seen in a moral light, as implied by the second epigraph.

A brief synopsis of the films may be useful for what follows. Both films are remarkable amongst other things for the soundtrack, the interior monologue of a Parisian horse butcher, a fascist ranting against everyone, especially women, gays and Arabs, in which there is much talk of arseholes, cunts, shit, cocks, fucking, and so on.

Carne, a 40-minute short, begins with an abattoir scene where a horse is killed and eviscerated, intercut with the birth of the butcher (Philippe Nahon)'s daughter, Cynthia (Blandine Lenoir), as she emerges from her mother (apart from Cynthia, none of the other characters is named). Short scenes with intertitles recount Cynthia's childhood as she grows up without her mother who left the butcher shortly after the birth. The butcher idolizes his daughter who is mute and retarded; we see him washing her, dressing her, feeding her, and, eventually, feeling ambivalent towards her sexually as she reaches adolescence. He mistakes the menstrual blood on her knickers for the blood of defloration by an Arab who works on the nearby building site, called 'le trou', or the hole; he plunges his knife into an unsuspecting worker's mouth (the wrong man, as it happens) and twists it around. He is jailed, and on release finds it difficult to get work. He leaves for a new life in Lille with the female owner of the café where he has been working (Frankye Pain) and whom he has made pregnant.

I Stand Alone reprises *Carne*'s narrative with a rapid-delivery monologue by the butcher overlaying stills of buildings. We learn more about the butcher's early childhood; he never knew his mother, was raised as an orphan, was sodomized by his teacher. The butcher, dependant on his partner's money, resents her, and drifts from job to job. He brutally attacks his pregnant wife when she accuses him of infidelity, and leaves for Paris once more, taking his mother-in-law's revolver. Jobless, and unsuccessful in his attempts to borrow money from acquaintances, he spends his last few francs on a coffee. At the end of his tether, he picks Cynthia up from the institution with the aim of killing her and himself. We see him doing this, but it turns out to be a fantasy, and the film ends as he extols the virtues of incest.

It may also be useful to define the abject briefly. Julia Kristeva characterizes it as a combination of fear and loathing, but also of attraction to the pre-Oedipal state, prior to the acquisition of language and prior to what Lacan calls the Law of the Father. The abject is therefore linked to the maternal, to lack of control and helplessness, to all the fluids we might associate with early childhood (vomit, blood, urine, excrement). The abject is a liminal state, an in-between, poised on the cusp of subject-hood, but not quite yet subjecthood.[5] There is an unsettling combination of fluidity and rigidity in our films, but it is no stereotyped female-male binary. The butcher is not so much contrasted with a female other, as presented to us as both rigid and fluid; and he hates both, as much as he is attracted to both. There is overlap between the whole (the wholeness and the singular) to which he aspires, and the hole (the oblivion contained within the whole) to which he aspires no less (hence the title of this paper). We can explore this issue by focusing on the three clear references to *Taxi Driver* (Scorsese, 1976), on which the last part of the film is obsessively structured.

'Taxi Driver' Variation 1: the Porn Film and the Butcher as Penis

In the first reference to *Taxi Driver* the butcher goes disconsolately to see a porn movie and watches stony-faced as a heterosexual couple perform on screen. The scene is a key one for the film, insisting on existential isolation and alienation, as well as on the radical separation of the sexes. As the butcher watches, he muses thus:

> Either you're born with a cock and you're useful if you behave like a good hard cock which stuffs holes, or you're born with a hole and you will only be useful if you are stuffed yourself. But in both cases you are alone. Yes, I'm a cock, a miserable cock, and to be respected I must always stay hard.

The 'hard body' desired here is Theweleit's 'fascist male warrior', who fears being overwhelmed by a feminising red flood.[6] It is hardly surprising that the butcher, who must draw blood as part of his job, feels repulsion for fluids spilling out of control from ruptured and distended bodies, whether those of slaughtered horses or women giving birth, or indeed a woman dying.

Nahon's body emphasizes the rigidity and aggression of the hard body. He is squat; he has bulbous glaring eyes, and a belligerently protuberant nose. His body is thus constructed as a threatening forward lunge, matched linguistically by the monosyllables he occasionally spits out vituperatively, his teeth and fists clenched. As Kristeva says of the abject subject, 'I expel *myself*, I spit *myself* out, I abject *myself* within the same motion through which "I" claim to establish *myself*' (*Powers of Horror*, 3). These seep across and through the entire film in a stream of consciousness, a linguistic fluidity, which contaminates the otherwise often neutral sights we see (a humdrum hotel room, empty streets). That linguistic fluidity suggests that the rigidity of the butcher is not quite what it seems.

Indeed, the butcher's observations as he watches the porn film are ambiguous. The subject of the utterance, shifting from male to female within the single 'you', suggests that the butcher himself is the one who needs to be 'stuffed', the hole made whole; in this fantasy he is both cock and hole at one and the same time. That whole combines both masculinity, and a femininity constantly repressed and represented as abject. It is a masculinity subjected hysterically to the Law, and a femininity abjected in the liminal spaces which border and burrow through the Law, like a network of arteries pulsating obscenely under skin stretched to breaking point, until a hole perforates the skin for the blood to gush out, as happens when the butcher fantasizes the murder of his daughter.

Words gush out in the butcher's stream of consciousness monologue, like the blood gushing out of Cynthia, like the blood which accompanies Cynthia's birth in *Carne*, gushing out of the vagina, and like the blood gushing out of the slaughtered horse's stomach in the scene intercut with Cynthia's birth. The films show an obsession with holes of all kinds. It is not just the vagina through which blood and baby Cynthia emerge, or the hole in Cynthia's neck spurting blood when she dies, or the horse's stomach from which blood and guts gush out, or the vagina in the porn film, but the repeated scenes where the butcher gropes for Cynthia's vagina as they sit on the bed, and the exterior shots of tunnels into which the butcher drives or emerges on foot. It is also the many shots of mouths, whether the mouth of the Arab worker into which the butcher twists his knife, or the shots of the butcher's own mouth with the eyes out of shot, cartoon-style.

Importantly, however, the mouth is not just vaginal, as the opening scenes of *Carne* might have suggested; it is also cloacal. A number of spaces function as holes, not least because of their linguistic associations. The word *trou* in French is used colloquially for both the vagina, and, in the expression which occurs several times in the films, *trou de cul*, for the anus as well. It is also a colloquialism for prison, and it is the word used in *Carne* to refer to the building site. In each case, these spaces referred to as holes (the building site and the prison) contain other sexualized holes; for the building site it is the worker's mouth penetrated by the butcher's twisting knife held at his crotch height; and in the prison, there is an implication that the butcher and his cellmate engage in gay sex.

But spaces are often also closed to the butcher; doors of buildings — the hotel, the butcher's shop, the café — are as frequently closed as open. Spaces are therefore as much cloacal as they are vaginal in the film. They are potential holes waiting to swallow him like the *vagina dentata*, or rejecting him because they are tightly closed like anxious anal sphincters.

This section has shown how the demarcation between rigidity and fluidity, which the butcher postulates as the marker of sexual difference, collapses under the weight of linguistic fluidity. The obsession with holes equally collapses the distinction between vagina and anus. The next section will explore the shift from the butcher as penis to the butcher as turd.

'Taxi Driver' Variation 2: the Gun in the Mirror and the Butcher as Turd

The self-disgust generated by the abject is made clear in the second *Taxi Driver* reference, when the butcher returns to his hotel room and looks at himself in the mirror with his gun, fantasizing that he will kill those who have crossed him, as well as killing himself. The violence he turns against himself bears out Kristeva's point that in the abject the subject struggles to disentangle himself from what lies within, the unnameable and horrifying maternal origin. As the butcher says in that scene, playing on the part-homonym *mère/merde*, 'my whole life has been a colossal turd, willed by a whore of a mother'; elsewhere in the film he refers to himself derisively as a 'trou de cul', or arsehole. He is both turd and hole, or, more precisely, turd in the hole, what Kristeva calls the anal penis, 'the phallus with which infantile imagination provides the feminine sex' (*Powers of Horror*, 71). The butcher, desperate to remain hard and penile, realizes that he is also fecal, *homo erectus*, but also *homo rectus*, whole and hole. There could be no clearer expression of what Calvin Thomas calls 'scatontological anxiety'.

Thomas brings together Freud's account of the *fort/da* game, and his theory of cloacal birth to suggest that the former 'is implicated not only with the boy's phantasy of having been produced through his mother's bowels, and his foreclosure of that phantasy, but also with his own struggles to secure identity through the control of his bowels'.[7] As Thomas points out, those struggles are never really successful, and all modes of representation are, to use his word, haunted by scatontological anxiety: 'The image of "unimpaired masculinity", the self-produced, self-representational image of the actively "self-made man", is haunted by the earlier phantasmatic image of having been a passively and cloacally (m)other-made child' ('Last Laughs', 29). Hence the aggression against women in the butcher's rambling monologue, and the fear of homosexuality, 'a fear of the anus as phantasmatic origin in the former instance and as destination of desire or locus of pleasure (...) in the latter' (Thomas, *Male Matters*, 88). The beginning of *I Stand Alone* makes it clear that the butcher was abused as a child, an event which posits the possibility of the pleasure to be gained from the anus, even if it is a pleasure only available to the abuser (we assume); the butcher's frequent references to sodomy suggest both repulsion and attraction, a fear of becoming feminized, but also the masochistic desire to return to be 'a passive object and slave to this jouissance, aggressed, sadisticized' (*Powers of Horror*, 183), as Kristeva writes of some of Céline's more racist and homophobic pronouncements.

Like Céline's work, the butcher's voice smears what we see in a fecal stream of consciousness, an effect all the more pronounced by the editing out of the pauses and breaths between statements. We are attracted to this abject anality, submerged in it, for very simple material reasons. The butcher's voice-over draws us close to him, for two reasons. First, because its almost continuous nature means that we are always with the butcher, 'forced to share permanently his states of mind and to follow him in his most frightening excesses', as Noé puts it.[8] Second, because the punctuating gunshots on the soundtrack interact with that voice-over, encouraging us to see that voice-over not for what it is, an extremely aggressive flow, but for what it is in relation to the gunshots, a more mellifluous flow, a refuge from what Noé calls the stress of those gunshots.[9]

Blood as a visual sign of rupture, rejected birth, menstruation, and death, mingles with the shit of the soundtrack. As Thomas suggests, the anxious subject 'collapses all those heterogeneous processes for which bodies are sites — fecal, urinal, seminal, fetal, menstrual, glottal, lingual — into an undifferentiated and abject flux' (*Male Matters*, 32); all of these are present either visually or linguistically in the two films. The borders between the visual and the aural are constantly shattered by explosions, whether aural, in the gunshots which punctuate the soundtrack, or the sudden zooms which jerk us forward dizzyingly from one plane into another. Sounds become signs, and signs become sounds, both signifying the horror of the abject with its fluid boundaries leaking into each other. Seeing and hearing melt into the searing light of a brilliant white fade-out at the end of the murder/suicide sequence, signifying apocalyptic failure, the blankness of an anger so excessive that the words strangle and extrude their obscene obverse, the silence of death, never so aptly named a pregnant silence, a silence full of what it cannot silence, a silence made of countless explosions paused as they are about to explode. Kristeva's comment on Céline's prose, which she describes as 'a thin film constantly threatened with bursting' (*Powers of Horror*, 141) is an apt analysis of the promiscuity between the visual and the aural in *I Stand Alone*.

This section has shown how the butcher's frame of reference is fecal and abject. The clean, hard body, or *corps propre*, as Kristeva calls it, collapses its boundaries and is invaded from within by abject fluids associated with the mother. Another boundary, that between seeing and hearing, is collapsed as the butcher's stream of consciousness permeates the image track, working both with and against it. The next section will explore the butcher's antithetical attempts to resolve the dissolution of the boundaries; first, through hysterical cutting, second through incest.

'Taxi Driver' Variation 3: Murder, Incest, Cannibalism

The final reference to *Taxi Driver* is the butcher shooting his daughter, which, as in *Taxi Driver*, is a bloodbath in a claustrophobic hotel space. This scene, no less than the first two replays, all differ from *Taxi Driver* in one significant way, however. They underline the butcher's failure, something he comments on in the fantasized murder scene: 'I've failed at everything. My birth, my youth, my love life, my shop. I should never have been born. My entire life is a mistake'. In the first film theatre scene, he is alone, and comments disconsolately on solitude, whereas Travis Bickle unsuspectingly takes his suitably offended girlfriend. In the mirror scene, like Bickle, the butcher fantasizes the death of others, but, unlike Bickle, also fantasizes his own death. And, finally, in the murder scene, Bickle murders a whole group of pimps and prostitutes, and is heroized for those murders, whereas the butcher merely fantasizes his daughter's murder, but does not go through with it, remaining the unheroic failure he commented on in the previous mirror sequence.

Arguably, his murderous fantasy is the logical conclusion to a series of insistent but ineffectual cuts practised in the two films. Cutting can be seen as an hysterical attempt to control time and the change which it brings, and to control space, most particularly to control the invasion of the fragmenting and hetero-dimensional abject into the monolithic and uni-dimensional *corps propre*. There is first the cut between the two films, which overlap with each other in terms of narrative. Then there are the very literal cuts we see as the butcher chops the meat at the beginning of *Carne*, these narrative cuts being mirrored by editing cuts as intertitles signal the passage of the years, as though the butcher were trying to control time. This sequence is echoed at the beginning of *I Stand Alone*, as the butcher recounts his life. His breathless, rapid-delivery monologue overlays a visual track consisting of photo-album stills of people and places, as if he were trying to staunch the flux of time by punctuating it with frozen images, familiar clichés providing havens of recognisability within the anarchic flux of life itself. The cuts we see at the beginning of the films are themselves echoed throughout by rapid edits accompanied by fast zooms and gunshot sounds, as previously mentioned. These procedures can be seen as attempts to separate body and sign, materiality and spirit.

These various types of cutting have the opposite effect to that desired, however; they undermine the coherence of the narrative, compounding the butcher's failure. As Kristeva points out in relation to Céline's writing, the narrative is carved up into choice morsels with which the butcher is fascinated, and that fascination dislocates the narrative, allowing the abject to emerge, disrupt, and occasionally to overwhelm. The films set up cutting as a kind of ritual, but the films are submerged in fluids, whether corporeal or linguistic. It is therefore logical that we should see images which suggest that the mother's body and the daughter's body can be eaten: the mother's body giving birth is intercut with a horse being slaughtered for the butcher; the butcher dreams of pink fleshy fillets which are shot and handled by the butcher in such a way as to suggest a vagina. It is therefore also logical that the butcher fails to kill his daughter, choosing instead the fantasy of incest, since incest represents the suspension of the Law of the Father, as Žižek points out,[10] in the return to the non-differentiation of the pre-Oedipal and the engulfment in the archaic mother. It is for that reason that we might disagree with reviewers who felt that the apparent redemption of the butcher through incest was a disappointing closure.[11] It is logical in terms of the butcher's project; and, more importantly, it is emphatically not a redemption, but, in appearance at least, a regressive return to the abject.

This section has shown how the third *Taxi Driver* reference emphasizes the butcher's failure, despite the cutting procedures which attempt to reinstate the control of the *corps propre*. Incest is no redemption, but forms an integral part of this failure, since it signals the return to the abject. *I Stand Alone* is neither joyous affirmation nor humdrum recognition of the abject, but a precarious balance between the two. The final section will suggest that this is figured narratively by incest, and metaphorically by something connected to it but which we do not see, at least not directly.

Coda: Semen

The radical potential of incest as break with the Law and return to the abject, as argued above, is destabilized by what is never shown in the film, although constantly gestured at: semen. In fact, semen *does* appear, but sublimated, figured both as closure, and as counter-weight to the abject (unlike other markers of the abject, such as excrement and menstrual blood, which are connected with the mother, semen, for obvious reasons, is paternal; see Kristeva, *Powers of Horror*, 71–2).

Arguably, there might have been plenty of opportunities for semen to be shown, whether prior to the birth scene in *Carne*, or as part of the porn film the butcher watches in *I Stand Alone*, or even as part of his incest fantasy. It is there nevertheless. It appears indirectly in the unexpected fade to white at the end of the film, where it is linked to the butcher's insistence that he will commit incest. It also appears indirectly throughout the film *as the film itself*. The constant cutting procedures described above are an attempt to keep the abject at bay, to impose meaning on the body. Whether cuts of meat or cuts of film, cutting tries to impose the phallic economy; and if the cuts are the process, then the product is, metaphorically speaking, semen, which is why semen is present liminally as the film itself, even if the butcher (and the film) to a large extent fail, because cutting releases the abject, figured by flux (of blood, of language).

Cutting is a constant struggle between the release of abjected blood and paternal semen; between red and white; between absence of meaning and meaning; between the hole and the whole. The final scenes of the film are crucial in this respect, since they contrast the murder of Cynthia and the rape of Cynthia as two alternative narrative economies answering the question 'how can this end?'. The first produces, literally, a gaping hole which gushes blood, as had the feminized holes of *Carne*: Cynthia's mother giving birth to Cynthia, intercut with the slaughter of the horse, could not make clearer the fear and fascination of the abject. But the final scenes take up another fascination, the fascination with Cynthia's invisible vagina. The butcher is often seen groping for Cynthia's vagina in *I Stand Alone*, fascinated by what is deceptive and doubly hidden from his gaze, first by her skirt, second by her flesh, the bleeding wound which deceives the gaze; neither we nor the butcher know in *Carne* whether the blood on her knickers signifies rape or menstruation.

Like semen, then, Cynthia's vagina is never seen, but we know that it is there, an object of endless fascination for the butcher, who wishes to implant his semen in it, to loop the loop. Why? As the final sentences of the final dialogue suggest — 'Between us, that's all I can see. I love you.' — the butcher seeks disappearance through identification with the same in a safe pre-Oedipal space where absent mother, mute daughter, and father collapse into a transcendent, phallicized space, no longer the messy corporeal space of the maternalized abject, but 'pure' emptiness. No blood, no words (the two are the same in these films, abject flux); just the blinding whiteness of the final money shot in fantasied copulation, figured by the slashing copula of my title, w/h, seen but not heard.

PHIL POWRIE
University of Newcastle upon Tyne

NOTES

1. Judith Butler, *Bodies That Matter: On the Discursive Limits of 'Sex'* (New York and London, Routledge, 1994), 3.
2. Kaja Silverman, *Male Subjectivity at the Margins* (New York and London, Routledge, 1992), 65.
3. Carlos Pardo, 'Crime, pornographie et mépris du peuple: des films français fascinés par le sordide' in *Le Monde Diplomatique* (February 2000), 28. All translations are mine unless otherwise indicated.
4. *Carne* is the French term for tough leathery meat; it is also used figuratively about a person, roughly translating as 'swine'.
5. Julia Kristeva, *Powers of Horror: An Essay on Abjection*, translated by Leon S. Roudiez (New York, Columbia University Press, 1982). Originally published 1980.
6. Calvin Thomas, *Male Matters: Masculinity, Anxiety, and the Male Body on the Line* (Urbana and Chicago, University of Illinois Press, 1996), 129.
7. Calvin Thomas, 'Last laughs: *Batman*, masculinity and the technology of abjection', *Men and Masculinities* 2:1 (1999), 26–46.
8. Philippe Rouyer, 'Gaspar Noé: Une mise en scène ludique', *Positif* 457 (1999), 29–33, 31.
9. Tristan de Bourbon, 'Gaspar Noé, la violence du quotidien', *L'Humanité*, 17 February 1999.
10. Slavoj Žižek, *The Art of the Ridiculous Sublime: On David Lynch's Lost Highway*, (Seattle, The Walter Chapin Simpson Center for the Humanities/University of Washington, 2000), 31.
11. Bernard Genin, 'Ecoeurant de complaisance', *Télérama* 2562, 17 February 1999, 1.

Queer Masculinity: The Representation of John Paul Pitoc's Body in *Trick*

One of the most troublesome aspects of homophobic discourse is the desire to read sexuality and gender as collapsible categories. I still shudder to hear the question 'Which one is the girl?' directed at a gay male couple. This should, of course, more correctly be termed 'effeminophobia' which, as Alan Sinfield points out, is rooted in misogyny. The effeminate male is not only in defiance of hegemonic gender roles and therefore 'wrong' but he is inferior because he is 'falling away from the purposeful reasonableness that is supposed to constitute manliness, into the laxity and weakness conventionally attributed to women'.[1] The classification of gay men as effeminate is a misogynistic denigration of their status.

There is historical precedence for this kind of thinking. David Halperin, in his study of sexuality in ancient Mediterranean cultures, pointed out that there was no homo/hetero binary as there is today:

> an adult, male citizen of Athens can have legitimate sexual relations only with statutory minors (his inferiors not in age but in social and political status): the proper targets of his sexual desire include, specifically women, boys, foreigners and slaves.[2]

Kaja Silverman therefore suggests that 'the classical affinities between women and boys in classical Greek society encouraged their conceptual alignment'.[3] Of course, the classical Greek boy will eventually become a man and then his position will change. As Gregory Woods summarizes:

> the moment of the boy's first stubble is so often conceived in poetry as a time of great loss, when a beloved boy is suddenly too old to be respectably the object of a man's passion, and must be allowed to find a boyfriend of his own.[4]

Sexual passivity, therefore, was conflated with the idea of femininity which signified lower social status.

However, as Sinfield argues, it was not until the Oscar Wilde trial that the modern day conflation of effeminacy with same sex passion solidified.[5] In the century following Wilde's public disgrace, the conflation of passive homosexuality with effeminacy became a virtual gay cliche. Understandably the gay craze for being 'straight acting' (most personal ads still demand that characteristic) is in direct reaction to the diachronic stigma of passive homosexuality as effeminacy. Homosexuality can now often be read not as gender transitivity but as gender intransitivity or gender liminality. However, as Sinfield points out, this simply shows that the obsession with conflating sexuality and gender is still burning: 'It seems clear, though, that macho-man is in reaction against effeminacy, and this means that the masculine/feminine binary structure has not gone away, only been redistributed' (*The Wilde Century*, 193). More specifically the conflation of sexual passivity with effeminacy is still viciously policed; Michael Warner, writing in 1999 New York, asserts:

(AIDS) Prevention researchers have often noted that when they survey men about the levels of risk in their sexual lives, the numbers never add up. Far more men admit to fucking without condoms than admit to being fucked. Even quite aggressively 'out' gay men often suffer from an intense form of what might be called 'bottom shame'. Their masculinity is more closely identified with insertive than with receptive anal sex.[6]

Even in 1999 New York (arguably the Western world's gay capital), Warner points out that sexuality is still being conflated with gender. Sexual passivity equals femininity which, regulated by effeminophobia, equals inferiority. Do we still therefore have a terror of being coded as feminine and do we still culturally believe that either gender performativity or gender performance are indicative of a specific sexual preference?

This question has haunted queer theory for years. How do we have a theory which addresses gay sexuality without resorting to reductivist terms of gender? As Sedgwick has argued sexuality is more fluid and moves in excess of these homophobic binaries such as masculine and feminine, top/bottom, or butch/femme.[7] As Judith Butler summarizes: 'There are no direct expressive or causal lines between sex, gender, gender presentation, sexual practice, fantasy and sexuality. None of these terms capture or determine the rest'.[8]

This question is subtly addressed by *Trick* (directed by Fall, 1999). The film unsettles the sexuality/gender continuum through the representation of the body of screen debutant John Paul Pitoc who plays gogo boy Marc. The term I want to use to describe his bodily representation is 'Queer Masculinity'.

234 *Paragraph*

Masculinity and femininity are epistemological rather than ontological. We no longer read them as stable binaries (if indeed we ever did) but see them as subsisting in a more dynamic relationship of cultural mutability. Queer is even more problematic and is still an edgy, fluctuating term which many people reject altogether.[9] Politically, the sexier more transgressive aspect of queer is in response to earlier gay politics which sought to challenge paradigms within a heterocentrist system while queer, 'the last gasp of post-structuralism'[10] tried to expose the system of homophobia as a cultural system. I am, therefore, particularly fond of Sedgwick's definition of queer in which she stresses the 'criss-crossing of the lines of identification and desire among genders, races, and sexual definitions'.[11] It should be remembered that queer originally meant 'across'. It comes from the latin 'torquere' (to twist), the Indo-European root 'twerkw' and the old English 'athwart'. I therefore want to argue that queer masculinity twists the binarized positions of gender connoted by such categories as active/passive, top/bottom or their more misogynistic counterparts butch/femme.

Trick is a romantic comedy although the title is ironically indebted to Renaud Camus's *Tricks* which is a narrative of twenty-five promiscuous gay encounters. Roland Barthes explains the meaning of a gay 'trick' as: 'Trick — the encounter which takes place only once: more than cruising, less than love: an intensity, which passes without regret'.[12] The trick in question is Gabriel — a shy, aspiring composer of Broadway musicals — picking up gogo boy Marc on a New York Subway train. The rest of the night the boys attempt to find somewhere to be alone together but never succeed.

The Cinematic Representation of Marc's Body

Returning once again to the homophobe's worrying question of 'which one is the girl' which I shall translate into 'who is coded as feminine and does that prescribe what someone likes to do in bed?' we come up against the question of what constitutes femininity or more specifically a feminized body?

It is immediately apparent that Marc's body questions the boundaries of masculinity and femininity within the rubric of the cinematic gaze. Bearing in mind that 'the gaze' is not a synonym for 'the look' — the former is associated with the phallus and the latter is associated with the eye — the canon of early feminist film criticism[13] dictated that men gaze at women who in turn look at themselves being gazed at. The male hero, who controls the gaze, also controls the film's narrative. As E. Ann Kaplan summarized in her much quoted essay 'Is the gaze male?': 'The gaze is not necessarily male (literally) but to own and activate the gaze, given our language and the structure of the unconscious, is to be in the "masculine" position'.[14] Although Mulvey asserted that 'the male figure cannot bear the burden of sexual objectification' ('Visual Pleasure', 20), Richard Dyer[15] and Steve Neale[16] have argued that the male body can, in fact, be the object of the gaze but only if viewed during activity, such as sport or fighting, which attempt to restore phallic dominance to the disempowered male body. Even when the male body is static, as in a pin-up, Dyer asserted that the model must either disavow the gaze by staring through it with a phallic defiance or ignore it, generally by elevating his eyes, to show an exalted indifference to the castrating gaze. Most importantly the nude or nearly nude pin-up can attempt to restore phallic mastery by tensing his pumped up muscles and so the image of the pin-up always contains 'clenched fists, the bulging muscles, the hardened jaws, the proliferation of phallic symbols' ('Don't Look Now', 71). If this is not the case, Neale asserts, as in the example of Rock Hudson, the body is 'feminized' ('Masculinity as Spectacle', 14) to allow it to become the object of an erotic look. Richard Meyer cites how Rock Hudson 'submits more readily to the camera, anticipating, even inviting its objectification'.[17] In accordance with Neale and Meyer, this is a feminized body or, more specifically, one that is cinematically coded as feminine.

However, as I have already pointed out, gay male culture still seems to maintain an almost pathological fear of being coded as feminine which signifies the ideological threat of misogynistic denigration. Signifying a feminized position through the body's cultural representation should be undesirable. The narrative of *Trick* stresses paranoid effeminophobia emphasized by the scene where Gabriel is asked, in a gay bar, what he does for a living. He replies that he writes musicals and subsequently apologises for this saying: 'It makes me sound like a queen — which I don't think I am. Not that there is anything wrong with that — It's just that I'm not.' Well, if there's nothing wrong with it why even bring the subject up? Being a queen signifies the most exaggerated or excessive form of feminine performance. In citing the most extreme example rather than just saying 'effeminate', Gabriel has signified an actual phobia of being seen as feminine.

The pick up scene, however, displays a particular twist on the cinematic gaze and whether or not a body is coded as passive and feminine or masculine and active. Marc enters the train carriage. The camera takes Gabriel's point of view and gazes at Marc who, while entering the carriage, does not reciprocate the gaze but lowers his eyes demurely. The camera continually locks us into Gabriel's point of view by showing us Gabriel, then what he looks at and then his reaction. Marc, meanwhile, is represented in slow motion so that the camera's gaze can take erotic pleasure in his luxurious gait and the insouciant way he lolls into a train seat.

Marc, after finding a seat on the train, then appears to sleep. Being asleep is the most vulnerable and passive position which a human body can occupy. Many horror films (recently *Hannibal*) offer the masochistic thrill of the monster gazing at the heroine while asleep, as the sleeping body signifies baby-like vulnerability. Marc is therefore gazed at while in a position of total submission. His muscle groups are not tensed but are relaxed and flaccid while he dozes. Gabriel's gaze, our gaze, drools over Marc's body.

However, the visual implication is that Marc is only feigning sleep although he vehemently asserts in the narrative that he was tired. If he is affecting sleep he has chosen to place his body in a position of submission with all the resonances of femininity or infancy which the image affords.

Images of the youthful male body in repose are not new. Classical art and statuary abounds with as many representations of sleeping fauns as the more famous, confrontational male heroic poses. The difference, however, seems to be one of age. As long as the body has not reached sexual, masculine maturity, then it can be coded as languorous and submissive. This further emphasizes the conflation between youth, femininity, social status and sexual passivity. Most recently Calvin Klein has exploited this visual trope in his *CK ONE* advertisements where youthful androgynes lean or recline languidly. Considering that CK One is a scent marketed for 'both men and women' the confusion of gender is one of the advertisement's priorities.

This, however, raises the question of whether a body objectified is necessarily a body disempowered? It should be remembered that the subject controlling the gaze is static and essentially locked in mesmeric control by the object at which he gazes. As Susan Bordo suggests:

'Passive' hardly describes what's going on when one person offers himself or herself to another. Inviting, receiving, responding—these are active behaviours, too, and rather thrilling ones.[18]

It is only by placing himself in the most vulnerable of positions that Marc can invite Gabriel's shy, reticent gaze and so, in a particularly queer way, is still actively controlling the action.

However, one of the most jolting scenes in the film is when Marc suddenly opens his eyes and aggressively returns the camera's gaze. He then proceeds to move from a position of objectified body into the subject of the action who instigates the 'trick'. While Marc is a body to be looked at, he is also a body which forwards the diegetic narrative. Within the space of a few seconds Marc's body shifts seamlessly from being a passive, feminized body into the traditionally masculinized, active body.

Marc's Physical Body

This criss-crossing of the binaries subject/object masculine/feminine is summarized by Marc's actual physical body. It is a muscular, built body. Although he does not possess the excessive muscularity of competitive bodybuilders it should be noted that he has a proportionate, harmonious physique and not just chest and biceps as can often be found in the gay scene.[19]

Bodybuilding is a culturally mutable term as the bodies of sumo wrestlers and powerlifters can also be accurately described as 'built'. These bodies, however, are judged on what they can do rather than on how they look. Competitive bodybuilding is different and arguably holds a queer sensibility.[20] Instead of emphasizing strength, the activity focuses on the appearance of the muscular, harmoniously proportionate physique. Bob Paris — the only openly gay professional bodybuilder to date, who was a top competitor in the Mr. Olympia for many years — used to become infuriated when people asked him how much he could bench or squat: 'I'm not really concerned with that. I work out with heavy weights but heavy single bench presses are more the concern of powerlifters. That's not really what bodybuilding is about'.[21]

Bodybuilding, therefore, curiously synthesizes both the codes of masculinity and femininity. While the built body is a body of dominance, strength and control, it is inevitably a smooth, hairless, made up body. Although bodybuilders claim that they only shave their bodies so as not to obscure any muscle groups this does not explain why they also shave their arm pits which are not the site of any muscle group. The reason is simply to convey an impression of feminine submission, or a body which is not to be feared for its dominance but rather a body to be gazed at and touched. Hairless femininity is, of course, a modern, bourgeois Western construct which is related to conveying an impression of youthfulness. Only a baby or very young child has hairless skin. This again reinforces the cultural elision between femininity, youth and social status.

We see this emphasized when Marc returns to Gabriel's flat. First he stands shirtless under the room's light so as to make his muscularity appear even more massive and intimidating. Then, however, he assumes a more passive position and, lying down on the bed (his hairless armpits clearly visible), draws Gabriel's hand across his chiselled abs emphasizing that he is a body to be touched and not feared. It is interesting to note that Marc draws Gabriel's hand across his abs and not any other muscle group such as biceps. Abs hold a curious position within bodybuilding culture. Professional bodybuilder Kevon Levrone talks of how 'any ab exercise sucks'.[22] The nature of training abs dictates that the bodybuilder must do high reps with very low weights and so there is little opportunity to demonstrate strength, and its disingenuous corollary — masculinity — while training this muscle group. Abs themselves are an oppositional muscle group which, although imperative for back support, do not increase overall strength.

The Sexualized Body

Trick does not show explicit sex scenes. The best we have is a teasing glimpse in Gabriel's apartment. After caressing Marc's abs, Gabriel infuriatingly flees to the safety of his piano claiming that playing will 'relax' him. Although Philip Brett has pointed out that being musical is a clichéd euphemism for homosexuality[23] (in *The Talented Mr. Ripley*, Peter Smith Kingsley's homosexuality is connoted simply by his musicality) playing the piano, by contrast, has actually been coded as feminine. In the film *Tootsie*, Sandy's redneck father points out that it is a 'great thing' for a lady to play a piano while in former, more genteel days, being a lady was virtually predicated upon the ability to play the piano. Jane Austen's heroines, when they weren't swooning (or if Sedgwick is to be believed — masturbating[24]) then they were playing the piano or harpsichord. The piano was a graceful instrument that did not require the lady to become contorted as in playing the violin or flute — and perish the thought that a lady should even consider the cello. More importantly the piano has not simply been conflated with femininity throughout history but is a virtual metaphor for female sexuality. The film *The Piano* is one of the most lusciously poetic explorations of the piano as a metaphor for female sexuality.

Gabriel, however, plays his piano while Marc stands behind him and massages his shoulders. The camera — from a low angle so as to heroicize the subject — shows us Marc's lithely muscled back flexing as he manipulates Gabriel's shoulders. Gabriel then admits that his fantasy has always been to have someone 'go down' on him while he plays the piano. Without hesitation Marc agrees to Gabriel's fantasy and prostrates himself, on his hands and knees, underneath Gabriel's piano. Visually the power dynamics of the scene are now coded differently. The active masculine body physically subordinates himself to the feminized body. The scene stresses the erotic lubricity of roles. As Alan Sinfield has asked in two of his books, 'Who is active, who passive, in fellatio'?[25] While 'suck it' is one of the most misogynistic insults which can be directed at a woman, the question of who is actually doing something during fellatio is ambiguous. The conventional binaries of active/inserter and passive/insertee become clouded. To elaborate on Sinfield's question, who is 'the girl' or who is coded as feminine or masculine in the scene?

This is further emphasized by a later scene when the boys run into Gabriel's friend and musical mentor Perry who has just split up with his long term boyfriend. Perry agrees to let the boys spend the night at his apartment but, on the way there, they run into Perry's ex. In order to make the ex-boyfriend jealous Perry snogs Marc who plays along with the game.

Marc points out that what he and Perry have together is not simply passion it is 'animal'. He therefore stresses the folk essentialist view that sexuality is something innate which explodes from within. However, he then juxtaposes this by saying that he and Perry are, unfortunately, both 'out and out tops, so we're doing the rounds looking for hot bottoms. We've got one', he says, indicating Gabriel. How unfortunate it must be to have an animal passion for someone, but not to be able to have sex because you are both 'tops' and so have to trawl the city hunting for 'hot bottoms'. The juxtaposition of Marc with the camply feminine, gender transitive Perry exposes how ludicrous the portrayal of sexuality within the matrix of gender really is. Likewise, is Gabriel just assumed to be a 'hot bottom' because of his gender presentation or was there an interview conducted beforehand? The scene satirizes the conflation of gender with sexuality and shows Marc to be a more astute cultural critic than his narrative background would imply.

But is it Queer?

Trick is a pretty film which features two young, cute boys who are attractive without being the Adonis-like figures which inflamed so much anti-gay criticism.[26] The story is sweet, inoffensive, sometimes funny and sometimes maudlin. However, is it worthy of the hefty title of 'queer'?

Marc flirts with the hegemony of masculinity and twists or queers the binary structure of masculine and feminine. This is subtly different from gay macho drag which tried to subvert heterocentrist paradigms through appropriation. Richard Dyer summarized this when he wrote: 'If that bearded, muscular beer-drinker turns out to be a pansy, however are you going to know the 'real' men any more'?[27]

On the other hand queer, rather than subverting or satirizing the paradigms, tried to expose masculinity and femininity as an actual system of cultural constructions. As Murray Healy suggests: 'The difference now is that, whereas straights used to define the cultural terms, the agenda is no longer determined by the dominant'.[28]

However, there is one other key aspect of queer which requires consideration. In reclaiming the insult 'queer' it is often wrongly assumed that 'to do so strips it of its homophobic power'.[29] However, as both Sedgwick and Butler have emphasized, queer can never be extricated from its memory of all those years of abuse.[30] The core of the word still bristles with shame.

In the subway pick-up scene we have one other gaze: a gaze of shame. For a split second the camera offers us the admonishment of a dour *hausfrau* — conservatism incarnate — whose stare implies, not so much the constative, as performative utterance 'Shame on you!'. (The film does soften this blow as the interpellation of witnesses, demanded by a performative utterance, is not facilitated by the train.) Gabriel, like any sufferer flooding with shame, quickly looks away. The shame is explicitly connected to the stigma of sex. As the narrative suggests, Gabriel's previous defense against this was a Larry Kramer style politics in which his sexual identity was sanitized and desexualized: a gay identity not predicated upon shameful sex but yearningly filtered through his songwriting.[31] He is the time-honoured 'gay friend' and 'the safe eroticism' for Katherine.[32]

Marc, in diametric opposition, seems to be a Tom of Finland style fantasy from some mythic gay pastoral, never tarnished by the stigma of shame, and who exists only for the pleasure of sex. He picks boys up in the subway, tells Perry how he indulges in threeways or fourgies and is animated only by sensual pleasure. However, it is curious that Marc does not invite Gabriel back to his place in Brooklyn and justifies this with some frail story of having an elderly landlady. By the end of the film, however, he admits to Gabriel that this elderly landlady is his mother and immediately follows the revelation with a sheepish, embarrassed smile which is his first expression of shame throughout the film. This is symbolic of the old fashioned trope of the closet in which an iron dichotomy condemned gay sex to lurking in a secret underworld (Chelsea and Greenwich) while supposedly 'normal' life continued elsewhere (in Marc's case Brooklyn). Marc therefore transcribed shame into a specific aspect of his life and maintained an ironic distance from it elsewhere. As Sally R. Munt suggests queer promiscuity is 'a radical challenge to heteronormative coercion' but it is simultaneously 'a reaction to that same repressed conservatism, thus continuing, by effect to be inscribed within it'.[33]

The all important kiss at the end of the film is therefore not simply a narrative convention but signals a transcendence of shame. In the penultimate scene the boys are finally alone in a café washroom. For a chilling moment it seems that they will finally kiss in that most Genetesque, illicit underworld. It is Marc, however, who breaks away and leads them both outside.

The kiss finally takes place on a sidewalk and, in that moment, Marc, in a gesture of affection, has escaped the promiscuity which is simultaneously facilitated but also regulated by the gay scene. It is extremely important that the kiss takes place on the sidewalk as, like the early days of Queer Nation, the kiss-ins were an 'infusion of consumer space with a queer sensibility'.[34]

As we have seen with the body of Marc, which is positioned simultaneously and consecutively within what we term masculine and feminine paradigms, there is no prescription of sexual activity by diacritical gender presentation which in turn is not predicated upon the physically sexed body. The film offers the reassuring image of mobile desire in which sexual roles are not prescribed by gender performativity. It is only, however, by fighting through the various cultural constrictions such as place, social relationships and queer shame, that desire can be fulfilled.

NIALL RICHARDSON
University of Ulster

NOTES

1. Alan Sinfield, *Cultural Politics: Queer Readings* (London, Routledge, 1994), 15.
2. *One Hundred Years of Homosexuality: And Other Essays on Greek Love* (London and New York, Routledge, 1990), 30.
3. 'A Woman's Soul Enclosed in a Man's Body; Femininity in Male Homosexuality' in Kaja Silverman, *Male Subjectivity at the Margins* (London and New York, Routledge, 1992), 341.
4. *A History of Gay Literature: The Male Tradition* (New Haven and London, Yale University Press, 1998), 30.
5. Alan Sinfield, *The Wilde Century* (London, Cassell, 1994).
6. *The Trouble with Normal: sex politics and the ethics of queer life* (New York, Free Press, 1999), 212.
7. Eve Kosofsky Sedgwick has argued: 'For meanwhile the whole realm of what modern culture refers to as sexuality and also calls sex — the array of acts, expectations, narratives, pleasures, identity-formations, and knowledges, in both women and men, that tends to cluster most densely around certain genital sensations but is not adequately defined by them — that realm is virtually impossible to situate on a map delimited by the feminist-defined sex/gender distinction' (*Epistemology of the Closet* (Berkeley, University of California Press, 1990), 29).
8. 'Imitation and Gender Insubordination' in *Inside/Out: Lesbian Theories, Gay Theories* edited by Diana Fuss (London and New York, Routledge, 1991), 25.
9. I am thinking especially of Paul Burston's deliberately polemical statement '"Queer" is simply "Gay" with knobs and nipple-rings on' *What Are You Looking At?* (London, Cassell, 1995), 101. Helen (charles) stresses the enigmatic, lubricity of queer when she writes 'I have not been able to come any closer to a clear definition of what Queer is or what it attempts to be', ' "Queer Nigger": Theorizing "White" Activism' in *Activating Theory: Lesbian, Gay and Bisexual Politics*, edited by Joseph Bristow and Angelia R. Wilson (London, Lawrence and Wishart, 1991), 97–106, 99–100).
10. Eric Savoy, 'You Can't Go Homo Again: Queer Theory and the Foreclosure of Gay Studies', *English Studies in Canada*, 20, (1994) 129–152.
11. Eve Kosofsky Sedgwick, 'New Preface' (1992) in *Between Men: English Literature and Male Homosocial Desire* (New York, Columbia University Press, 1986), viii.
12. Preface (1979) to Renaud Camus *Tricks: 25 Encounters* translated by Richard Howard (New York, Saint Martin's Press, 1981).
13. Laura Mulvey, 'Visual Pleasure and Narrative Cinema' published in *Screen*, 16:3, Autumn (1975), 6–18, and also 'Afterthoughts on 'Visual Pleasure and Narrative Cinema' inspired by King Vidor's *Duel in the Sun* (1946)' published in *Framework*, 6 (1988), 15–17, Summer (1981).

14 'Is the Gaze Male?' in E. Ann Kaplan *Women and Film: Both Sides of the Camera* (London and New York, Routledge, 1983), 30.
15 'Don't Look Now: The Male Pin-Up' *Screen* 23:3–4 (1982), 61–73.
16 'Masculinity as Spectacle: Reflections on Men and Mainstream Cinema' in *Screen* 26:6 (1983), 2–16.
17 'Rock Hudson's Body' in *Inside/Out: Lesbian Theories, Gay Theories*, edited by Diana Fuss, (London and New York, Routledge, 1991), 259–88, 261.
18 'Beauty (Re)Discovers the Male Body' in *Beauty Matters*, edited by Peg Zeglin Brand (Bloomington and Indianapolis, Indiana University Press, 2000), 112–54, 133.
19 To the untrained eye one relatively well-developed physique can look very similar to another. It is possible to create the illusion of a built body through only training the muscles which are on display such as chest and biceps. A competitively validated bodybuilder's physique, however, is one where all the muscle groups are harmoniously proportioned. The upper chest must sweep into the deltoids, the triceps must match the biceps and the traps should blend into the rear deltoids.
20 I have deliberately chosen 'queer' as opposed to 'homoerotic' as bodybuilding is obviously predicated upon its homoerotic appeal. As Alan Ellenzweig explains: 'The homoerotic engages in varying degrees those feelings of desire, intimacy, admiration, or affection between members of the same sex, whereas the homosexual engages the actual physical or, more properly, the sexual — the genital — expression of those sentiments' *The Homoerotic Photograph* (New York, Columbia University Press, 1992), 2. Queer, by contrast, stresses the simultaneously dissonant masculinization and femininization which bodybuilding renders on the body. As Margaret Walters has affirmed: 'for all his super-masculinity the bodybuilder's exaggerated breast development, as well as his dedicated self-absorption, can make him look unexpectedly, surreally feminine' (*The Male Nude: A New Perspective* (New York and London, Paddington Press Ltd., 1978), 295.
21 Bob Paris, *In a Gorilla Suit: My Adventures in Bodybuilding* (New York, St. Martin's Press, 1997), 140.
22 'The Big Picture: The Kevin Levrone File' compiled by Jim Rosenthal, *Flex*, June, (1999), 138.
23 'Musicality, Essentialism and The Closet' in *Queering the Pitch: the New Gay and Lesbian Musicology* edited by Philip Brett, Elizabeth Wood and Gary C. Thomas (London and New York, Routledge, 1994), 11.
24 Eve Kosofsky Sedgwick, 'Jane Austen and the Masturbating Girl' in *Tendencies* (London, Routledge, 1994), 118. In humble defence of Sedgwick's argument (and as a graduate of the Julian Clary school of literary criticism) I noted that, in the the 1992 BBC adaptation of *Sense and Sensibility*, one of Marianne Dashwood's favourite piano pieces was 'The Thickety Bush'.

25 *The Wilde Century*, 170 and *Gay and After* (London, Serpent's Tail, 1998), 49.
26 'Anti-gay' was predominantly a journalistic backlash movement which objected to the body fascism of the gay scene and its idealization in the photographs of Bruce Weber, Tom Bianchi and Herb Ritts. For stirring anti-gay criticism see *Anti-Gay* (London and New York Cassell, 1996), edited by Marc Simpson. I particularly like John Weir's acid comment explaining that 'He isn't gay anymore; he can't afford the gym membership' (viii).
27 'Getting over the rainbow: identity and pleasure in gay cultural politics' in Richard Dyer *Only Entertainment* (London and New York, Routledge, 1992), 165.
28 'The mark of a man: masculine identities and the art of macho drag' *Critical Quarterly* 36: 1 (Spring), 86–93, 92.
29 Julia Parnby, 'Queer Straits' *Trouble and Strife* 26, 13–16, 14.
30 Eve Kosofsky Sedgwick: 'The main reason why the self-application of 'queer' by activists has proved so volatile is that there's no way that any amount of affirmative reclamation is going to succeed in detaching the word from its associations with shame' ('Queer Performativity: Henry James's *The Art of the Novel'*, *GLQ: A Journal of Lesbian and Gay Studies*, 1:1 (1993), 1–18, 4; Judith Butler: 'Queer' derives its force precisely through the repeated invocation by which it has become linked to accusation, pathologization, insult' (*Bodies that Matter: On the Discursive Limits of 'Sex'* (New York and London, Zoetrope, 1993), 226).
31 The playwright Larry Kramer who, despite receiving a lot of bad press, has for decades been calling for a desexed gay movement.
32 Baz Dreisinger, 'The Queen in Shining Armor: Safe Eroticism and the Gay Friend' *Journal of Popular Film and Television* 28:1 Spring (2000), 3–11, 6.
33 'Shame/Pride dichotomies in *Queer As Folk*' *Textual Practice* 14:3 Winter (2000), 531–46, 534.
34 Lauren Berlant and Elizabeth Freeman, 'Queer Nationality' in *Fear of a Queer Planet: Queer Politics and Social Theory*, edited by Michael Warner (Minneapolis, University of Minnesota Press, 1993), 213.

Racing Forms and the Exhibition(ist) (Mis)Match

In my dreams, everyone has read my book *Male Matters* closely, repeatedly, and with unalloyed pleasure.¹ Since the reality is doubtless otherwise, I will open by rehearsing the book's main argument and revisiting a few of its most pertinent theoretical scenes — pertinent, that is, to the question of men's bodies and visual culture. I will then turn to some examples from visual culture in order to consider, in a rough and admittedly inadequate way, a question that the book itself failed to raise at all: the question of race, of the forming of race and of the racing of forms, particularly — or markedly — the visualized forms of 'the male body'.

In *Male Matters*, I attempt to trace cultural anxieties about the productions of men's bodies, anxieties that come into play whenever such productions exceed the hetero-masculine economies of visibility that work to contain them. Taking the word 'production' from *pro-ducere* — 'to render visible, to cause to appear and be made to appear'² — and taking the preposition 'of' in the phrase 'productions of men's bodies' as a double genitive, the book explores, on the one hand, anxieties about the ways male bodies *are* produced, visibly rendered, caused to appear, both physically and in representation, and, on the other, anxieties about the matters that male bodies themselves *do* produce, visibly render, cause to appear, both physically and in representation.

Of course, the very distinction between the physical and the representational has become problematic; indeed, the distinction has been effectively dissolved by politically inflected psychoanalytic theory, which tells us not only that the physical, the material, the anatomical, are, for us as specifically human beings, always matters of psychical representation, but that psychical representation is itself inextricable from social and cultural production and reproduction. As speaking subjects, we lose whatever pure, unmediated physicality we retroactively had from the representational and symbolic get-go, at the moment of Lacan's mirror stage, followed by accession to the symbolic order of language, which is also the ideological moment of Althusser's policeman's interpellating hail, or, if you prefer, the always already of what Foucault calls 'social orthopaedics', what Judith Butler refers to as 'regulatory regimes'.[3]

If, however, the distinction between the physical and the representational cannot be humanly maintained, neither can it be utterly collapsed nor dialectically sublated. Each is the other's mutual, albeit often anguished, support. Moreover, their interaction can be foregrounded in the phrase 'productions of men's bodies' taken as a double genitive — taken, that is, in the sense of the manner in which men's bodies *are* produced and in terms of the matters that men's bodies *do* produce, physically and in representation. Thus, exploring the productions of men's bodies, and related anxieties, as *Male Matters* attempts, leads us to four related corporeo-discursive fields.

First: the field of the physical production of male bodies by and through female bodies. *Male Matters* speculates on the psychical consequences of one particular phantasy regarding the way female bodies 'render' male bodies — to wit, Freud's notion of the child's 'cloacal theory' of its own body's origin, a theory which links the process of childbirth to defecation. The book explores the repression or suppression of what might be called the actively cloacal or 'abjecting mother' in the formation of the Oedipalized, hetero-masculine subject. Drawing mainly from the work of Julia Kristeva, *Male Matters* examines the anxieties on the part of this subject regarding its own phantasmatic construction of the pre-Oedipal mother, whose body is not 'lacking' but excessive, expressive, productive. In relation to this productive maternal body, the fledgling hetero-masculine subject can hardly phantasize its own body as the phallus that — if it only it were not for paternal prohibition — would make good her 'lack'. Rather than 'being the phallus' of the mother's symbolic lack or desire, the subject's body becomes the abject 'anal penis' of her unthinkable semiotic excess. In this phantasmatic scenario, the Name-of-the-Father does not *bar* the subject's access to the mother's body but rather *saves* the subject from that body's expulsion and material re-engulfment. The subject's 'anxiety of production' with respect to the abjecting mother is prior to any 'castration anxiety', and indeed, the book argues, the latter can be the former's symbolic remedy.

Second: the field of the representational production of men's bodies by and through the various apparatuses and technologies of culture — art, media, literature, film; the way men's bodies appear, are displayed, or, more significantly, do *not* appear, are *not* displayed, in the dominant economies of the visible. *Male Matters* explores the structural conditions of possibility for such economies; their role in the formation of hetero-masculine subjectivity; and the privileges granted to that seemingly disembodied subject by virtue of its desired (and, largely, granted) immunity from being 'marked'. The book examines, and even hopes to intervene in, the asymmetrical power relations between that subject and its variously marked, embodied, or visibly represented 'others'.

Third: the physical matters that men's bodies produce, cause to appear, or, given the reigning specular economies, conceal from appearance: semen, urine, blood, sweat, snot, shit, tears, words. Granted, only the first item on the list is specifically, physically male. And yet, drawing from Luce Irigaray's work on fluids and solids, Linda Williams' treatment of the ejaculation scenes or 'money-shots' in hard-core film pornography, and one exceedingly curious moment in Hegel's *Phenomenology of Spirit* (which is among the theoretical scenes to be revisited here), *Male Matters* examines the way this essentially male matter can appear to be feminine. Indeed, the book argues, if ejaculate appears at all it tends to do so, abjectly, on the side (so to speak) *of* the feminine.[4] The book further suggests that anxieties about the gendered duplicity of the visibly disseminated trace may have played their part in the whole troubled history of the relation between idealized masculinity and the degraded realm of the visible.

As for the last item on the list of bodily productions — 'words' — its appearance there will seem less surprisingly out of place if one takes the well-known phrase 'the materiality of language' as I do, literally; or if one grants that at this very moment I am producing words through an opening in my body; or, again, if one recognizes what is at stake in the following well-worn but crucial quotations from Kristeva and Lacan. From Kristeva: 'I expel *myself*, I spit *myself* out, I abject *myself* within the same motion through which "I" claim to establish myself'.[5] And from Lacan: 'This subject, who thinks that he can accede to himself by designating himself in the statement, is no more than such an object. Just ask the writer about the anxiety he experiences when he faces the blank sheet of paper, and he will tell you who *is* the turd of his phantasy'.[6]

If nothing else, these quotations provide a point of transition, if not collapse, not only between the oral and the anal, or between the motion of speech and the movement of writing, but also between the third corporeo-discursive field (the physical matters that men's bodies produce) and the fourth: the representational matters that men's bodies produce by and through the various apparatuses and technologies of culture — again, art, media, literature, film. At the crux of *Male*

Matters' polemic is a conception of language, and particularly of writing, as a bodily function; the book's main concern is with the gendered ambiguities and possibilities for abjection inscribed in the unavoidable self-alienations of language, what Lacan calls 'the self's radical ex-centricity to itself' (*Écrits*, 171) in the insistence of the letter. The book itself insists on reading this literal self-alienation as a self-excorporation and a self-abjection that is potentially gender-bending, feminizing, queering — in any case, both absolutely necessary and profoundly disturbing to hegemonic masculinity.

If, however, the book's main focus is on language and writing, the larger problem it attempts to address involves productions of bodies, regimes of visibility, and relations of power. Although I have here designated four corporeo-discursive fields of inquiry, I should stress that, for me, feminist and queer politics remain the untranscendable horizon of those fields and of any inquiry into them. One cannot meaningfully address the productions of men's bodies — masculinized, empowered, superordinated bodies — without also addressing the production and the oppression of women's bodies, feminized bodies, queered bodies, raced bodies — disempowered or subordinated bodies all — without, in other words, addressing the various mechanisms of displacement, projection, and abjection that govern and support the dominant regimes of the visible. To address those mechanisms here, I want to revisit, as I said, several pertinent, fairly well-known theoretical scenes that *Male Matters* cites — formulations, that is, that pertinently theorize both sight and the scenic.

First: from John Berger's *Ways of Seeing*, the pithy assertion that 'Men act and women appear'.[7] Here one might elaborate by saying that masculinity is conventionally constituted as and by action or activity, while femininity is conventionally constituted as and by the appearance of passivity and the passivity of appearance. One might give an example of the convention by pointing, as does Linda Williams, to the very origins of the motion picture: Eadweard Muybridge's photographic motion studies, in which nude male figures are generally represented only in vigorous athletic action while nude female figures often tend (even though these are motion studies) to stand, sit, or lie still, luxuriating in the aura of their 'to-be-looked-at-ness' — if not inviting erotic contemplation, then at least 'doing nothing' to dispel it. But one might also point out the fairly obvious ways in which this action/appearance binary is undone. Any *represented* action, for example, is rather inevitably an appearance, while some modes of appearance, particularly those staged for erotic contemplation, can be quite active, if not frenetic (nude dancers and porn performers are often much more vigorously active than their passive, voyeuristic counterparts).

Of course, it could be argued that the underlying purpose of masculine activity-in-appearance is precisely to avoid giving the appearance of appearance, to dispel erotic contemplation, to deflect the gaze. This is the point, to move to the second theoretical scene, that Laura Mulvey simultaneously gets and misses when, in the famous essay 'Visual Pleasure and Narrative Cinema,' she writes, 'According to the principles of the ruling ideology and the psychical structures that back it up, the male figure cannot bear the burden of sexual objectification. Man [writes Mulvey] is reluctant to gaze at his exhibitionist like'.[8] Reluctant, to be sure, but not absolutely unwilling; and perhaps all of the following is implied in the phrase 'the ruling ideology,' but Mulvey's formulation does need amending so that it is more clearly the *straight* male figure, perhaps the straight *white* male figure, that cannot bear the burden of sexual objectification, the straight white man who is reluctant to gaze at his exhibitionist like. Correspondingly, women would not be the only ones made to bear the burden of representation, embodiment, sexual objectification. Obviously, or perhaps covertly, men gaze at other men, their 'likes', but only under certain conditions of exhibition—generally, those, such as sports and cinematic or videographic warfare, that guarantee competitive violence, or at least actively dispel erotic contemplation, deflect the gaze. If the terms of these conditions are somehow broken, then there may indeed be exhibition, but there will be no identificatory match. In other words, the man's exhibitionist 'like,' by virtue of exhibition, becomes un-liked, dis-liked. The exhibited male body is almost the same, but not quite—or, in some cases, to quote Homi Bhabha, 'almost the same, but not white'.[9] As Sally Robinson puts it in her recent book *Marked Men: White Masculinity in Crisis*, because 'male power is dependent on stalling the recognition of male embodiment, and particularly, white male embodiment, (...) nonwhite men have been forced to carry the symbolic burden of *over*embodiment'.[10]

I will return to the specifically racial forms of this exhibition(ist) (mis)match. Here I want to touch on a third pertinent scenic formulation, Lacan's assertion that the phallus 'can only play its role when veiled' (*Écrits*, 288) and that, consequently, any 'virile display in the human being [will] seem feminine' (*Écrits*, 91). Never mind for the moment the opacities of Lacan's argument that the phallus is not the penis but the 'signifier of lack': quite clearly, the restrictions placed on the phallus in terms of its display hold good for the penis and for seminal fluid alike. In the restricted visual economy of procreative heterosexual copulation, aka straight sex, the penis and its transmitted product can indeed play their proper roles only while veiled, or, to use a more unfortunate word, 'sheathed', but in any case hidden, contained, prevented from appearing, kept out of the picture.

And if one has any doubts that this physical restriction effects psychical representation and larger specular economies, one might consider that moment in the *Phenomenology of Spirit* wherein Hegel likens the difference between properly conceptual thinking and representational or 'picture-thinking' to two different forms of urethral discharge. Properly conceptual dialectical thought, says Hegel, must temporarily descend into and merge with mere picture-thinking, but, ideally, the concept, the *Begriff*, the infinite judgement, will sublate and work its way through *Vorstellung*, or picture-thinking, on its long march to what Hegel calls 'imageless truth'. The temporary conjunction of *Begriff* and *Vorstellung* in consciousness, Hegel asserts, is the same conjunction of the pure and the crude, the high and the low, that 'Nature naively expresses when it combines (...) the organ of generation with the organ of urination. The infinite judgement *qua* infinite [says Hegel] would be the fulfillment of life that comprehends itself; [but] the consciousness of the infinite judgement that remains on the level of picture-thinking behaves as urination'.[11]

Examining this urethral passage in the *Phenomenology* at some length, *Male Matters* suggests that when Hegel compares the difference between pure concept and crude picture in the *psychical* organ to that between semen and urine in the *physical* organ, he may also have another difference somewhere in mind: namely, the difference between insemination and dissemination, between a veiled seminal production that remains proper to a heterosexual dialectical economy and an unveiled production that exceeds it — or, to put it in other words, between ejaculation as dialectical *action* and ejaculate as unsublatable *appearance*. Implied here, by me, is the classical deconstructionist argument that the putative difference *between* semen and urine can be read as a difference *within* seminal fluid; that the putative difference *between* the conceptual and the merely pictorial is *internal* to the conceptual; that the difference between action and appearance is comparably unstable and collapsible, as is that between other arguably related binaries, such as masculine and feminine, straight and queer, white and black. The fact that these differential relations are stabilized and maintained as oppositions has nothing to do with their 'essential nature', since they haven't any, and everything to do with ideological structures, with social and psychic mechanisms of displacement, projection, and abjection, and with the various apparatuses and technologies of visual culture that depend upon and support those mechanisms. In any case, Hegel's linking of picturation with micturition allows us to consider the ways hetero-masculinity can become anxious, if not quite pissed off, whenever it gets 'inappropriately' put into the picture. It allows us to consider the cultural mechanisms of displacement, projection, and abjection that work to arrange masculine icons, assuage masculine anxieties, and channel masculinist rage.

Before turning to some specific iconography, however, I would like to linger over some duplicities or ambiguities inscribed in the very mechanisms of visual production. Ever since Freud elaborated on the *fort/da* game in *Beyond the Pleasure Principle*, the underlying principle of representation itself has been related to the movement from passivity to activity, has been ascribed to the desire for a symbolic mastery upon which nothing less is staked than ego coherence itself. Since the activity, the mastery, and the coherence are all conventionally registered to the masculine, correspondingly, the principle means or 'tools' of representation or visual production — the brush, the pen, the camera, the gaze itself — have been conventionally likened to the phallus. Here one mentions their shape, the way they are handled, their seeming capacity to 'penetrate' into reality, and the more salient fact that historically it has been men who have possessed and attempted to control them.

But there are problems with this conventional phallicizing of representational acts and means. Or, one might say, there are ways in which the means themselves can be said to de-mean the phallic claims that are sometimes made on them and through them. In *Male Matters*, the dominant strategy for de-meaning or deflating the phallus is by way of an abjecting carnal irony, an aggressive analization or fecalization of phallic claims. Thus, in regard to the painter's brush, a carnal ironist might repeat with a certain relish Lacan's claim that 'the authenticity of what emerges in painting is diminished (...) by the fact that we have to get our colours where they're to be found, that is to say, in the shit (...). The creator [says Lacan] will never participate in anything other than the creation of a small dirty deposit, a succession of small dirty deposits juxtaposed'.[12] In regard to the pen, the carnal ironist might help breed the suspicion that we sometimes have to get our ink and our letters in the same way Lacan suggests we get our colours, the suspicion that our writings may be less monuments of unageing intellect than small dirty deposits juxtaposed, or what Leo Bersani, writing about Jean Genet, refers to as 'cultural droppings'.[13] As for the camera, the sphincterish character of its shutter and lens complicates any notion of that apparatus as perpetrator of the penetrating gaze, since the camera must in effect *be* penetrated by light to capture what the gaze 'takes in'. In other words, *pace* D.A. Miller, the camera may not be 'so total a prick' after all.[14] And this duplicity extends to the gaze as well, for as Slavoj Žižek contends, writing about Hitchcock in *Looking Awry*, there is an 'intimate connection between the gaze and the couple power/impotence. The gaze [writes Žižek] denotes at the same time power (it enables us to exert control over the situation, to occupy the position of the master) and impotence (as bearers of the gaze, we are reduced to the role of passive witnesses to the adversary's action).'[15]

Caught up, then, in the intimate duplicity of the gaze, the abject ambiguities and carnal ironies of visual production itself, we find that there is no symbolic power that cannot also be read as impotence, no top that cannot be bottomed, no *act* of seeing that does not also *appear* to be subject to what Lee Edelman nicely calls '(be)hindsight'.[16] And unless these ambiguities are merely the obsessive concern of this particular carnal ironist (though I have trundled out all these names and citations to suggest otherwise), spectres of abjection, powerlessness, and penetrability can be said to circle and haunt all scenes of heteromasculinist representation, any visible production of the male body whatsoever. Nevertheless, despite the increased proliferation of images of men's bodies in the past decade or so, these ambiguities are for the most part safely contained, the ironies glossed over. The recognition of male embodiment, particularly white male embodiment, remains stalled, and masculinist power is thereby largely recuperated.

To get a sense of this stalling, let's consider the cover photographs of two books concerning 'the male body' that were published in the United States in the mid 1990s. The first is my own book, the cover photograph of which I actually had no role in selecting. What I had wanted was a very suggestive detail from the hell of Hieronymus Bosch's 'Garden of Earthly Delights'. A large bird-like creature sits on a toilet-throne, devouring male bodies whole and then excreting them into a dark pit: in what might be called a sort of hideous pre-parody of dialectical synthesis, the big bird is shitting men while the partially devoured male body is shitting a flock of birds. As much as I wanted this image, however, I was told by my publisher that reproducing it would cost too much money. I should say, however, that I'm quite pleased with what the publisher did select, particularly with the pornographic luridness of the blue tint, and that I'm sure this cover sold more copies of the book than would have Bosch. But let's have a look. What might appear at first glance to be a contemporary image drawn from a Calvin Klein underwear advertisement is actually a photograph from the nineteenth century. Two shirtless men are locked in a twisted embrace. One's bicep bulges into the other's crotch. Their eyes are directed at each other's behinds. The man in the foreground can be called sexually attractive, or at least impressively torsoed, while the backgrounded man seems less so, or is at least, noticeably, inelegantly coiffured. They are, of course, wrestling, or pretending to wrestle, and this athletic action is what both permits and represses the erotic contemplation of the foregrounded man's appearance, as does, I think, the discrepancy in beauty between him and his partner (that is, the appearance of two equally beautiful men in such an embrace might have been 'too much,' might have overwhelmed the staged action meant to contain it). This photograph, then, both elicits and represses or deflects what Diana Fuss calls the 'homospectatorial look'.[17] It represents both the possibility of recognizing male embodiment and the possible stalling of that recognition.

But onto what or whom is that look typically deflected? Where is that recognition generally stalled? Let's consider the cover of another book about 'the male body,' this one actually entitled *The Male Body*,[18] a cover that I think suggestively exemplifies, and perhaps even comments upon, the 'almost the same but not white' dynamic of the exhibition(ist) (mis)match. Here Robert Mapplethorpe's 1983 photograph of Ken Moody serves to represent what purports to be a textual uncovering of '*the* male body'. The racial dynamics of this 'service,' however, can be noted with some irony. Most typically, when dominant white culture desires to instantiate itself and universalize its interests, it attempts to do so by coupling a generic definite article—'the'—with some general noun and with some image of itself in which and by which it recognizes itself. Think, for example, of phrases such as 'the family' or even 'the human' and of the blanched images they unfortunately but most likely conjure up, and not only in white minds. Here, however, when it is *male* embodiment that is to be recognized, when 'male body' is the phrase to which the definite article is attached, a black man stands in, does representational service. Because this 'servant' is not engaged in any particular athletic activity, his image appears to be more open to erotic contemplation by other male spectators; moreover, that very appearance of openness works to 'feminize' Moody's image, despite his impressively defined musculature. But because straight white men are still reluctant to gaze upon their exhibitionist likes, Moody's blackness provides the reluctant with a comforting and distantiating dissimilitude, an anxiety-assuaging opportunity for projection, displacement, and abjection, or, at the very least, the reassurance that one's 'own' white male body is not on the line. If, however, Moody's shoulders seem almost poised to accept 'the symbolic burden of overembodiment,' we might instead read the raised right hand as a gesture of refusal. We might see Moody as not simply standing before our gaze in submission but walking away from it in defiance. On the other hand, we have to ask which of our own anxieties might be assuaged by this interpretive translation of sexualized appearance into politicized gestural action.

If, for whatever reason, we do read refusal into Moody's raised hand—and there are good reasons for such a reading—we can certainly locate instances of visual culture in which black men are represented as accepting the burden of overembodiment quite happily. For an example, consider the Herb Ritts's Mapplethorpe-inspired video for the Janet Jackson tune 'Love Will Never Do Without You'.

At the beginning of this video we see, in black and white, six medium-close shots that alternate between two silhouetted, erotically moving bodies, one Janet Jackson's, the other a shirtless black man's. In the seventh shot, we see Janet's body, still largely silhouetted, in profile, her hand making the standard soft-porn move from her breasts (about which I'll have something to say in a moment) down to her crotch. At the moment of crotch-caress, however, we cut to a fully-lit long-shot of a shirtless and very black-skinned male figure running away from us across the white sands of a desert (fig. 1), and now we begin to alternate between long-shots of this black male body receding into the distance, and medium-close shots of Janet coupled with and orbiting a stationary male body that turns out to be white (fig. 2).

As, arguably, does Janet's *own* body, for, when we cut to the brightly-lit close-ups that alternate between her face and the profile of her grinning white admirer (I'm told he's a well-known soap-opera star), we see that the black and white videography, which works to *accentuate* the difference between the white man's skin and that of the receding runner, more effectively *negates* the difference in value between the white man's skin and Janet's. Moreover, if we compare this Janet Jackson video to earlier examples (such as 'Nasty Boys', 'The Pleasure Principle', and 'What Have You Done For Me Lately?'),

Racing Forms and the Exhibition(ist) (Mis)Match 255

Figure 1. Still from Herb Ritts, video for Janet Jackson, 'Love Will Never Do Without You'.

Figure 2. Still from Herb Ritts, video for Janet Jackson, 'Love Will Never Do Without You'.

we see not only a noticeable lightening of her skin tone, but also a politically readable transformation of the shape of her body. For 'Love Will Never Do Without You' is the first video to feature Janet's newly enhanced breasts, and feature them it certainly does, while it also draws our attention to the notable diminishment of what had previously been a more generously proportioned behind. And if we are familiar with the rap-artist Sir Mix-a-Lot's video 'Baby's Got Back,' we know what *he* would have to say about the racial politics of this shrinkage (for the unfamiliar, 'Baby's Got Back' registers a protest against the imposition onto black women of white male standards of female booty-size).

In 'Love Will Never Do Without You,' then, Janet Jackson is softened and whitened, reproportioned and realigned. Missing here is any of the abrasive 'urban' edginess of the earlier videos — the staccato storm-trooper dancing in 'Rhythm Nation,' for example. Newly breasted, butt-shrunk, bleached, and blanched, Janet is now positioned as an idealized fantasy object of comfortable straight white male desire. However, I would argue, in order to position her so, the black male has to be, as it were, removed from the equation, which removal or driving out is implicitly and explicitly what the video dramatizes. The video, that is, labours to lift 'blackness' — perhaps even to lift 'phallic blackness,' the aforementioned urban edginess — off of Janet, to place it onto the back of the running black man, and to neutralize it there. But 'blackness' isn't simply expelled from the picture; rather, it is retained as a comfortably distanced but necessary backdrop for this bleached-out sexual fantasy. The running black man, as we soon discover, is withdrawing from us neither to escape or *refuse* our gaze, as might be Ken Moody in the Mapplethorpe photograph, but merely to be better positioned to *receive* it, and more. Distantiated object, this black man, and the nearly naked others whose bodies the video exhibits, will receive not only the 'burden' of the blackness that has been withdrawn from Janet's body and redoubled onto his own; he will also receive, has already received in advance, the burden of the white man's embodiment as well. For conspicuously enough, and unlike either Janet or the black men, the white man's body is never shown by itself in its entirety (granted, there are some torso shots of what may be a white male body — it is difficult to tell — but the visual connection between that body and the grinning white male head is never established). He isn't even required (or permitted) to take off his white shirt. Identificatory pivot for the white male spectator, the white man is shown as the exclusive subject of desire for Janet — gazing at her, holding her, rubbing up against her — while the black men are consigned to representational fates (distantiation, objectification, fetishization, decapitation) to which the white male hero's body is never subjected. Unlike Whitey, none of the black men ever occupies the same frame as Janet.

Moreover, there are a number of shots in this segregating video that work to 'feminize' the appearance of the black male bodies, moments when the camera cuts from close-ups of Janet's body-parts to full body shots or close-ups of (usually faceless or headless) black men. These cuts, I would argue, do not dramatize heterosexualized encounters among these part-objects but rather attempt to establish an equivalence between Janet's feminized body and black men's bodies which, by virtue of their very display, are thereby demasculinized, disempowered, perhaps even 'queered' to the extent that their utter unimportance to the heterosexual encounter between Janet and Whitey (and by extension the white male spectator) is stressed (although this stress may have the unintended effect of revealing the way straight 'importance' utterly depends upon its own staging of queer 'triviality'). In addition, the bodies themselves are positioned and posed in ways that suggest a willingness if not an abundant happiness to bear the symbolic burden of overembodiment. Arms are repeatedly raised and spread like those of an Atlas, or a crucified Jesus. And when we do finally get close-up shots of the lip-synching, blissfully smiling black male face, the signal fact that his eyes remain *closed* works to assure us that the object of our gaze will not turn his on us. The carefully established aura of his visual objectification, his 'to-be-looked-at-ness,' his castration, remains completely undisturbed — as, by extension, do 'we'.

All eyes are wide open, however, in the next visual sequence I want to consider, a scene from Oliver Stone's football saga *Any Given Sunday*. In this film, the protagonist is an aging white professional football coach, played by Al Pacino, who struggles against a disempowerment that is represented both, on the one hand, by the team's new owner, a ruthless young white woman, played by Cameron Diaz, who has inherited the ownership of the franchise from her father, and, on the other, by an uppity young black quarterback, played by Jamie Foxx. The narrative conflict is resolved when the coach subdues both threats: after defying the odds and putting together a winning season, the coach leaves Diaz's team for another, taking the star black quarterback with him. Or, to put it in other words, the narrative conflict is resolved when the coach, facing his own castration, saves himself from that fate by recovering the phallus, here represented by the black quarterback, taking that phallus away from the woman who has attempted inappropriately to wield it and restoring it to himself. Of course, that a black man's body can be used in such a symbolically narrative form — as a phallus exchanged between a white man and a white woman — itself speaks volumes: the inverse (a white male body exchanged between a black man and a black woman) is practically unthinkable in dominant cultural terms.

The sequence I want to examine begins when the white woman owner, as yet still 'phallic', penetrates the sweaty recesses of the racially mixed but all-male post-victory locker-room to congratulate the team. She casually approaches a naked and (of course) impressively built black player, noticeably noticing his penis (though I myself didn't notice her notice the first half-dozen times I viewed the clip, since I was busy noticing the same thing as she). Reaching to shake his hand, she briefly gives the impression that she's reaching to grab his crank (fig. 3).

Now, perhaps it is needless to say that instances of full frontal male nudity in mainstream American cinema are infrequent — indeed, virtually non-existent. And though Oliver Stone's films are usually

Figure 3. Still from Oliver Stone, *Any Given Sunday*.

replete with female nudity (*Any Given Sunday* is no exception), and are always on some level about recuperating the phallus, this is, I'm fairly sure, the first time he's ever shown us a dick. Of course, it isn't *his* dick that we see (though he does appear in the film), and, significantly, it isn't even a *white* dick that we see. More significantly, it also isn't the phallus that we see. Even though both the black man's body and his penis are impressively proportioned, the very virile display of that body has, as Lacan promised it would, the effect—I would say, the *intentional* effect—of feminizing or dephallicizing it. The very composition of the shot, which positions the black male body and the white female body alongside each other, can be read as suggesting a sort of visual equivalence between them.

As if this 'feminization' of the black male body at the moment of its virile display needed underscoring, this scene, like Herb Ritts's video, ends on a note of raced castration. A hulking white man (with eyes cosmetically blackened, accentuating their openness), is dancing in the shower-room with a group of black players. Insulted by the black mens' assertion that he (being white) can't dance, he leaves the shower with a Schwarzneggerish 'I'll be back'. When he does came back, he hurls an adolescent alligator into the shower-room where the black men who had dissed him are still bathing. Calling the naked black men 'pussies', the triumphant white hulk pumps his arms in the air—somehow, I guess, having proven that he *can* dance. One of the black men is shown cringing and apologizing, holding up his hands, not in refusal of our gaze, but to protect himself against the alligator's gaping jaws (fig. 4). On one level, these jaws and their intrusion might be read as a metaphor for the *vagina dentata* of the phallic and hence castrating female owner. On another level, we might read this long phallic snout that opens to reveal a devouring orifice as a metaphor for the camera itself, particularly since here the alligator is threatening to 'take' or even to 'snap' exactly what Stone's snapping apparatus has already taken. Since it is delivered by a white man, and posed as a threat against a black penis, the alligator may serve to further reassure white male viewers about the spectacle earlier taken in. In other words, although Stone's camera inevitably opens us up to penetration, the alligator assures us that at least no black phallus will ever pierce the whites of our eyes, much less any of our darker orifices.

I want to conclude with a brief anecdote. Not long ago, in Atlanta, following a friend's recommendation, I went to get my hair cut in what turned out to be a gay male bath and barbershop. The walls of this shop were decorated with, among other more or less pornographic

260 Paragraph

Figure 4. Still from Oliver Stone, *Any Given Sunday*.

images, framed covers of vintage male body-building magazines from the forties and fifties. As I conversed with the barber, Randy, about these images, and about my job teaching critical theory and gender studies, I told him a little bit about the conference on 'Men's Bodies' for which this essay was originally written, and about the essay itself. When it was time to pay up, I needed a pen to write Randy a cheque. He first handed me your basic unadorned ball-point but then said that, given the topic of my paper, he had a different implement that might be more appropriate, and he then presented me with a pen that had as its cap a miniature rubber penis and balls. They — the penis and balls — were what a white person would call 'flesh-coloured'. I was about to take hold of this item when, with the words 'or perhaps even better', Randy held up yet another pen, this one capped by a what a black person would call a 'flesh-coloured' rubber penis and balls (same size, by the way), and we shared a laugh as I wrote out the cheque. The point of this story, and of my comments here, is that perhaps no act of writing or of identification or of representation is immune from the embodied production of social and cultural meaning. As Stuart

Hall puts it, 'The world must be made to mean'.[19] Complex issues of gender, sexuality, race, representation, and ultimately power, are always in play whenever meaning is made, and although the meaning is rarely made so apparent, the appearance of an 'other' — of the other that 'I' inevitably is[20] — always caps off any self-identificatory act, even if it is only the signing of one's own name.

CALVIN THOMAS
Georgia State University

NOTES

1 *Male Matters: Masculinity, Anxiety, and the Male Body on the Line* (Urbana, University of Illinois Press, 1996).
2 Jean Baudrillard, *Forget Foucault* (New York, Semiotexte, 1987), 21.
3 Michel Foucault, 'Truth and Juridical Forms' in *Power: Essential Works of Michel Foucault 1954–1984*, Volume Three, edited by James D. Faubion, translated by Robert Hurley et al. (New York, The New Press, 2000), 57; Judith Butler, 'Imitation and Gender Insubordination' in *Inside/Out: Lesbian Theories, Gay Theories*, edited by Diana Fuss (New York, Routledge, 1991), 13.
4 In the Farley Brothers' film *There's Something About Mary*, for example, the post-masturbatory cum that we first see hanging lugubriously from Ben Stiller's ear is eventually distributed into Cameron Diaz's hair (she mistakes it for styling gel). In Todd Solondz's film *Happiness*, a young boy, standing on the balcony of his apartment building, masturbates while watching two women sunbathing in the courtyard below. His semen, which lands on a guardrail and is lapped up by the family dog, is transferred to his own mother's mouth when, in the very next scene, she kisses the dog at the dinner table.
5 Julia Kristeva, *Powers of Horror: An Essay on Abjection*, translated by Leon S. Roudiez (New York, Columbia University Press, 1982), 5.
6 Jacques Lacan, *Écrits: A Selection*, translated by Alan Sheridan (New York, Norton, 1977), 315.
7 John Berger, *Ways of Seeing* (New York, Viking, 1973), 47.
8 Laura Mulvey, 'Visual Pleasure and Narrative Cinema,' *The Sexual Subject: A Screen Reader in Sexuality* (New York, Routledge, 1992), 27–8.
9 Homi Bhabha, *The Location of Culture* (New York, Routledge, 1994), 89.
10 Sally Robinson, *Marked Men: White Masculinity in Crisis* (New York, Columbia University Press, 2000), 43.
11 G.W.F Hegel, *Phenomenology of Spirit*, translated by A.V. Miller (Oxford, Oxford University Press, 1971), 243.

12 Jacques Lacan, *The Seminar of Jacques Lacan, Book XI: The Four Fundamental Concepts of Psychoanalysis*, edited by Jacques-Alain Miller, translated by Alan Sheridan (New York, Norton, 1998), 117.
13 Leo Bersani, *Homos* (Cambridge, Harvard University Press, 1995), 181.
14 D.A. Miller, 'Anal Rope' in *Inside/Out: Lesbian Theories, Gay Theories*, edited by Diana Fuss, 139.
15 Slavoj Žižek, *Looking Awry: An Introduction to Jacques Lacan through Popular Culture* (Cambridge, MIT Press, 1998), 72.
16 Lee Edelman, '*Rear Window*'s Glasshole' in *Outtakes*, edited by Ellis Hanson (Durham, Duke University Press, 1999), 101.
17 Diana Fuss, 'Fashion and the Homospectatorial Look,' *Critical Inquiry* 18:4 (Summer 1992), 713–37.
18 Laurence Goldstein, editor, *The Male Body: Features, Destinies, Exposures* (University of Michigan Press, 1994).
19 Stuart Hall, 'The Rediscovery of "Ideology"' in *Literary Theory: An Anthology*, edited by Julie Rivkin and Michael Ryan (New York, Blackwell, 1998), 1050.
20 Cf. Rimbaud: '*Je est un autre*'. *Complete Works and Selected Letters*, translated by Wallace Fowlie (Chicago, University of Chicago Press, 1966), 304.

Mainstreaming the Money Shot: Reflections on the Representation of Ejaculation in Contemporary American Cinema

Although by no means universal there is a propensity in Western culture, both popular and theoretical, to frame masculinity, especially normative heterosexual ideology's notion of masculinity, in what could be broadly described as economic terms; that is, to offer a conception of masculinity as a quality based on quantity — something one has rather than something one is. This effectively downgrades the notion of there being a masculine ontology, an open and non-excluding experience of being masculine, in favour of masculinity as an epistemological category, something known, excluding and countable. As reliance on the epistemological is necessarily temporal, this effectively promotes a notion of masculinity as somehow gained by the male subject and hence something that can in time be accrued, counted, hoarded and, of course, lost. However, this economistic model is not limited to masculinity as a concept but also informs attitudes towards more prosaic and material facets of male bodies, including attitudes surrounding male sexual function. This paper focuses on how economistic notions of value are inscribed in representations of both ejaculate and ejaculation, and how this further encourages economistic readings of masculine value in general.

The origins of this propensity to make masculinity something other than men's experience of their own bodies, or to render the experience of being that body as secondary to the notion of the masculine, are undoubtedly many, ancient and complex. Although this paper cannot describe them all in any detail, it will distinguish between two major interrelated economic modalities that seem both archaic and fundamental to such metaphorization. First, semen's value within a reproductive economy, the progenitorial role of semen as the very seed corn of society, and second, the physical effect of semen on the body as a vital fluid within an economy of masculinization. The former is most clearly found in the generation narrative of Genesis[1] whilst the later informed the ancient Greek medical model of the humours.[2]

The seed corn value of semen present in the Bible is also expressed negatively by one of the oldest representations of ejaculate in the western tradition, in the 3,000-year old story of Onan (Genesis 38:4–10).[3] Onan infamously spilled his seed on the ground rather than inseminate his dead brother's wife — for which God slew him.[4] It is worth remembering that the previous thirty-seven chapters of Genesis have reported endlessly on humanity's primary and fundamental duty — God's demand that his creation should be fruitful and multiply. This cannot be stressed enough. The Old Testament is nothing if not a breeder's manual in which phallic-function-as-law and phallic-function-as-insemination are inseparable.

Likewise the notion that semen literally made men masculine has a long heritage. According to the second century physician Aretaeus the Cappadocian, for example, semen was not merely manufactured by the male body but vital to its well-being, because 'it is the semen when possessed of vitality which makes us to be men, hot, well braced in limbs, hairy, well voiced, spirited, strong to think and act' (cited in Allen, *The Wages of Sin*, 83). This concept of semen manufacturing masculinity rather than the other way around persisted well beyond the ancient model of the humours on which Aretaeus drew. It was still employed as one of the main arguments for the nineteenth and early twentieth-century anti-male masturbation hysteria.[5] In both models semen's value is negated by it being seen or made visible, and it would therefore be expected that both modalities would negatively inflect representations of ejaculation.

Indeed, the representations of ejaculation under consideration — from *There's Something about Mary* (Bobby and Peter Farrelly, 1998) and *Happiness* (Todd Solondz, 1999) — undoubtedly present narratives of masculinity that draw heavily on these traditional economistic models of masculinity. Of particular note is the importance both texts attach to spermatic exchange, despite staging the required visibility of ejaculate via masturbation narratives. Notwithstanding the reliance on a masturbatory climax, the act as represented is not strictly solitary and both texts represent the further transfer of the ejaculate to a woman. This has distinct resonance with the usual pornographic representation of ejaculate — the 'money shot'[6] — that also customarily demonstrates ejaculation and then requires that the ejaculate be transferred to a woman. However, whilst the story of transfer might be a familiar one, the location of its telling is not.

It would be naive to argue that such representations suggest an increased ideological comfort in making the male body visible. The male body has always been a site of mainstream cinematic spectacle, which cannot but screen the male through the hegemonic prism of dominant ideological discourses.[7] However, it is equally simplistic to assume the relationship between the representation of masculinity on screen and the masculine gaze[8] (that the cinematic apparatus is often claimed to elicit and promote) is unproblematic or fixed. Masculine narcissistic pleasure always risks descent into a homosexual erotic gaze at odds with the perceived notion of the heterosexist masculine subject of the gaze for it has to make the masculine itself an object. Therefore, once screened, masculinity cannot but partake of spectacle.[9] Furthermore, the gap that inevitably opens up between any ideological notion in its more sublime or idealist state and the inherent shortfall of the material representation of this idea is always historically located. Hence, although a repetition of the subject-object distinction lies at the heart of ideological discomfort—from the Bible to Hollywood—its expression is far from static. An analysis of what appears as new forms of representation must take account of this underlying repetition, whilst simultaneously remaining open to the effect of sedimentation, in which the attempt to carry forward the same ideological perspective buckles the ideological intention under its own historical weight.

It is this translocation from one medium to another that both reveals and creates tension between representational form and contemporary ideological meaning. In the attempt to say the same thing but in a different voice new meanings emerge. Indeed, rather than a reference to a timeless essence, it is a specifically contemporary expression of historicized meaning that comes into play. Hence, although neither of these representations in itself offers a revolutionary revaluation of the value of ejaculate, the fact that they employ a representation that has been confined to, if not definitional of, hardcore pornography is revealing.

Representations of the penis are still uncommon in cinema, whilst the direct representation of the erect penis is still prohibited. Despite these films appearing at opposite ends of the spectrum of contemporary American film—one a mass-market teenage sex comedy, the other an art-house-distributed tragic-comedy—both comply with this censorship. However, in choosing to represent ejaculate with varying degrees of verisimilitude, they equally seem to question the spirit if not the letter of this prohibition by referencing themselves to pornographic representation. In pornography, the value of ejaculate is as proof of the actuality of the male performer's climax, and hence the viewer is assured of getting their money's worth, that this is genuine hardcore. This suggests the following interrelated questions. What is the value of such a representation in non-pornographic cinema, where the prohibition on representing the erect penis ensures that no such certainty exists? In this respect, is the money in these money shots the same as in pornography, and if so what is it attempting to purchase? Why should this particular and profound material truth of masculine being lend itself to this specific metaphorization of value in the first place, and how far does the metaphor extend?

In *There's Something About Mary*, Ted (Ben Stiller) is depicted masturbating in a hotel bathroom prior to a date with Mary (Cameron Diaz). The act is pragmatically rather than erotically motivated — Ted has been advised by Dom (Chris Elliot) that masturbating before an important date is recommended, if not in fact vital, if one is to remain calm and attentive. Although the positive benefits of both reduced nerves and reduced sexual tension are presented as a given, it is the negative psychological effect of accumulated semen on the psyche — 'baby batter on the brain', as Dom defines it — that promotes the urgent need for the masturbatory act. Indeed, to go out without first ridding oneself of ejaculate is like 'going out with a loaded gun'. Although the aggression of the metaphor is telling, its main narrative purpose is to suggest that in such a 'loaded' state the male subject is incapable of engaging in an honest or open communication with a woman as all he can think about is having sex. Dom contrasts this state to the relaxed, communicative attitude demonstrated immediately after sex, which, he suggests, is the one sought by women in a partner. He even claims that once a man rids himself of semen, he can, if only temporarily, 'think like a girl'. The act of 'cleaning out the pipes', therefore, rids the male subject of that which paradoxically renders him masculine while simultaneously hindering the formation of a heterosexual relationship. It is semen that must be given up or exchanged if the positive benefits of homosociality to the formation of the heterosexual couple are to be realized. This effectively identifies semen (rather than the body that produces it) as the source of sexually aggressive masculinity.

Interestingly, *There's Something About Mary* agrees with the humours model over the effects of seminal loss, but validates rather than fears them. Masculinity remains a quality based on quantity, an economic form, but masculinity itself is no longer valued. However, the ideological validity of such a radical rejection of the masculine principle is brought into question by the representation itself which is unable to simply dispose of the offending substance. In the masturbation scene, the non-diegetic music, Bizet's 'Danse bohème' from *Carmen*, matches the frantic diegetic slapping and gasping sounds. While the former is dramatic and the latter pornographic, their combination is undoubtedly comic. We see Ted from just above the waist, leaning forward over the sink, a newspaper advert for a bra sale acting as a pornographic prop. The furious jerking of his left elbow and his expression half-way between pain and deep concentration leave us in little doubt as to his act. Only through the frenzy of masturbation can he lose the frenzy of masculinity. This is emphasized through the scene being intercut with Mary's composed arrival at the hotel, her relaxed pace again matched by the non-diegetic music — a lounge-jazz rendition of Cole Porter's 'I've Got You Under My Skin', which seems to ironically mock Ted's — and masculinity's — situation. We return to a close up of Ted's grimacing face, but climax is confirmed by his grasping of the newspaper, the one spasm indexing the other. At this stage the music stops and Ted begins to clean up. However, he cannot locate exactly where his ejaculate has gone, and looks around himself in some confusion as Mary arrives outside his room. Assuming the problem is confined to the bathroom, and after checking his clothing, he opens the door to her. It is only then that the ejaculate is located, when Mary spots it hanging from Ted's left ear. Sight-gag rather than physiology dominates the *mise en scène* (the ejaculate is far too rubbery to claim much verisimilitude). Indeed, Mary herself mistakes it for hair-gel, so preparing the way for the next scene and sight-gag, in which after taking and applying the 'hair-gel' her hair stands stiff and vertical.

It could undoubtedly be argued that this transfer is motivated by a misogynistic desire to make Mary abject in revenge for Ted's own feelings of abjection towards his own ejaculate.[10] This is both in the sense of a state of base subjectivity, of feeling abject, but also in the more direct sense of an act in which to abject is to throw away or cast down. However, it could equally be claimed that Mary's gesture demonstrates an immediate easy intimacy with Ted and despite her ignorance as to the true nature of this substance, her taking freely of that which had clearly been in direct contact with Ted's body, represents a more utopian fantasy. The acceptance of the substance by another in its materiality negates ejaculate's power of abjection. Both readings however suggest the value of masculinity to itself remains within the logic of a moment of exchange, rather than the monadic experience of a body.

The same logic of exchange applies in *Happiness*,[11] but the epistemological value of visible ejaculate is opposite to that intended by Ted. On this occasion rather than a reduction or negation of phallic masculinity ejaculation is taken and longed for as proof of its presence. The reason for this is it is a representation of the first ejaculatory orgasm of Billy (Rufus Reed), a thirteen year old boy who has been gravely concerned by his previous inability to ejaculate. Once again, however, the logic of a sight-gag eschews both neutral or celebratory expression of what is after all a profound moment for the subject, and instead employs a comic form again dependent on economistic logic. Once more the external substance is devalued and then subsequently revalidated through a process of exchange in which the ejaculate takes on value when once again it is transferred to a woman. Whatever else this suggests about hegemonic masculinity's attitude to the feminine, it does demand an economistic attitude to the self *qua* masculinity.

Billy has explicitly expressed a normative desire to 'grow up', to know orgasm in the ontological sense. That such a desire for knowledge of self comes before knowledge of other seems a developmental inevitability and therefore suggests a properly historic interface between the actualities of male bodies and the specific somatic individual prior to any exchange. Likewise, the accidental voyeurism that initiates his masturbation — from the safety of a balcony several floors up he spies a bikini-clad woman sunbathing below — does not in itself demand an exchange. Billy is instead accidentally possessed by the body of this other. However, a number of narrative strategies are employed to refute this possibility and again conflate masculinity, ejaculation and exchange. In particular, both the *mise en scène* and music deny either celebratory or innocent readings of his masturbation by deploying specifically pornographic tropes through which Billy buys his orgasm.

Although the casting of a believable woman who could erotically arouse Billy offers a wide range of body-subjects, the woman cast clearly partakes of the excessive semiotic of the female pornography performer. In a film in which casting is a major narrative strategy,[12] such a choice cannot be accidental or incidental: the bikini is particularly small while her breasts appear to be surgically augmented, and she is, of course, blonde. The kitsch non-diegetic muzak is also reminiscent of that used in pornographic movies and although we see nothing of Billy below the waist and merely see him slightly swaying, we are presented with a realistic shot of his ejaculate. However, this epistemological verification of his masculine status comes at a price.

With the decision to realistically demonstrate his tiny dripping ejaculate on the balcony railings, and the family dog licking it up, Billy has clearly entered an adult world where the male body-subject is once again seen to be in a state of abjection. As in *There's Something About Mary*, this is the truth of male sexuality in *Happiness*. At the end of sexual fantasy lies not phallic Mastery but brute substance, a reminder of the mocking limitations of the material remainder. That is, phallic sexuality creates its own leftover, or excess, which cannot be accounted for. Indeed, Billy seems far more mesmerized by the sight of his own ejaculate than he does by the woman below. The actions of the dog, itself driven by a base brute nature, further intensifies his sense of abjection. However, in again choosing to demonstrate a spermatic transfer (the dog wanders back into the flat where Billy's mother insists on a 'kiss', letting the animal lick her face), a value, if only a negative one, is assigned to brute substance. When Billy returns to the dinner table and announces 'I came', his family sits in dumb silence and the film ends. While attempting to suggest that nothing can be said of this, the implication being that male abjection is essentially inexplicable yet inescapable, the sight-gag again insists on an exchange which undoubtedly creates meaning beyond this silence.

Although the film ends with Billy's first 'successful' masturbation, it is accompanied by a tremendous sense of anti-climax, suggesting only the victory of idiot, dumb desire. Billy's 'achievement' is to have entered the banal prison of adult male desire, which likewise suggests that adult male desire never develops beyond the masturbatory behaviour of thirteen year old boys. The narrative demands that not just a woman, but his mother, chooses in ignorance to accept this substance seems even more overtly misogynist in intent than in *There's Something About Mary*. The inclusion of the agency of the dog adds a level of alienation that reduces the possibility of the representation appealing to any underlying masculine desire or fantasy of acceptance. The money shot is so devalued by the representation, so negatively over-determined, it is a currency that seems almost worthless. This is not the case in pornography, and a comparison with the representation of valued semen is instructive.

In her study of pornography, *Hard Core*, Linda Williams attempts to analyse the value assigned to the phenomenon of the pornographic money shot in terms of both 'the Marxian fetish of commodity capital' as well its convergence with 'the Freudian fetish of castration disavowal' (118). According to Williams, the pornographic form doubly fetishizes the value of external ejaculation. First, it is valued as proof of the status of the representation, that this movie is genuine hardcore, and the purchaser has therefore got his money's worth. Second, the overwhelming and irrefutable visual evidence of male climax itself is over-valued as a representation of sexual knowledge *per se*, such that the very existence of a female partner and female pleasure is rendered absent from the epistemological framework. However, as Williams points out, the logic of 'this visual evidence of the mechanical truth of bodily pleasure' (101) suffers an antinomy. 'For to show the quantifiable, material "truth" of his pleasure, the male pornographic film performer must withdraw from any tactile connection with the genitals or mouth of the woman so that the "spending" of his ejaculate is visible' (101). Williams argues that the money shot is therefore a perversion from more direct forms of genital engagement, or exchange, because pornography's focus on quantification renders ejaculate, the stand-in or fetish object for what cannot be shown, visible. We see the cash but not the purchase, which remains priceless.

According to Williams, the visual domination of the money shot 'only calls attention to the impossibility of representing the climax as experienced in the "wonders of the unseen world", the climax that is represented becomes a new figure of lack' (119). It is at this point that her convergence between the Marxist and Freudian model of the fetish comes under strain and tends towards the psychoanalytic rather than materialist. In concentrating her argument on how the money shot is in effect a solution to the impossibility of representing either the sex act *in toto* or female sexual pleasure, Williams seems to imply that the money shot *does* account for phallic pleasure in its entirety. It is as if the visibility of ejaculation itself renders phallic, and hence male, sexual pleasure an epistemological category, as unlike Sally, Harry cannot both show it and fake it.[13] However, this description of the money shot relies rather heavily on what it is not, the representation of the pleasures of the unseen world, whilst simultaneously over-valuing what it is as 'the "truth" of his pleasure'. That is, Williams claims that the money shot 'represents the climax of a heterosexual act in entirely phallic terms' (119). If this is the case, it does so by (as with Onan) offering direct evidence of the negation of the phallic function *qua* insemination, and hence the money shot is also a clear demonstration of valuing phallic pleasure over sexual function. In this sense the money shot problematizes the relationship between the notion of the phallic and the concept of patriarchy. The money shot buys and hence values phallic pleasure by selling and hence devaluing phallic function.

Furthermore, this over-validation of the 'frenzy of the visible'[14] ignores the impossibility of actually representing the equally invisible male orgasm, and hence Williams seems to accept the money shot's collapse of ejaculation and orgasm into the same phenomena. Ejaculation does not merely reference phallic pleasure — it seems it *is* phallic pleasure. If this were the case, however, the spectacular epistemology of both phallic pleasure and the pornographic form would value the sight of masturbatory ejaculation if not quite as highly as the 'meat shot' or penetration shot, then at least more than it does, for the masturbatory ejaculation is equally spectacular. This, however, is not the case as the dominant form of heterosexual pornography Williams describes features couples or groups rather than individual masturbating men. Proof of orgasm in itself seems far less valued than some notion of exchange that legitimizes the phallic value on display. Like money it is a promise to pay, a credit note of patriarchy, and hence a stand-in or fetish.

However, as Marx's description of money reveals, the fetishized value of money is not merely a facilitator of exchange, it is created in the very act of exchange. Williams's incredulity towards the money shot as a suitable explanatory climax to a copulative sexual act seems entirely reasonable. The money shot is not that valuable. Indeed, it makes the money-shot *qua* Freudian fetish even more extraordinary and inexplicable. However, if the money shot is referencing a masturbatory act a different reading presents itself. Indeed, I would suggest that we need to take Williams's point as to the elision of the female sexual partner literally and to argue that what the money shot claims as its money's worth is not knowledge of the invisible but the visible. The representation of an intersubjective sexual act is in fact a cover to stage a masturbatory practice, not the other way around. Whilst withdrawal and external ejaculation represents a failure of representation of sexual intercourse it fully succeeds in representing a masturbatory climax. Whilst this may seem a perverse aim in terms of the supposed narrative, a partnered sex act, it is not in terms of the use of pornography as an aid to masturbation. In Hegelian terms one could almost claim that the development of the money shot is exemplary of the dialectical *Aufhebung* in which the pornographic form has undergone a sublation in which it become even more like its notion. The truth of the value is not intrinsic to what it buys in the narrative but extrinsic in the expenditure of the reader. The money shot does not try to paper over a void, to make up for a lack, but instead attempts to re-connote an excessive material denotation of masculinity, to render mythic and to mystify the subject's relation to his lived body. To prevent the gaze falling on semen in itself, a process that would threaten it with scopic feminization, a myth of transfer revalidates the substance *qua* potentiality. It thus renders the 'true' value of ejaculate immaterial while conferring value on the actual material stuff as represented.[15]

The problem with Williams's analysis arises in the attempt to converge the Marxian and Freudian notions of the fetish over actual material relations as expressed in the money shot. Central to the notion of the Freudian fetish is its role in castration disavowal and as such the money shot *qua* fetish undoubtedly represents it own lack. However, for the Marxist notion of the fetish, the transcendent element of commodity exchange is not based on lack but on a misinterpretation of a presence, a thing or use value that partakes of the commodity form. Although Marx emphasizes that fetishism relates to the form of the commodity as an expression of social relations separate from the physical properties of the object, he does not dismiss the existence of the object. However spectral the commodity form may be, it is not immaterial. Rather than something lacking, there is something hidden and mystified. With commodities 'there is a definite social relation between men, that assumes in their eyes, a relation between things'.[16] If the money shot partakes of this form of fetish, the commodity producer, the male performer, seems just as alienated from that which is produced as the female performer. The value is not therefore in his money but in the exchange.

In Marx, the value which is immanent to the commodity form is labour time, where money far from being that which merely 'renders commodities commensurable' (94) is instead the fetishization of that human labour. Furthermore, money is a universal measure of value that is 'the phenomenal form that must of necessity be assumed by that measure of value which is immanent in commodities' (94). Although it would seem something of a category error to conflate economic and spermatic production, it is possible to argue that their mechanisms of abstraction and fetishization are formally related. Without daring to suggest that one can demonstrate the 'exchange value' of masculinity, one can suggest the 'value'—indeed, the fetishization of exchange—inherent to normative notions of masculinity that are made explicit by this particular metaphorization of masculine identity.

The appeal to the psychoanalytic logic of the fetish as a signifier of lack, however, blocks this manoeuvre as it lacks a suitable anchorage in the material world. The emphasis on meaning, knowing and counting seems inherent to the form of analysis as opposed to the phenomena itself. Whilst ejaculation is undoubtedly a signifying process, it is also a phenomenal event that cannot be so easily described or dismissed. By accepting the logic of the metaphor, Williams's analysis of external ejaculation as a money shot takes the metaphor at its word and ignores the pre-reflective ontological aspect of this profound truth of male being that is both unaccounted for and uncountable in her description of phallic pleasure, divorced as it is from its relation to phallic function.

The money shot offers a rather obvious economic metaphor of masculine value and therefore it could be argued cannot but lend itself to the economistic model. However, in her attempt to converge Marxist and Freudian notions of the fetish, Williams's argument exposes psychoanalysis at a more general theoretical level to this particular materialist criticism. Beyond whether the analysis offered by the Freudian field is description or proscription, it seems to partake of the same propensity to render masculinity as something the subject has rather than in any way is. From a materialist perspective the problem would appear to be in the psychoanalytic separation of pleasure from function, in which the desire for pleasure does not merely mystify the actual material body, but disavows it entirely in favor of a spectral body free of a material referent. Whilst this imaginary presence is specified by Freud as the mother's penis,[17] the concept develops under the influence of Lacan into a generalized theory of lack in which the subject's experience of the absence of this imaginary presence becomes the proof of its psychic existence. Of particular note is that the signifier of this lack is the infamous phallus. Although Lacan insists that the phallus here is not a biological organ but an abstract signifier, and that masculinity's having or ownership of the phallus *qua* signifier is itself illusory, he still seems to insist on a material effect 'of giving reality to the subject in this signifier'.[18] The reality of biological sex and anatomy only matters in relation to the subject's position as a speaking being. In Lacan, as with the money shot, the experience of anatomy as a signifier seems uncannily similar to the experience of things as commodities. However, unlike Marx's model of commodity fetishism, the fundamental material reality or use value of anatomy is excluded from the model.

Furthermore, Lacan's description of the relationship between the sexes turns 'around a "to be" and a "to have"' (289) in relation to this phallus, the fetish object *par excellence*, with his notion of femininity corresponding to the former position and masculinity to the latter. Any notion of pre-linguistic masculine ontology is doubly rejected here. First, being, and the inherent impossibility of ever fully saying what *being* is, seems strictly feminine. In his formulae of sexuation in Seminar XX,[19] Lacan claims epistemological ignorance of the feminine, a 'not all' which is itself logically necessary to the existential conception of the feminine. The feminine, as with the very notion of ontology itself, stays unknowable due to the symbolic impossibility of forming a boundary around the concept such that one may describe all that lies inside. The feminine is not a description but the limit or impossibility of description as such. If the feminine is infinite content, it seems masculinity on the other hand is the very form of the finite, of the one. On the masculine side of his formulae the subject either does or does not conform to his notion of the phallic function immaterial of the content of the notion. Indeed, masculinity is effectively contentless, rendered a function to which the subject either does or does not submit. Hence, as with the less theoretically sublime description of the money shot, masculinity again is rendered accountable, a binary and quantifiable event rather than a quality.

Second, and even more fundamentally, in the insistence that the phallus is not the erect penis, and that the immaterial reality of the phallic function *qua* law takes precedence over the material reality of phallic function *qua* insemination, the profound ontological 'truth' of erection and ejaculation seems ignored, if not denied. It is one thing to avoid the pitfalls of biologism; it is another to disconnect meaning from matter. Yet a simple charge of idealist reduction would actually miss the appeal to the material inherent in the Lacanian notion of masculinity, particularly in regard to the masculine or phallic pleasure that is smuggled back into his model. As with these cinematic representations, Lacan also suggests in seminar XX that phallic pleasure outside a system of exchange — masturbation — can offer nothing but 'the jouissance of the idiot' (81). As Jacques-Alain Miller has described it, masturbation is the archetypal *doing* related to this phallic *having*. Miller states that 'having is clearly linked to masturbation. Phallic *jouissance* is proprietary *jouissance* par excellence'.[20] Whilst this offers a more visceral existential grounding for masculinity, one that undoubtedly appeals to the material existence of masculine being over the masculine as pure (mis)signification, it is hardly presented as either a positive ontological foundation or politically appealing. Moreover, he describes masturbation as a form of satisfying impotence. While appealing to the material truth of both sexual satisfaction and impotence in terms of the impossibility of potency *qua* insemination, this equally suggests that no actual man in isolation can ever account for his masculine being as he is divorced from the possibility of fulfilling his function. Masculinity exists not as it is but as what it gives or, indeed, withholds. Again, masculine sexual pleasure is defined in a zero sum relationship with patriarchal function. Reading Williams's argument in relation to the money shot via Lacanian conceptions of masturbation highlights their shared difficulty in imagining phallic pleasure other than in a politically negative binary of being either repressive phallic mastery or selfish idiotic and masturbatory. Without exchange, masculinity is masturbatory; with exchange, it becomes patriarchal domination.

Therefore, Onan's mortal sin, his crime against patriarchy in this particular instance, has less to do with illicit pleasure than with contraception as a direct disavowal of his father's law to multiply. In this respect, Lacan's critique of masturbation seems to follow the same logic of God's in relation to Onan, that it is wasteful or profligate, but the question is why? The reason lies in the psychoanalytic notion of a primordial father,[21] who initiates the realm of phallic law but remains outside it; that is, a sublime initiating masculine subject who begins, but does not himself submit to, the phallic function. In the masturbator, however, we meet this mythic alpha male's ridiculous counterpart who likewise resists submission. If phallic law is so easy to disobey it begs the question as to its continued domination.

Phallic pleasure in both the biblical and the psychoanalytic sense is inherently miserly and selfish, and anathema to the biological phallic function. Indeed, Miller specifically describes both masculinity as a notion and actual male subjects as the most unwilling inseminators and hence potential patriarchs. 'When he does finally give, it is as if he had been robbed, to the point that he reserves masturbation as the refuge of *jouissance* for himself: *one for her, one for me!*' (21). Free of the wrath of God, if not necessarily the religious logic, apparently there is still not enough of this stuff to go around. Masculinity exists in an either/or condition between function and pleasure. It is, of course, only the denial of the possibility of seminal abundance that determines this logic. Why masturbatory *jouissance* could not lead to three for her, five for me and nine for us, or any other combination physiologically imaginable, remains unexplained.

If Lacan subsumes the significance of the materiality of erection and orgasm as a form of being in favour of a process of signification, Williams collapses male orgasm into the signifying event of ejaculation so that the material truth of the equally *invisible* male orgasm is again dismissed. The 'not all' of the masculine *qua* ontological category, the opacity of male sexual being, is in both cases ignored in favour of a reduction of masculinity to a quantifiable function explicable in economic terms. While the pitfalls of a reductive anatomy-as-destiny argument must be avoided, it must equally be remembered that masculinity, beyond being a set of ideologically-motivated signifying practices, is also a lived experience. Men are embodied in a particular way that, while not exclusively so, is literally phallic. This is not to claim that masculinity can be accounted for solely through physiology, or that the social value of masculinity is reducible to biological maleness. It is instead to suggest that to divorce masculinity as an historic ideological construct from the limitations and possibilities of the experience of the lived flesh of the male body is to confine one's explanation to an idealist realm of signification. In erection and ejaculation the male body may indeed be in sympathy with the very process of signification — particularly its marking of difference within a temporal flow — but this is to reduce being to being seen. If not behind then certainly beyond these signifying events is an experiencing subject and an active material body that remains unaccounted for. Masculinity *qua* subjectivity is, therefore, neither simply a material essence nor an ideological construct for it cannot be divorced from its status as the historical material expression of a particular man's life any more than the individual somatic body can express masculinity's meaning outside history.

Therefore, although masculinity is not reducible to a biological event, the profound meaning for the subject of this event is undoubtedly central to masculine identity. Likewise the gap between pleasure and purpose is such that one cannot assume the phallic is necessarily patriarchal. Indeed patriarchy seems well aware of this, hence the ideological propensity to lock the meaning of ejaculation into a reproductive economy. In this sense, challenges to normative notions of masculinity that remain essentially anti-phallic miss this point. On their own it is difficult to see how they encourage sexual political revolution as they neither address nor believe in other more liberatory possibilities linked to what men's bodies actually do. Therefore, a more pre-reflective description of male being and male bodies, one that articulates the potential for a revaluation or repositioning rather than a rejection of the phallic and the concomitant value of ejaculate, suggests itself as a political task. Rather than a call for male subjects to be other-than-men, it instead is an appeal to the potentiality of men-being-other. Despite their ideological intention and narrative determinations, representations of the male body in its most phallic moment open the male subject, if only temporarily, to another possibility, another reading, of material masculinity — pleasure without mastery, production without ownership, abundance outside of profligacy.

GREG TUCK
Buckinghamshire Chilterns University College

NOTES

1. Although typically translated as seed, the Hebrew term 'zera' means both semen and offspring. See Robert Alter, *Genesis: Translation and Commentary* (London, W.W. Norton & Co, 1996), 31.
2. Starting with Hippocrates in the fifth century BC and codified by Galen in the second century AD, humoral medicine stressed the need for balance between the four humours or bodily fluids — blood, phlegm, yellow bile and black bile — for the maintenance of good health. Semen was considered a highly refined form of blood and hence its loss should not be taken lightly. See Peter Lewis Allen, *The Wages of Sin: Sex and Disease, Past and Present* (London, Chicago University Press, 2000), 6–7 and Roy Porter, *The Greatest Benefit to Mankind: A Medical History of Humanity from Antiquity to the Present* (London, HarperCollins, 1997), 56–8.
3. See Robert Alter, *Genesis: Translation and Commentary*, 218.
4. Whilst this relegation of the mother to the status of a vessel, a suitable field for cultivating, allows for a notion of her as not dissimilar to her husband's fields, and hence her husband's property, who owns the semen seems more ambivalent and confusing. Onan is specified as fearing he will give seed unto his brother. As semen in itself it seems to be Onan's, whereas from the moment of conception or birth, the seed will grow with his brother's name, and therefore the semen seems to belong to another, or at least another name, more than the body from which it came. Thus semen is doubly owned. In its gross physical nature it belongs to the individual but in its status as seed corn, as sublime object, it quite literally belongs to the named father not the biological one.
5. Starting with the commercial success of an anonymous pamphlet *Onania, or the Heinous Sin of Self-Pollution* first published in 1710 and the integration of its claims of moral and physical degradation by the nascent medical profession (most notable in the writings of a Swiss physician Samuel-Auguste Tissot), masturbation became the target of specific vilification as a dissipation and degradation of both personal and social vitality. As late as 1845, consulting surgeons R.J. Brodie and Co. not only claimed that masturbation lead to 'nervousness, hypochondriacism, depression of spirits, melancholy mania,

epilepsy, hysteria, paralysis, dimness of sight, difficulty in hearing (…) it weakens the function of the reproductive organs, and produces temporary or permanent impotency'. Furthermore, they still made direct appeals to the model of the humors by stating that 'the seminal fluid is the very essence of the vital principle, the most essential part of the blood'. See R.J. Brodie & Co., *The Secret Companion, or a Medical Work on Onanism or Self Pollution* (London, published by the Authors, 1845), 9–11.

6 See Linda Williams, *Hard Core: Power, Pleasure, and the 'Frenzy of the Visible'* (London, University of California Press, 1999), 93–119.
7 See *Screening the Male: Exploring Masculinities in Hollywood Cinema* (London, Routledge, 1993), edited by Steve Cohan and Ina Rae Hark, 1–8.
8 Laura Mulvey's analysis of the visual pleasure created and offered by classical Hollywood Cinema as in itself a masculine formation is obviously foundational in this regard. See Laura Mulvey, 'Visual Pleasure and Narrative Cinema' in *The Sexual Subject: A Screen Reader in Sexuality* (London, Routledge, 1992), 22–34.
9 See Steve Neale, 'Masculinity as Spectacle: Reflections on Men and Mainstream Cinema' in *Screening the Male: Exploring Masculinities in Hollywood Cinema*, 9–22.
10 Although Kristeva's notion of abjection is of obvious relevance here, the detailed attention it undoubtedly deserves is beyond the scope of this essay (although it presents itself as necessary future task); therefore it is in the more familiar usage of the abject that the term is employed here.
11 Prior to this scene there is in fact another representation of ejaculation in *Happiness*. Although on this occasion the text does not demonstrate the direct material transfer of the ejaculate to a woman, it occurs whilst the male subject is making an obscene telephone call, a virtual transfer that I would argue follows the same logic as described here. It is still the woman who is rendered abject whereas once again the man is represented as distanced from his ejaculate.
12 For all the realism of its shooting style and locations the casting of this film offers a litany of stereotypes. We have, for example, amongst others a computer-geek, a frigid-housewife, a sick-therapist, and a poetess-femme fatale.
13 It should be remembered that the main point of the infamous faked orgasm scene in *When Harry Met Sally* (Rob Reiner, USA, 1989) is to demonstrate that the faked representation of the act was identical to a genuine observation of a female orgasm. That is, its representation demands an inherent invisibility that forever renders the visual evidence epistemologically dubious.
14 Frenzy here refers to the sub-title of Williams's book.
15 In this precise sense, *contra* Andrea Dworkin, pornography is more akin to a theory of masturbation than of rape.

16 Karl Marx, *Capital*, Volume One, translated by Samuel Moore and Edward Aveling (Moscow, Foreign Languages Publishing House, 1961), 72.
17 See 'The Sexual Theories of Children' in *On Sexuality*, Pelican Freud Library No. 7, translated by James Strachey (Harmondsworth, Penguin Books, 1977), 193–6.
18 *Ecrits: A selection*, translated by Alan Sheridan (London, Routledge, 1977), 289.
19 *Encore: The Seminar of Jacques Lacan, Book XX*, translated by Bruce Fink (London, W.W. Norton & Co, 1998), 78–89. The formulae of sexuation are a set of four logical propositions, two on the masculine side, two on the feminine side, which attempt to articulate four possible relations of the subject to the phallic function. Although borrowed from classical logic, it could be argued that it is illegitimate for Lacan to employ a negative copula over the existential quantifier on the feminine side of his logical schema as the existential quantifier already contains its own inherent ambivalence (standing as it does for terms such as some, certain, most) such that it is illogical for it to submit to a universal negation.
20 Jacques-Alain Miller, 'The Relationship between the Sexes' in *Sexuation: Sic 3*, edited by Renata Salecl (London, Duke University Press, 2000), 20.
21 Freud's arguments as developed in *Totem and Taboo* and *Moses and Monotheism* are foundational in this regard (See Volume 13 of the Standard Edition).

Homosexual Prototypes: Repetition and the Construction of the Generic in the Iconography of Gay Pornography

In 1970, quite late in his illustrious career, Tom of Finland produced an image depicting 13 variously attired, handsome, muscular and well endowed young men appraising the merits of a nude, square jawed Adonis standing on a rock in the middle of an unspecified forest glade. (Fig. 1) The setting recalls the idealized generic landscape of renaissance art. The elongated rectilinear composition of the image is reminiscent of Botticelli's *La Primavera* and the bronzed god, the focus of the desiring gazes of both the subjects in the illustration and presumably the viewers, assumes the pose of Michaelangelo's *David*. The image wittily suggests that this woodland arena is the art gallery of the urban gay male, where living statuary, breathing works of art are assessed and admired. Though the figures depicted in this illustration sport costumes and accoutrements that afford them some sense of individualism, some sense of a social location, they simultaneously act as exemplars, they have a generic sameness. It is this very sense of sameness that I identify as one of the defining characteristics of the iconography and types deployed in contemporary American gay video pornography.

My analysis concerns itself with the homosexual Prototypes in the texts of American gay pornographic videos. I am referring here to the recurrent deployment of an idealized, generic, muscular, male performer typifying what Richard Dyer has described as the 'Californian ideal of a sort of clean anonymity'.[1] I propose the concept of Prototype as an active and dynamic model that presupposes an agency to the readers of cultural texts, though my emphasis is on textual qualities rather than the responses to them. What is at stake here for the gay reader is the construction of an iconography and set of identities that speak to and are made by gay men; sexualized identities based on, as Jamie Gough observes 'masculinity as a sexual fetish'.[2] In this paper I will develop the concept of Prototype out of a re-evaluation of approaches to generic forms of representation and outline the particular relevance that this concept has to the study of gay pornography.

Repetition and Construction of the Generic in the Iconography of Gay Pornography 281

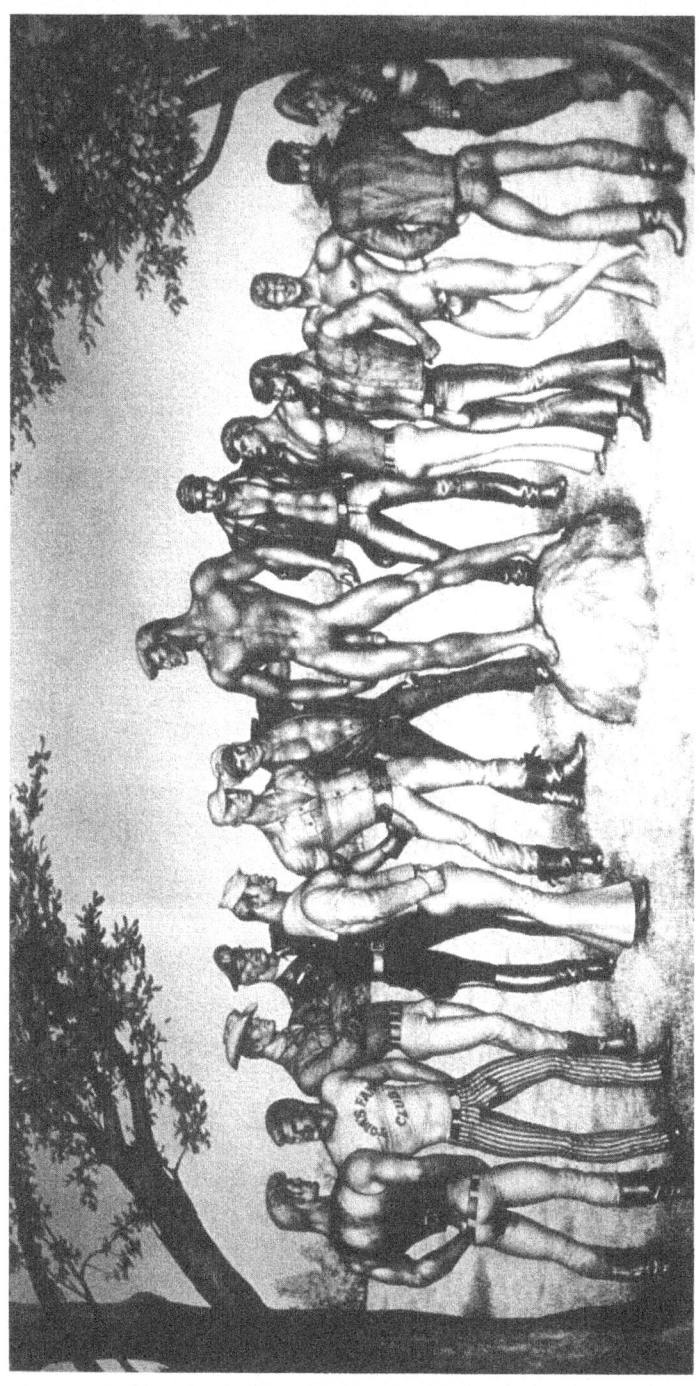

Figure 1. Tom of Finland, *Untitled*, 1970.

The study of genre and generic conventions has been a consistent concern for academics in film and television studies yet the analysis of generic iconographic types has been relatively overlooked. I would suggest that this is due, in no small part, to the dominance of the concept of stereotype as the primary tool for the analysis of the representation of recurrent character types and their function within texts. It is the theoretical model of stereotype that I will take issue with initially. It is a fundamental axiom that the texts of gay porn are constituted of stereotypical representations of homosexual personae, practices and milieux. The problem with stereotype as an analytical tool arises predominantly from this apparent simplicity, this common sense quality. The study of stereotypes generally presupposes that the processes of mediation and representation lead to distortion and oppression. When Walter Lippman coined the term stereotype in the 1920s Richard Dyer notes 'he did not intend it to have a wholly and necessarily pejorative connotation'.[3] However, in its contemporary application, the study of stereotypes is almost entirely predicated on this assumption.

A stereotype is widely understood as a view held by one homogeneous group about another that reveals evidence of prejudice. In the first instance this raises problematic issues about the extent to which notions of consensus or homogeneous groups are feasible within a fractured culture such as ours. With particular reference to the images we can observe in the texts of gay porn, the extent to which any group can be seen to stereotypically represent members of their own group must also be called into question. Given these reservations I would suggest that it is still relevant to address the generic constructions evident in contemporary culture.

Stereotype was widely incorporated into cultural studies debate during the 1960s and 1970s by culturalist academics inspired by the work of European structuralists and has become more widely assimilated into popular debate around representation and the media as the work of second wave feminists gained influence. Stereotype was and for many still is a useful and highly persuasive model, enabling scholars to identify and account for prejudiced attitudes within culture exemplified through negative representations of minority groups. It is a concept broadly predicated upon a notion of the subject as sutured and coerced into a dominant reading of a text. It posits the subject as both passive and homogeneous. Even later writing on feminism and stereotypes such as Tessa Perkins' article 'Rethinking Stereotypes'[4] in which a level of complexity and ambiguity is acknowledged, still presupposes a dominant preferred reading and, by association, therefore a more or less passive reader.

In a fractured and ethnically, socially and ideologically mixed society, the relevance of the notion of stereotype and the attendant assumptions upon which it is predicated must be questioned. What is proposed here, as an alternative, is a concept that encompasses the active agency of the reader of media texts and the ambivalent nature of signs and symbolic exchange in contemporary society. Steve Neale's critique of stereotyping, in which he emphasizes the importance of concentrating on a concept of 'difference' when studying representations, is valuable when considering the limitations of stereotype as theoretical model.[5] Given this, however, I agree with Richard Dyer that: 'it is still worthwhile to look at the relatively unified, repetitious representations we get of groups' (unpublished interview).

We need not reject the study of stereotypes out of hand. The study of stereotypes has been of crucial importance in identifying how prejudice is perpetuated in cultural texts, however, these concerns are not the focus of my research. Rather than dismissing the concept of stereotype, I am suggesting that the repetitious iconography of gay pornography is something more than just stereotypical. As a theoretical model stereotype does not and cannot fully account for what is taking place in the texts of gay pornography. I propose a model to explain these repetitive constructions in a way that is dynamic rather than static and deterministic. It is this dynamic model, this evidence of Prototypes that can be observed in the texts of gay pornography.

A Prototype is a generic iconographic construction in a cultural text. A Prototype has an ambivalent quality it is not deterministically inscribed with oppressive or coercive connotations. The reading of a Prototype is an active process. The reader engages with the text to identify those meanings that have resonance for the individual subject. An exposition of the qualities of the Prototype enables us to identify five key characteristics. Critically it is not the performers in gay porn videos themselves who are Prototypes. The Prototype is rather more a conjunction of specific presentational characteristics, iconography and physical attributes that emerges within the location of a specific text.

An Ideal

The Prototype is a fantasy object. It is possessed of an extreme or exaggerated iconography. The Prototype, due to its construction and iconography, is both distant and unobtainable. The rhetorical strategies of pornography privilege this sense of idealism, this exaggeration of the eroticized male form. Pornography's role is to construct sexual fantasies whilst simultaneously and paradoxically producing an illusion of reality: we are presented with *real* sexual encounters in mythologized fantasy scenarios. In the case of the homoerotic Prototype this results in masculine iconography that is overdetermined, fetishized and excessive. We are presented with fantasized hypermasculine men apparently desiring each other and engaging in explicit homosexual encounters for our close inspection.

Manufactured

Perhaps an obvious point but significant nonetheless: the Prototype is the product of a manufacturing process and subsequently a system of exchange and consumption, whether that be in the realm of the arts or popular culture. What is perhaps less clear and I would like to place particular emphasize on here is, to use Baudrillard's terminology, the quality of simulation that results from the manufactured nature of the Prototype. Baudrillard's development of the theoretical model of the simulacra heavily informs the construction of the concept of Prototype here. The study of stereotypes has previously been based on the assumption that there is a clear link between represented groups and their stereotypical representation. Stereotypes can be seen as evidence of Baudrillard's second order of simulation. Stereotype 'masks and denatures a profound reality'.[6] In the Prototype a direct relationship to an objective reality diminishes. The Prototype, in gay porn does not function to represent reality moreover it is constructed out of exaggerated and mythic signifiers that have only an indexical relationship to real conditions of existence. The Prototype in this sense belongs to Baudrillard's third order of simulation where as Mike Gane has noted 'Produced objects begin to be modelled not from a real basis but from an artificial nucleus of characteristics'.[7]

Repetition

As a corollary to the above, the concept of repetition is a vital characteristic of the Prototype. As a result of mass production but also at the level of subjective reading, Prototypes proliferate in gay pornography. For example, American gay video pornography is a relatively marginal form of cultural production, effectively illegal in the UK yet the prototypic constructions that it produces are ubiquitous both in the gay media and increasingly can be observed infiltrating mainstream culture's representations of the eroticized male. Once more Baudrillard's dual concepts of hyper-reality and simulation come into play. As Gane observes: 'The hyper-real is the simulation form which dominates and as such defines itself in relation to that which is always already reproduced' (*Baudrillard's Bestiary*, 102). Prototypes are simulations in Baudrillard's terms: they are copies without originals.

A Machine

Borrowing terminology rather than a theoretical position from Gilles Deleuze and Felix Guattari, I see the Prototype as a machine of desire; a manufactured construct that is the dynamic object of the subject's desire. The Prototype is intended to be desirable and is mechanically constructed, in a sense to mechanically produce desire in the subject. The relevance to homoerotic representation here is clear, the Prototype is a construct in gay pornography that is created to act as the object of the reader's sexual fixation. The Prototypes that are evident in the texts of gay pornography are constructed as the repositories of the sexual investments of gay men. In his essay 'The Body' in *Symbolic Exchange and Death* Baudrillard observes:'The homogenized body as the site of the industrial production of signs and differences, mobilised under the sign of programmatic seduction'.[9]

Incomplete

Related to the quality of dynamism that is a feature of the Prototype it is important to stress the incomplete nature of prototypic construction. The Prototype is in a stage of transition waiting to be appropriated, redefined, remodelled and added to. In gay pornography, changing cultural trends, fashion, attitudes to norms of sexual conduct all influence prototypic construction. This is perhaps best exemplified in the changing nature of the Leatherman's iconography from a conflation of Fascist and biker imagery during the 1950s and 1960s to the inclusion during the 1970s and 1980s of leather and rubber fetishism. Similarly, the presentation of the porn bottom, perhaps most simply defined as the performer who gets fucked in a sexual encounter, has evolved during the course of the past 20 years. The iconography of the smooth, blond pubescent and post pubescent bottoms of 1970s and 1980s porn, such as Kurt Marshall and Kevin Williams (perhaps the most famous porn bottom of the 1980s), has been supplanted in the 1990s and twenty-first century. First, by the return of Kevin Williams to the porn industry in the late 1990s as an older, muscular and distinctly more aggressive performer, and then by performers like the tattooed, muscular Caesar, described in the industry as a *power bottom*. The prototypic bottoms of 1980s pornography have mutated into power bottoms redefining the deterministic passive/active hierarchies of gay porn roles by virtue of their aggressive performance of the so-called passive role in gay sex.

So what then of the significance of the concept of Prototype for homosexuals and in particular the function that Prototypes perform as constructs in gay pornography? It should be noted here that pornography occupies a central place in gay culture as perhaps the predominant expression of a gay identity, constructed by and for gay men. In this sense we can see the Prototype, the generic, idealized, beautiful man as occupying a pivotal position in gay culture as the expression of ideals, fantasies and desires and also as a composite of a paradigm of mythological homoerotic signifiers. This homoerotic Prototype can be seen as the result of the shift in identity of the gay man in post Stonewall gay urban culture. Whereas the classical ideal of male homoerotic beauty had long been a fetish in homosexual circles (most notably in the French Homophile movement of the 1940s) the politicization of the gay rights movement from the late 1960s onwards resulted in the rejection by significant numbers of gay men in the developed scenes of major cities in the USA and Europe of established categories of the homosexual and homosexual conduct (effeminacy, flamboyant dress and so on) and the adoption of a stridently male and sexually promiscuous persona. As a persecuted subculture, gays have historically had to construct an identity, to reinvent themselves, often out of a paradigm of referents belonging to an oppressive heterosexual culture. Ironically, this has resulted, in gay pornography, in the adoption and fetishization of the signifiers of macho masculinity. It is even more ironic then that when, within the current realm of cultural debate, masculinity is seen as in crisis, many of the signifiers of virile male heterosexuality have become, in the homoerotic Prototype, inverted. In the texts of gay porn masculinity serves at some level, even whilst it frequently fetishizes the straight man as fantasy object, to signify the *other*, that is, the homosexual.

Two broad questions are raised then with reference to the homosexual Prototype of gay pornography. Firstly, what forms do these

Prototypes take in the texts of gay porn and secondly, why does a homoerotic Prototype exist and what is its function?

Representations of soldiers, sailors, construction workers, body builders, a veritable cornucopia of types that act as exemplars of strident masculinity, all exhibiting the prototypical characteristics identified previously, populate the texts of gay pornography. Perhaps the most influential proponent of the homoerotic Prototype is the illustrator Tom of Finland, whose work, along with such illustrators as George Quaintance, Harry Bush, Rex and others, published initially in the magazine *Physique Pictorial*, has had a profound impact on the formulation of a paradigm of erotic Prototypes in gay porn. The generic nature of the square jaw, muscular body, direct gaze and large penis, (all characteristics of prototypic construction) can be found in Tom's work. Perhaps Tom of Finland's most singular contribution to the range of homoerotic Prototypes and the one which has had the most sustained influence in gay popular culture, is the development of the Leatherman. The Leatherman is of crucial significance to gay porn and is one of the genre's most recurrent Prototypes. True to my analysis of the Prototype as a construction, manufactured as a machine of desire, the Leatherman had no explicit representational existence until Tom of Finland's illustrations of the 1950s and 1960s, which were to inform the clone iconography of the post Stonewall era. Tom was to articulate a particular form of homoeroticism, eliding biker iconography with militaristic motifs, effectively conflating the signification of the rebel with that of the authoritarian figure. It would be a grand and essentially flawed claim to attribute the creation of the Leatherman to Tom alone. The skin magazines of the late 1960s and 1970s, biker and leather bars in Urban USA, London and Berlin and the graphic artists Rex and Ettienne were all equally significant. But it was Tom who was able to coalesce these disparate influences into a coherent sexualized identity that has an enduring potency. Today, the Leatherman is a central figure in the repertoire of homoerotic Prototypes that proliferate in media representations and nowhere more so than in gay porn.

To move on to the ideological function or imperative of the Prototype in gay porn it is possible to identify two potential lines of argument. Whilst I acknowledge both as valid, the emphasis of my study focuses on the more generative and positive inflection of the second approach identified. Firstly there is what might be described as the exploitative discourse of pornography. Under the terms of this argument, the generic, highly manufactured and mediated nature of the homoerotic Prototype can be seen as evidence of the homogenizing imperatives of capitalism. The nature of homosexual desire can be regarded as contained and delineated through a process of capitalist manipulation. Clearly there is some worth in such a line of argument however, within such a discursive framework a paradox emerges that not only undermines this position but also calls into question fundamental assumptions, such as the implicit though complex and at times contradictory relationship between capitalism as a process and patriarchy as a system of knowledge/power. We see evidence, in the proliferation of homoerotica and gay prototypes, of the assimilation of homosexuality into the discourse of capitalism: a process that a traditional understanding of patriarchy cannot countenance. This seems at some level to indicate an ambivalent dimension to capitalism: capitalism as a dynamic process rather than determined and determining.[9]

The second line of argument, and the one that is privileged here is an approach that might be regarded as an empowering discourse of gay pornography. Such a line of argument acknowledges the nature of capitalist production and the extent to which a degree of exploitation is intrinsic to such a process. It is axiomatic that the gay pornography industry exists for commercial gain and economic as well as cultural imperatives drive the agenda that underpins pornographic production. We cannot however dismiss pornography generally and gay pornography more specifically as mere exploitation. The exploitative nature of pornography is perhaps more evident than that of other cultural commodities. This is partly to do with the often clandestine nature of production, distribution and consumption of pornographic texts, and partly to do with the extensive body of academic work that aims to position pornography as exploitative. Furthermore, textual qualities such as the frequently low production values and an aesthetic that Constance Penley, writing about heterosexual pornography, has noted offends bourgeois sensibilities, combined with the explicit content of the pornographic text itself and its equally explicit form of address and aim to elicit desire in the viewer all seem to situate pornography as a textual commodity that is peculiarly exploitative.[10] Pornography, however, is a complex form of text and no less so than any of the other products produced under capitalism in a patriarchal society that are consumed and made use of to define both our identities and desires as individuals. Gay porn, I would argue is doubly complex because it exists in a wider patriarchal culture that rejects and to a large extent attempts to deny the existence of gay desire, and yet it is simultaneously a product of the capitalist process which though ambivalent and amoral, is one of the key processes by which patriarchal order is maintained.

We see in the gay Prototype a subculture appropriating the signifiers of a supposedly oppressive culture and, in some cases, overturning their original dominant significations to such an extent that the popular and dominant signification is altered. It is reductive to see gay pornography in general, and the gay Prototype in particular, as merely the fetishization of oppressive patriarchy and as in some way intrinsically homophobic. I would rather suggest that, in gay pornography the polysemic potential of masculine signification is to some extent realized. Macho signifiers are played with, released from their dominant and increasingly redundant associations: they are exaggerated, eroticized and fetishized.

The homoerotic Prototype is the idealized object for the gay reader. It provides a clear, identifiable object that through its function as a machine of desire has a regularizing and normative role. Simultaneously, the Prototypes of gay pornography subvert dominant modes of address: hypermasculinity and machismo become the signifiers of gay sexuality as well as the object of gay desire. Ultimately, it is this conflict between generic, normative imperatives and the subversion, eroticization and appropriation of masculine signification that makes the Prototypes of gay pornography both problematic and intriguing.

JOHN MERCER
Buckinghamshire Chilterns University College

Acknowledgements

I would like to pay special thanks to Dr Martin Shingler and the Department of Film and Cultural Studies at Staffordshire University for supporting this research, Tom Waugh at Concordia University for his kindness and encouragement, my colleagues at Buckinghamshire Chilterns University College for their comments and suggestions and Matthew Blouin of the Tom of Finland Foundation for his assistance in securing the illustration that accompanies this paper.

NOTES

1 I should take the opportunity here to thank Richard Dyer for sparing the time to speak to me on several occasions about my research. The references here relate to an unpublished interview.

2 Jamie Gough, 'Images of Sexual Identity and the Masculinization of the Gay Man' in *Coming on Strong. Gay Politics and Culture*, edited by Simon Shepherd and Mick Wallis (London, Unwin, 1989), 121.
3 *The Matter of Images* (London, Routledge, 1993), 11.
4 'Rethinking Stereotypes' in *Ideology and Cultural Production*, edited by Michèle Barratt et al. (London, Croom Helm, 1979).
5 Steve Neale, 'The Same Old Story', *Screen Education* 32/33 (1979).
6 Jean Baudrillard, *Simulacra and Simulation* (Ann Arbor, University of Michigan Press, 1994), 6.
7 Mike Gane, *Baudrillard's Bestiary* (London, Routledge, 1991), 97.
8 Jean Baudrillard, *Symbolic Exchange and Death* (London, Sage, 1993), 112.
9 John D'Emilio, 'Capitalism and Gay Identity' in *The Lesbian and Gay Studies Reader*, edited by Henry Abelove, Michèle Aina Baraile & David M. Halperin (New York, Routledge, 1993). D'Emilio's excellent article debates these issues in much greater detail than time will allow here.
10 Constance Penley, 'Crackers and Whackers: White Trashing of Porn' in *White Trash: Race and Gender in America*, edited by Wray & Newitz (New York, Routledge, 1997).

EU Authorised Representative:
Easy Access System Europe Mustamäe tee 50, 10621 Tallinn, Estonia
gpsr.requests@easproject.com

Printed and bound by CPI Group (UK) Ltd, Croydon, CR0 4YY